The Dogged Victims of Inexorable Fate

BY DAN JENKINS

A FIRESIDE BOOK
Published by Simon and Schuster Inc.
New York • London • Toronto • Sydney • Tokyo • Singapore

Fireside
Simon & Schuster Building
Rockefeller Center
1230 Avenue of the Americas
New York, New York 10020

First Fireside Edition 1990
Published by arrangement with the author.

FIRESIDE and colophon are registered trademarks
of Simon & Schuster Inc.

Designed by Irving Perkins Associates
Manufactured in the United States of America

10 9 8 7 6 5 4 3 2 1

Library of Congress Cataloging in Publication Data
Jenkins, Dan.
The dogged victims of inexorable fate / by Dan Jenkins.
p.   cm. — (Fireside sports classics)
Originally published: Boston : Little, Brown, 1970.
"A Fireside book."
1. Golf—Anecdotes.   2. Golf—United States—History.   3. Golfers—
United States—Biography.   I. Title.   II. Series: Fireside sports
classic.
GV967.J4   1990
     796.352'02'07—dc20   90-30293
                                                                         CIP

ISBN 0-671-66750-5

For the gorgeous June Jenkins, of course,
who hates golf but loves Palm Springs;
&
For Bud, Seth, Whit, Mac and all of the
other dogged victims of 5:42 P.M.

Golf may be . . . a sophisticated game. At least, it is usually played with the outward appearance of great dignity. It is, nevertheless, a game of considerable passion, either of the explosive type, or that which burns inwardly and sears the soul.

—BOBBY JONES

Tommy Bolt's putter has spent more time in the air than Lindbergh.

—JIMMY DEMARET

Contents

Foreword

To those writers who spend weeks in an agony of composing sentences and making them into paragraphs that fit with other paragraphs to form a page and eventually a story, being in the company of Dan Jenkins at a sporting event can be a humbling experience. At a golf tournament, for example, Dan is usually to be found in good weather on the veranda, probably at a table with an umbrella over it and a waiter nearby. All day Dan may sit there as the other chairs at the table are occupied in turn by golfers, golfers' wives, tournament officials, gamblers, actors, club members, millionaires, pro football players, newspaper columnists, television commentators and various of Dan's friends who have no connection with the tournament beyond a clubhouse badge and an eagerness to tell what they have seen out on the course. Sometimes a table for four will have fourteen people at it, with Dave Marr discussing the town's restaurants, Arnold Palmer mulling over a flight plan, Don Meredith checking his grip on a teaspoon, George Low smiling at the size of the check someone other than he will get stuck with, and the rest rattling on about one thing or another while Dan, who has never been seen to take a note in his life, acts as chairman of the recreation committee.

Someone has said that the trouble with sitting around is you never know when you're finished. But Dan has a sense for it. He will rise and wander off and return in a while, having watched several of the tournament's more consequential shots being played. The sitting will resume, and the cast at the table continue to change, and the waiter keep shuttling, and then Dan is gone again. Two or three hours later he will turn up at a restaurant where thirty or forty of his day's companions are having an impromptu banquet, or at a party in someone's hotel suite, and inevitably he will be asked where he has been.

"Had to write a story," Dan will say if he feels like explaining.

In the interim Dan has slipped off to the press room or to his hotel and has written perhaps three thousand words of prose that is perceptive, funny, evocative, informative and so well organized that an editor scarcely ever needs to touch it. Dan does this thirty or more times a year for *Sports Illustrated,* frequently working against a Sunday night deadline that he never fails to make. He writes about golf, football or skiing for the most part but occasionally turns to the pop-sociology study of the surfing life in Hawaii, the high life in Hollywood, or any interesting style of life anywhere. Meanwhile, Dan manages to produce a book every year or so, such as the best-selling novel "Semi-Tough," and he can be seen regularly with his beautiful wife June at P. J. Clarke's or Elaine's in Manhattan or at dozens of other places from Beverly Hills to Kitzbühel.

One reason Dan is able to live this way is that when he gets at a typewriter he knows what he is talking about. Using golf again as an example—since golf is the subject of the stories in this collection—when he writes of George Low being beaten by a cross-handed Scot in the British Boys championship, Dan understands what such a defeat can do to a person. Dan was beaten in the Texas State Junior by a cross-handed Mexican who wore high-top tennis shoes and a baseball cap. If Dan ever had any notions of a career in golf, that helped dissuade him. But he used to be an excellent player and still would be except that he rarely plays. Dan was runner-up in the Fort Worth city championship—a distinction he shares with Ben Hogan and Byron Nelson—and was captain of the golf team at Texas Christian University, lofty achievements for one whose idea of practice was to drive a couple of balls into the woods before a match.

In those days we hung around Herb Massey's cafe in Fort Worth eating chicken fried steaks with cream gravy and hot biscuits, drank coffee and beer alternately, and played absurd games on a puck-bowling machine. There was one game in which you put your shirt and pants on backwards, faced away from the pins and slid the puck down the board behind you, as Dan reveals in this book in "The Glory Game," which is his memoir as a municipal course hustler. In another version you stood in the hedge and reached your arm in through the window for a blind shot. Dan was good at all the games we played but best at golf. I recall a match when he arrived at the course wearing a suit and tie just as his opponent was stepping onto the tee. Dan hit one practice putt and it went into the hole. Convinced he was ready, Dan trotted to the tee, shedding coat and tie and rolling up his sleeves. He had already been announced and without a warm-up swing he racked a mighty duck hook into the forest. "You're in for it today," he told his opponent from the University of Texas. "When I come out of there, we'll have alligators and bears chasing us."

While in college Dan played against Don January, Billy Maxwell, Wesley Ellis, Miller Barber, Ernie Vossler, all of whom have done rather well at the game as Professionals. He also played against Earl Stewart, Don Cherry, Joe Conrad and many other names on the Texas amateur circuit, which still offers pretty good schooling for someone trying to learn how to play. The dozen times a year that Dan now plays golf, he still breaks 80. I was playing with him on the great course at Merion a while back when he was researching his book *The Best 18 Golf Holes in America,* and Dan, who had not picked up a club in weeks, shot a 76 in a light drizzle. He has won the National Golf Writers tournament twice, and some other lesser events. But what used to impress us most about Dan Jenkins's connection with the game of golf nearly twenty years ago in Fort Worth was that Dan was the only one of us Ben Hogan would acknowledge. Whenever he saw Dan, Hogan would nod and smile tightly and say, "Hi, fella." We didn't see how you could hope to get any more recognition than that.

Clearly, Dan has done so. After many years as a daily col-

umnist in Fort Worth and Dallas and now as a senior writer
for *Sports Illustrated,* Dan is one of the country's most widely
known writers. A look at the prose that flows on the following
pages will show you why.

—EDWIN SHRAKE
Austin, Texas

Acknowledgment

In one form or another, and usually in typeface of the English language, most of the material in this book appeared originally in *Sports Illustrated,* which sent the author into a lot of country club bars to gather the information. It is not true that in order for these stories to be published in the first place the magazine had to cancel several thrilling layouts on ice boating, beagling and orienteering. That would have been the guess of a subscriber in the 1950's.

I am particularly grateful to the managing editor of *Sports Illustrated,* Mr. Andre Laguerre, for holding to the belief that I know more about the game of golf than anyone in P. J. Clarke's. I hereby thank the managing editor as well as the mother company, Time Inc., for permitting these essays to be expanded and embellished, and thus to gain the permanence of a collection.

The Dogged Victims of Inexorable Fate

The Dogged Victims of Inexorable Fate

> *On the golf course, a man may be the dogged victim of inex-*
> *orable fate, be struck down by an appalling stroke of trag-*
> *edy, become the hero of unbelievable melodrama, or the clown*
> *in a side-splitting comedy—any of these within a few hours,*
> *and all without having to bury a corpse or repair a tangled*
> *personality.*

—BOBBY JONES

It first occurred to me that golf was not particularly the grimmest game in the world one afternoon when I was reading *The Brothers Karamazov* on an electric cart. There is nothing in *The Brothers Karamazov* about golf, of course, and very little in the novel about electric carts. But I happened to be reading it, studying for an exam in comparative literature, as I came up the 18th fairway of the Worth Hills municipal course in Fort Worth several years ago. This struck some of my friends as being kind of funny, although not as funny as the fact that I was out of the hole and stood to lose at least fifty big ones.

At any rate, one of the thieves I played golf with in those days said, "I'll tell you one thing, Jankin. You'd be a lot better

off if you worked on your golf and paid less attention to them
Nazi Roosians."

He was probably right, I said, but it certainly was a bum
rap they were trying to pin on Dmitri Fyodorovitch.

My friend laughed, grabbed the crotch of his trousers, and
said, "I got your da-mitty damned old dorry-vitch right here.
I also got you out, out, out and one down."

Nobody has a soul, I said.

"Naw, they mostly usin' MacGregors and Spaldings now,"
he said.

A chapter in this book titled "The Glory Game" contains
a lot more exciting repartee like this, and it also describes in
detail why the author gave up a promising career as a tournament player, a career which might well have led him to the
zenith of an assistant pro's job in the lake regions of Wisconsin.

There was another time, later on, when it occurred to me
again that golf need not be so grim. This was one day in 1952
when I was covering the Masters tournament for the *Fort Worth
Press,* a daily newspaper which folded a long time ago but
hasn't realized it yet. A typewriter I was using in the Augusta
press room did a quaint and curious thing. On a hasty deadline,
it wrote, "Sam Snead won the Masters yesterday on greens
that were slicker than the top of his head."

My editor said he thought that was pretty foolish, what I
had done, leaving out the where, how and why in the lead,
and insulting Sam Snead. Where had I ever heard that this
was journalism, or, to use his terms, "good newspapering?" I
told him from reading *The Brothers Karamazov,* the new Daphne
Du Maurier he most likely had not read yet. So I wrote an
example to prove to him that I could do it his way. It went:

"Sam Snead, champion golfer, won the Masters, a big golf
tournament, yesterday, which was yesterday, on a golf course.
Mr. Snead is losing some of his hair but not all of it."

The final, crushing proof for me that golf should be taken
light-heartedly came in the spring of 1960. I was sitting
comfortably in the men's grill of Colonial Country Club in

Fort Worth, vividly describing the moment that Harry Vardon invented the grip, when Arnold Palmer and Dow Finsterwald entered the room. They strolled over and invited me to join them in a practice round before the Colonial National Invitation.

No thank you, I said. There will be a large gallery and I don't want to dazzle the crowd with my buttondown shirt and my shank. I'm a writer, not a golfer, I said. Palmer said he wasn't sure about that last part, but come along anyhow because it was late in the day and the people had gone home. So I weakened, unfortunately.

There were, of course, at least five thousand people lining the 1st fairway and gathered around the tee, waiting for Palmer and Finsterwald. When I walked timidly onto the 1st tee with my tie off, my sleeves rolled up, and the caddy carrying my white canvas bag, the only thing I overhead in the gallery was a man ask a friend, "Who's this geek?"

Hoping to put myself at ease, I went briskly over to Arnold and Dow, took the driver from Palmer's hands, as if to examine the all-weather grip on it or perhaps the swing weight, and tried to say something snappy.

"Who's away?" I said.

Palmer drove about 290 yards down the middle, and Finsterwald drove about 260 yards down the middle, and then it was time for me to tee off. I had always suspected that trying to play golf in the company of big time pros and a gallery would be something like walking naked into choir practice. And it was. In that moment on the 1st tee, I suddenly felt blinded and flushed, and that I would like to be somewhere else. Bolivia, maybe.

As I bent over to tee up the ball, I could barely see my hand shaking. I remember being able to taste a giant cotton rabbit in my mouth as I addressed the shot. I remember catching a glimpse of my shoes and wishing they had been shined. And I remember that as I took the club back, I overheard another comment in the gallery.

"No livin' way," a man said, quietly.

The drive went somewhere down the fairway, rather remarkably, but the next shot went only fifteen or twenty feet. I topped it. The next one went about ten yards. I topped it again. And the next one went about fifty yards. I hit a foot behind it. Eventually, I managed to pitch onto the putting surface, a feat that was greeted with a ripple of applause, which I took for what it was: a slightly unnecessary sarcasm from a few of my own friends in the crowd.

For a moment or so, I felt all right. I was on the green at last where I could stand around with Arnold and Dow, lean casually on my putter, and smoke. Except when I walked onto the lovely bent grass, I accidentally dragged one foot and my cleats carved a horrible divot out of the turf.

Humiliated, naturally, I quickly got down on my hands and knees to repair the divot. But when I got back up I noticed that the moisture of the green had implanted a huge damp splotch on each knee of my trousers. I leaned over and stared at the splotches, and began to give each leg a casual ruffle. When I raised up, my head hit something hard. It was my caddy's chin. He had come over to hand me the putter.

I took the putter and went over to my ball. I marked it and tried to hand it to the caddy so he could clean it. I dropped it. We both bent over to pick it up, bumped shoulders, and then got our hands on it at the same time. I dropped my putter. He dropped the towel. I picked up the towel. He picked up the putter. We exchanged them.

At this point, I thought I would light a cigarette to steady the nerves. I removed the pack from my pocket and tapped it against my left hand the way one does to make the cigarettes pop out. About four of them squirted out and onto the green. I picked them up and lit one. But when I went to remove it from my dry lips, it stuck, my fingers slid off the end, knocking the burning head down onto my shirt front. This forced me into a bit of an impromptu dance, which, in turn, resulted in my cleats taking another huge divot out of the green.

When that divot had been repaired, when I had successfully lighted another cigarette, and when I had a firm grip on the putter, I glanced around to see where Palmer and Finsterwald were and realized they had been staring at me, along with the other amused thousands, for God knows how long. It had been my turn to putt.

I won't go on about the rest of that round, or about the blue-red-purple funk that I played in. The point is made. I will say that because of the experience, and many others, I now know most of the pros pretty well. For example, I know Arnold Palmer well enough to call him Arnold. And Ben Hogan, with whom I have also played golf, has become a close enough friend that he never fails to phone me up to chat whenever we happen to wind up in Mratinje, Yugoslavia, at the same time.

This book is about professional golfers for the most part, and about the unique world around them. It is not a book with a continuing story line, except that modern golf itself is something of a story. But Arnold Palmer does not divorce Winnie and run off with Raquel Welch in the end. He marries his three-wood.

There is sometimes a temptation on the part of a writer putting together a collection to try to hang all of the stories on one line, to shape them into something larger and more meaningful than they are. This book doesn't do that any more than it pretends to tell the desperate slicer where his V's ought to point. It is not a history, though there is history in it, and it is not an instructional, though there are theories expounded.

If anything holds the book together other than the binding, it is the fact that a great many fascinating people play this game unconscionably well, and talk about it even better; and most of the more interesting personalities are examined within these covers, playing as I saw them play, and talking as I heard them talk.

The book takes its title from the words of Bobby Jones, who was often capable of writing about the game as well as he played it, which was not exactly with a 12-handicap. Speaking on the topic of golf's pressures, whether in championship competition or in one's normal Sunday foursome, Jones once wrote, "On the golf course, a man may be the dogged victim of inexorable fate, be struck down by an appalling stroke of tragedy, become the hero of unbelievable melodrama, or the clown in a sidesplitting comedy—any of these within a few hours, and all without having to bury a corpse or repair a tangled personality."

We golfers are all of those things at different times, I think. But since I have never known one who did not complain largely and most constantly about bad luck, I believe that we are mostly just the dogged victims of inexorable fate.

Why else, on occasions all too numerous, would we three-putt?

The Glory Game at Goat Hills

Clutch, Mother Zilch.

—MORON TOM,
standing on the 18th tee at Goat Hills

Goat Hills is gone now. It was swallowed up a few years ago
by the bulldozers of progress, and in the end it was nice to
learn that something could take a divot out of those hard
fairways. But all of the regular players had left long before.
We had matured at last. Maybe it will be all right to talk
about it now, about the place and the people and the times
we had. It could even be therapeutic. At least it will help
explain why I do not play golf so much anymore. I mean, I
keep getting invited to Winged Dip and Burning Foot and
all of those fancy clubs we sophisticated New Yorkers are
supposed to frequent, places where, I hear, they have real flag
sticks instead of broom handles. It sounds fine, but I usually
beg off. I am, frankly, still over-golfed from all those years
at Goat Hills in Texas. You would be too if . . . well, let me
tell you some of it. Not all, but some. I will try to be truth-
ful and not too sentimental. But where shall I begin? With
Cecil? Perhaps so. He was sort of a symbol in those days,
and. . . .

• • •

We called him Cecil the Parachute because he fell down a lot. He would attack the golf ball with a whining, leaping shove—more of a calisthenic than a swing, really—and occasionally, in his spectacular struggles for extra distance, he would soar right off the end of elevated tees.

He was a slim, bony, red-faced little man who wore crepe-soled shoes and heavily starched shirts that crackled when he marked his ball, always inching it forward as much as possible. When he was earthbound, Cecil drove a delivery truck for a cookie factory, Grandma's Cookies, I think, and he always parked it—hid it, rather—behind a tall hedge near the clubhouse. When the truck was there, out of sight of passing cars, one of which might have Grandma in it, you could be pretty sure that not only was Cecil out on the course but so, most likely, were Tiny, Easy, Magoo and Foot the Free, Ernie, Matty, Rush and Grease Repellent, Little Joe, Weldon the Oath, Jerry, John the Band-Aid and Moron Tom. And me. I was called Dump, basically because of what so many partners thought I did to them.

There would be an excellent chance that all of us would be in one hollering, protesting, club-slinking fifteensome, betting $800 million. Anyhow, when Cecil the Parachute had the truck hidden, you knew for sure that the game was on.

The game was not exactly the kind of golf that Gene Sarazen or any of his stodgy friends ever would have approved of. But it was, nevertheless, the kind we played for about fifteen years, through a lot of the 1940's and most of the 1950's, at a windy, dusty, indifferently mowed, stone-hard, broomstick-flagged, practically treeless, residentially surrounded public course named Worth Hills in Fort Worth, Texas. Goat Hills we called it, not too originally.

It was a gambling game that went on in some fashion or another, involving from two to twenty players, almost every day of every year. If someone missed a day, it could only have resulted from the fact that he got married or found a pinball

machine he could beat. In any case, he would be back tomorrow. The game thus survived—overwhelmed, outlasted—
not just my own shaftbending, divot-stomping presence, but
heat, rain, snow, wars, tornadoes, jobs, studies, illnesses, di-
vorces, births, deaths and considerations of infinity. If there
were certain days when some of us thought the game might
help pay part of our tuition through Texas Christian University, a jumble of cream brick buildings across the street from
the course, there were other days when it seemed we had
plunged into a lifetime of indebtedness. Either way, you were
emotionally if not financially trapped, incessantly drawn back
to the Hills, like Durrell to Alexandria.

Nearly all of the days at the Hills began the same way. We
would be slouched in wicker chairs on the small front porch
of the clubhouse, smoking, drinking coffee, complaining about
worldly things, such as the Seventh Street Theater not changing its movie in weeks. Say it was August. We would be
looking across the putting green and into the heat. In Texas
in August you can see the heat. It looks like germs. In fact,
say it was the day of the Great Cart Wreck.

A few of us were collapsed on the porch. Matty, who had
a crew cut and wore glasses, was resting against a rock
pillar, playing tunes with his fingernails on his upper front
teeth. He could do that. Learned it in study hall. For money
he could play most any tune and it would be recognizable.
I had heard him play "Sixty-Minute Man" and "Rocket 88,"
both of which were popular at this time and place on jukebox
at Jack's out on the Mansfield Highway. Jack's is where we
went at night "to hustle the pretties," as Moron Tom would
phrase it, or watch truck drivers fight to see who bought
the beer.

I was reading. Something light, I believe, like *The Brothers
Karamazov*. Any kind of book brought out in the presence of
Tiny, a railroad conductor, or Weldon the Oath, a postman,
or Grease Repellent, who worked at a Texaco station, would
prompt a whoop.

"Hey, Dump," one of them would say. "What you gonna do with all them book things clangin' around in your head?"

Be a writer, I would mumble, and grow up to marry Marlene Dietrich.

"That's good," another would say. "All I know is, you ain't gonna be no golfer."

Foot the Free, which was short for Big Foot the Freeloader, would be present, practice-putting at a small, chipped-out crevice in the concrete of the porch, a spot that marked the finish of the greatest single hole I ever saw played—but more about that later. Little Joe would be out on the putting green, trying to perfect a stroke behind his back that he felt might help him rob somebody. Magoo would be talking about how unlucky he was and how there couldn't be any God after the way he played the back nine yesterday.

Presently, on the day of the Great Cart Wreck, John the Band-Aid showed up, striding grimly from the parking lot, clubs over his shoulder, anxious to go play. He had whipped a Turf King pinball machine somewhere over on University Drive, and he had some money.

"You, you, you and you and you and you, too," said John. "All of you two, two, two. Automatic one downs and get-evens on nine and eighteen. Whipsaw everybody seventy or better for five." John had lost the day before.

We began tying our shoes.

Magoo said, "I don't guess anybody's gonna let me play since I didn't drop but a young fifty yesterday."

"You're here, aren't you?" said John, removing three clubs from his bag, which he dropped in the gravel, and swinging them violently in a limbering up exercise. "Me and Joe got all teams for five match and five medal. Dollar cats and double on birdies."

Little Joe, who played without a shirt and had a blond ducktail haircut, said, "Sure wish I'd get to pick my own partner someday. You gonna play good, John, or scrape it as usual?"

"Ain't no keep-off signs on me," said John. "You want some of your young partner?"

"I try five," said Little Joe in a high-pitched voice. "Five and a R-ra C." It was caddy talk, meaning Royal Crown Cola, the champagne of Negro caddies.

Little Joe and I took an electric cart, one of those two-seaters with three wheels, and John and Magoo took one. The rest, walked carrying their own clubs. We were an eightsome, but if others showed up later they could join in, and there would be plenty of action for them. It was not unusual for two or three players to catch up to us, or drive their cars around the course until they found us, park, hop out and get into the game right then. It was Matty one afternoon, I remember, who drove his red Olds right up near the 3rd green, leaped out with his golf shoes and glove already on, and said, "Do I have a duck in the car?" He had driven straight to the game from the University of Oklahoma where he was enrolled, a distance of about two hundred miles. And he had a live duck in the car in case anyone wanted to bet the couldn't hit a duck hook.

With only eight players this day the game was fairly simple to bookkeep. It worked like this. You played each of the other seven individually on the front nine, the back and the eighteen. And you and your partner played all other two-man combinations, or nine other twosomes, the same way. Any man or team who got one down automatically pressed, which meant starting a new bet right there. And everything was doubled, tripled, quadrupled—whatever it took—to get you even on the 9th and 18th holes if you were losing. It was certainly nice to birdie the 9th and 18th holes sometimes.

Naturally, there would always be a long, long pause on the ninth tee while everybody figured out how they stood, like this particular day. John the Band-Aid, who earned his nickname from bleeding a lot, had shot even-par 35, but he was down to everyone.

"All right, Magoo," said John. "With you I'm out, out,

out, even, even, one down and one down. I press your young ass for ten. Let's see, Foot. You got me out, out, out and one down with your friggin' birdie on seven. I'll push you eight." And so it went.

John the Band-Aid, who wore a straw hat and kept a handkerchief tied around his neck to protect him against sunburn, rarely observed honors on the tee. In fact, the game sort of worked in reverse etiquette. The losers would jump up and hit first.

The 9th tee at the Hills was on a semi-bluff, above a rather desperate dropoff into a cluster of undernourished hackberry trees, a creek, rocks and weeds. It was a par-four hole, going back toward the clubhouse and slightly uphill. The drive had to carry the big ravine, and if you hit it straight enough and far enough you could get a level lie, about a seven-iron from the green.

John the Band-Aid was teed up first, after all of the figuring out about scores, and as he addressed the ball, spreading his feet, he said, "I'm gonna hit this young mother right into Stadium Drive."

"Outhit you for five," said Magoo.

"You're on," said John, tightening his lips, gripping the driver. "Anybody else?"

"Hit it, Daddy," said Little Joe, his partner.

John the Band-Aid then curved a wondrous slice into the right rough, and coming off of his follow through he slung the club in the general direction of Eagle Mountain Lake, which was thirty miles behind us. He just missed hitting Little Joe, who nimbly ducked out of the way.

"Man, man," said Joe. "They ought to put you in a box and take you to the World's Fair."

John folded his arms and stared off in another direction for a moment, burning inside. Then, suddenly, he dashed over to his bag, jerked out his two-iron and slung it against the water fountain, snapping the shaft in half.

"That ass hole friggin' club cost me a shot back on the fourth," he explained.

I was fairly outraged, too, as I remember. Not at John. I had broken more clubs than he had ever owned. It was because I was one under and no money ahead. Maybe that's why I pointed the electric cart straight down the hill and let it run, putting Little Joe and myself instantly out of control, and headed for oblivion.

Over the rocks and ditches we were speeding, breaking the sound barrier for carts, and when the front wheel struck a large stone, sending us spiraling into the air, all I recall was hearing Little Joe's voice.

"Son of a young . . ." is all I heard him say.

We both went over the front end, head first, the bag and clubs spewing out behind and over us. I suppose I was out for ten seconds, and when I came to the cart was heaped on my left leg, battery acid was eating away at my shirt, and gnarled clubs were everywhere. Little Joe was sitting down in the rocks examining his skinned elbows and giggling. The others were standing around, looking at us, considering whether to lift the cart off my leg—or leave me there to lose all bets.

Magoo glanced down at Little Joe's white canvas bag, already being eaten into by the battery acid.

"Two dollars says Joe don't have a bag before we get to eighteen," he said.

My ankle was so swollen I had to remove my golf shoe and play the remainder of the round in one shoe and one sock. Little Joe's bag lasted until the 14th green where, when he went to pick it up after putting out, nothing was left but the two metal rings, top and bottom, joined together by a wooden stick and shoulder strap. And most of his left trouser leg was going fast.

"Two says Joe is stark naked by the seventeenth," said Magoo.

We finished the round, somehow. I do remember that both

Little Joe and I managed birdies on the last hole because Magoo and John the Band-Aid talked for weeks about the time they got beat by a cripple and a guy who was on fire.

In or out of a runaway cart, our game frequently took on odd dimensions. Utterly bored, we often played Goat Hills backwards, or to every other hole, or to every third hole, or entirely out of bounds except for the greens, which meant you had to stay in the roads and lawns, with only one club, or with only two or three clubs, or even at night, which could be stimulating because of all the occupied cars parked on the more remote fairways.

One of the more interesting games we invented was the Thousand-yard Dash. This was a one-hole marathon, starting at the farthest point on the course from the clubhouse—beside the 12th green—and ending at the chipped-out place in the concrete on the porch.

I have forgotten who invented it. Most likely it was either Foot the Free, Matty or myself, for we had once played from the old Majestic Theater to the Tarrant County courthouse in downtown Fort Worth without getting arrested. We had been driving around town, scraping fenders and breaking off radio aerials, when we stopped the car near the Majestic. Matty hopped out, opened the trunk of my car, got out a club and a ball and smashed a drive straight down Throckmorton Street, wonderfully straight, over automobiles and people. It rolled forever. Foot and I did the same. We played on with putters to the courthouse lawn, frequently falling down and flopping over like laughing fish. But, anyhow, they were about twelve of us who each put five dollars in the pot one day for the Thousand-yard Dash.

And off we went, flailing away, cutting across fairways, intruding on other foursomes, cursing and carefully counting the strokes of those who had chosen the same route as us. Some went to the left of the stone outhouse that perched atop the highest point of the course, and some played to the right of it. I followed Foot the Free because he could never afford to lose. He carried the same five-dollar bill for about eight years, I think. So we hooked a driver, hooked another driver, hooked a third driver, then hooked a spoon—you had to hook the ball at Goat Hills to get the roll—and that got us within pitching distance of the clubhouse porch. The others were out of it by now, lost in creeks or the flower beds of apartment houses which bordered the No. 1 fairway.

My approach shot carried the porch, hit hard against the clapboard wall of the clubhouse, chased Wells Howard, the pro, back inside the front door, brought a scream from his wife Lola, glanced off one of the rock pillars supporting the shingled overhang on the porch, and finally came to rest— puttable if I moved a chair—about twenty feet from the crevice.

Foot played a bounce shot, lofting a high wedge, letting it plop in front of the porch on the gravel. It hopped up beautifully over the curb and skidded against the wall, ricocheted off a chair leg and slammed to a halt only ten feet or so from the hole. Hell of a shot.

We quickly got a broom and began sweeping dirt particles off the porch to improve our putting lines, and we took off our shoes because cleats are very bad for putting on concrete. The other players gathered around and started making side bets. We put Wells and Lola at ease by convincing them that this would look good in our biographies one day after we had all gone out and won the young National Open and got ourselves famous.

A couple of rent-club players strolled out of the golf shop, and Foot asked them kindly not to step in his line. "Smart-ass punks," one of them said.

My putt offered one distinct danger, that of tapping it too hard and having it roll past the crevice and into a row of pull carts lined up at the far end of the porch, which is precisely what happened. I tried to argue that the carts were an unnatural hazard and that I deserved a free lift, but Wells Howard, no doubt believing the game to be my idea, ruled I had to play it. On in five, I eighteen-putted for a 23. Against anyone else I might still have had a chance, but Foot was one of the greatest putters in history on any kind of surface. He calmly tapped his ten-footer and it dribbled slowly, slowly over the concrete, wavering, wobbling—and in.

Foot's six was about the best hole I ever saw played, and I have seen several Odessa Pro-Am's. The only thing I have even heard about that came close to equaling it happened in Austin, Texas, a year or so later. A friend of mine named Bud Shrake, a Hills man on and off, a novelist and *Sports Illustrated* writer and the author of this book's Foreword, made a 517 against another friend, Jerre Todd, from the Lake Austin Inn to a brown leather loafer in the closet of Todd's apartment near the University of Texas campus.

I am sure that the longest hole we ever played was from the 1st tee at Goat Hills to the 3rd green at Colonial Country Club, roughly fifteen blocks away, regardless of whether one played down Stadium Drive, past the TCU football field, left on Park Hill and over the houses, or down Alton Road and Simondale, past the homes where wealthy roofing company owners and Rotarians lived.

The first time we played it, Tiny wore his bright red, elastic-waisted slacks—he was six foot three and weighed close to three hundred pounds—and Rush's dad, a retired oilman, caddied for him in a big black Lincoln, and Cecil the Parachute got bit by a cocker spaniel.

Playing through neighborhoods requires an unusual shot. The trick, we learned, was to stay in the streets as much as possible to get distance, so a good club to own was a blade putter. You can swat the ball low with a blade putter, guide it pretty well and get lots of extra roll on the pavement. We all kept one around.

I happened to have sliced a putter shot into a bed of iris on Alton Road and was searching for it when I noticed Cecil down the driveway, contemplating a difficult shot. It would have to rise quickly to clear a backyard cyclone fence, and then duck sharply to get under an oak, and then hook more severely to get around a tile roof and then slice back to land in the street. As he studied the shot a dog was barking at his ankles.

Cecil leaped at the ball in his customary manner and drove the shot straight into the Cyclone fence, about eight feet in front of him, and his follow-through carried him forward onto his elbows and stomach, like a man being dragged behind a team of horses. He slid head first into the fence, and the spaniel quickly chased after him as if it were retrieving a sock.

Cecil scrambled up and came tiptoeing back toward me down the driveway, saying, "Hurried the shot. That sucker was a-growlin' at me, and just when I started to swing I seen a lady cussin' me through the kitchen window."

We picked up—"I.P.'d," as one said at the time, meaning the ball was "in pocket"—and began looking for all the other competitors in backyards along the way toward Colonial. Tiny had quit at a fishpond. Grease Repellent had struck a sundial and lost his ball. Easy Reid had met a fellow and stopped to sell him some insurance. John the Band-Aid had broken his blade putter by throwing it against a chimney. The only two still in contention were Foot and Magoo, whom we found hitting seven-irons out of Bermuda grass lawns over the rose-covered fence and onto Colonial's 1st fairway. They had to play out fast because some Colonial members had sent a caddy back to the clubhouse to get the club manager, Vergal Bourland, who would call in the 82nd Airborne. Foot and Magoo each wound up with a nineteen and hustled back over the fence before Vergal could get their names.

Quite an argument followed, I recall, about the play-off. Magoo suggested playing back to Goat Hills, to the soft drink box in the lunchroom. Foot wanted to play to Herb Massey's restaurant on Eighth Avenue, only three miles away, because he felt like a chicken-fried steak with cream gravy and playing the shuffle bowl machine. Herb's is where we spent almost as much time as we did at Goat Hills, playing gin, betting football games, drinking beer, talking about girls and God, about the thirteen roads leading out of town and wagering on the pinball and shuffle bowl machines. It was where I once saw Matty come in one day with his pants and shirt on backwards and his glasses on the back of his head, and shoot 280 on the shuffle bowl—backwards. Foot and Magoo finally wound up splitting the money from Colonial, and we all went back to the Hills and got in a putting game that lasted until midnight.

To at least partly understand why anyone would hang around a municipal golf course for one-third of his life playing games such as these, you have to understand something about the town and the state and what golf means there.

First of all, Fort Worth is basically a quiet place. It is an old country town with a flexible society (anyone with money can join), a river, the Trinity, a fragrant stockyard on the North Side where no one ever went except to eat Mexican food at Joe Garcia's, a General Dynamics plant, a couple of newspapers, a lot of beer taverns, a downtown area sparkling with loan companies, a few elegant neighborhoods and a university, TCU, which was and is primarily noted for turning out Sam Baugh, Davey O'Brien, Jim Swink and Bob Lilly. It is a town where little has happened, outside of a few big college football games, since Vernon Castle, the dancer, was killed during World War I when his training plane crashed in a suburb. Nor has anyone cared to make something happen except, occasionally, on the golf courses.

Fort Worth is where Ben Hogan and Byron Nelson grew up, and this is one of the first facts a kid learns. There you are one day, out in the front yard brandishing a yardstick like a sword, playing Errol Flynn in *The Sea Hawk,* when, suddenly, your parents decide you have a natural swing. They then tell you about Hogan and Nelson, about Jimmy Demaret, who came from Houston, and about Lloyd Mangrum, Ralph Guldahl and Harry Cooper, who came from Dallas, and they shove you onto the nearest course and tell you not to come home until you're ready for the Ethiopian Four-ball. So you stay twenty years trying to cure a shank and learning to love a duck hook.

Essentially because of the climate—there are few weeks in any year when a man would not play golf in Texas—the sport for about thirty or forty years has been second in importance only to football. This is true throughout the state: in the north-central area of Fort Worth and Dallas, through the heavy pines of East Texas, and in the hills and woods around Austin, along the arid, palmed coasts of Houston and Corpus Christi and all across the peach-colored plains of West Texas and the Panhandle, where the fairways wind around mesquite and oil pumps and players can be seen wearing glistening tool dresser's helmets and coveralls, or Stetsons and khakis.

Golf has always received luxurious attention in the newspapers. As soon as you were old enough to read you could see headlines about people like Gus Moreland and Harry Todd playing in some fascinating thing called the Ranger Invitation. Just about every town with a service station clock used to have some kind of invitation tournament for amateurs. All kinds of places—Abilene, Lubbock, Tyler, Longview, Eastland, Waxahachie, Dublin, Midland. They would begin in mid-March and continue through mid-September, there being from ten to twenty each week, scattered all over, and it was possible, and I presume still is, for a good high school or collegiate golfer to play competitively for twenty or so weeks every year, winning, if he was talented enough, more sets of clubs, TV sets, silver trays and wristwatches than he could ever sell to get money to gamble with.

It was this vast amateur circuit that gave us Hogan and Nelson and Demaret, and then Jackie Burke, Jr., Tommy Bolt, Billy Maxwell, Don January, Wes Ellis, Earl Stewart, Shelley Mayfield, Don Cherry, Dave Marr, Bobby Nichols, Miller Barber, Charley Coody, Ernie Vossler, Don Massengale, Homero Blancos, Rex Baxter, Jacky Cupit, Dudley Wyson, Joe Conrad and dozens of others who made it and dozens who didn't.

I can relate with a certain amount of pride that Goat Hills produced its share of touring pros, not the least of which were Vossler, Coody, Massengale, Jack Montgomery and Jerry Edwards. Coody, Massengale and Montgomery came along after our goofy games were over, but Vossler and Edwards came right out of them. Ernie was a relentless competitor who could never understand why anyone other than he ever sank a putt. Sometimes, when a player like Weldon the Oath would hole one, Ernie would stalk straight to the clubhouse and brood. Vossler was never as proficient as, say, myself at breaking club shafts. In one streak I broke my eight-iron every day at the 17th tee for a week because I couldn't make a ball hold that dinky, par-three green. But Ernie had his moments. He bladed a six-iron one afternoon at the 6th hole, I remember, and almost killed us all. He hurled the club straight into the brick fairway, and the shaft snapped. Both parts of the club bounced into the air. One jagged end sprang back and hit Ernie in the palm, causing five stitches. The other glanced toward Weldon and myself, sending us sprawling, as if threatened by repetitious lightning bolts as the steel shaft sparkled in the sun and danced around us.

Later that same day Weldon the Oath had one of his talking fits—talking to the ball. He took oaths on the golf course. Outrageous vows and oaths. Wearing his postman's cap and playing without golf shoes, he had rushed to the game so quickly, I can still hear him giving the ball a wonderful lecture on the 14th tee. The 14th was the easiest hole on the course, a downhill, with-the-wind par four you could drive. If you didn't birdie this hole you broke at least three clubs. But here was Weldon on the tee, fearful of his usual slice.

"This is your last chance," he said to the ball, addressing his drive. "You lousy little crud. If you slice on me one more time I'm gonna bite you right in half and chew your rubber guts up. Now you go straight! You hear me? Do you *hear me* tellin' you this? There's no by God reason why you got to slice on me ever' time, damn it. Grreeeoood daaaammmm, you, aaaiiii!"

And Weldon hit a world-record slice.

It crossed at least two fairways to the right, a marvelous half-moon of a shot. The ball had scarcely left the clubhead before Weldon was spinning around in circles, pawing at the air with his driver, slugging at imaginary evils, whining and cursing. He ran over and started beating the driver head against a wooden tee marker. He hauled off and beat the ground with it, over and over. He stomped on the face of the club and wished he were wearing cleats to scar it forever. Then he suddenly stopped and got morose.

"Let me hit one more, just for practice," he said, calmly. "I got to figure out what I'm doing wrong."

Weldon hit another glorious slice and simply bent the shaft of the club over his knee and broke it.

"Gaaaaaa, rrreeeee, aaaddd," he exploded again. "I'm bamdad finished. This is my last day on any gaaad rrraaapp golf course son of a badddeerd bat rop ditch bastard crapping pee." He was so mad he couldn't make his words come out right. "You picks have guyed me damn stick. This rotten stinking miserable low-life friggin' spick nigger whore game."

Weldon the Oath hiked to the clubhouse, but he was, of course, back the next day.

After I holed out a thirty-foot putt to halve a gimme birdie one afternoon on the 14th, Vossler left for good. He moved on to more glamorous things, to the big money games at Ridglea, to become city champion, state amateur champion and ultimately onto the PGA tour. He won a couple of tournaments out there, made good money and finally settled down to a fine club job at Quail Creek in Oklahoma City. I have always considered Ernie our honor graduate.

For a while, all of us thought Jerry Edwards would make it, giving Goat Hills another star in pro golf. Jerry would go around shooting things like 29's and 30's on the back nine at the Hills, driving the ball four miles, or roughly the distance to old Paschal High School (now Tech), a Gibraltar of education that turned out most of us with diplomas in Library Pass Forging, Double Lunch Period Registration, Boiler Room Smoking, Basketball, Abortion Arranging, Tire Screeching and Secret Marriage. Jerry got in the money pretty often on the tour but never managed a win and eventually gave it up. His greatest publicity came when he was rumored to have gone AWOL from the army in 1962 to play in the U.S. Open. "A true Hills man," Magoo said.

Although Vossler and Edwards were the only two who succeeded, unless you want to count Coody, Massengale and Montgomery who came later, all of us at one time, I believe, envisioned a pro career. Easy Reid, for example, bought a huge black bag and an umbrella and some alligator shoes and turned pro, but the closest he came to the big time was missing the cut at the Odessa Pro-Am with me as a heavy partner. Grease Repellent turned pro one day after he shot 62 at the Hills, eight under par, breaking the course record that five of us had shared at 65. But Grease didn't go on the tour, and he didn't take a club job. He only refused to play in any more amateur tournaments, which he didn't enter anyhow.

Sadly, my own dreams were constantly spoiled by collisions with reality. The first time it happened was when I went to the State Junior tournament in San Antonio convinced I would win only to get beat three and two by a cross-handed Mexican wearing tennis shoes. I returned, thirsting for revenge, the following year and lost to a barefoot fourteen-year-old who had only five clubs.

But if those experiences were not enough to convince me, the Waxahachie Invitation should have. The Waxahachie Invitation was not exactly the Masters of Texas, but it had a lot of entries every year that we thought were awfully dazzling; players like Don Cherry, Earl Stewart, Don January, Billy Maxwell and Joe Conrad, to name a few. It was a real privilege to get beat 6–5 by any of them, we felt. I remember an unusually strong field one year at Waxahachie because it took a 70 to qualify for thirty of the thirty-two places in the championship flight. Unluckily, I shot 71 along with eleven others, so there had to be a sudden death play-off—swatfest, it was called—for the last two spots. A swatfest meant a gallery. Bad deal.

One by one we teed off on the 1st hole, a par three, and nine players bogeyed and were eliminated. I envied them all. One player got a birdie and was in. Two of us made pars and had to go another hole for the remaining berth, or the honor of being buried by a Cherry, a January or a Maxwell the next day.

The other fellow was a tall, twangy Texan named Shelby, and I did not realize until a few years later that it was the same Carroll Shelby who raced automobiles. This might have been the traumatic experience that made him change sports. The small crowd hung around to watch us play another hole, the 2nd, a par-five that bent around a deep cavern and was bordered on one side by a wire fence that separated the course from a cotton field. I recall teeing up my ball and overhearing a couple of spectators behind me.

"Who you want?" one said.

"Aw, neither, axe-you-ly. They both chili dippers," said the other.

Whatever Shelby did, I did better. He hooked, I hooked. He hit one over the fence, I hit one over the fence. He got lost in the cavern, I got lost in the cavern. He landed in a bunker, I landed in a bunker. At one point a man in the gallery said, "Well, I been to two county fairs and the Dublin Rodeo, but I ain't seen nothin' like this." I finally won the hole with a ten to Shelby's eleven most likely on a bookkeeping error.

One did not have to venture out of town—out on the *tour*, so to speak—to enrich the game back at Goat Hills. You could go across town to any of a dozen other courses that Fort Worth had. You could certainly sneak onto any of the country clubs and play from No. 2 through No. 17 frequently replacing all of the flagsticks in the bunkers instead of the cups for reasons which seemed hilarious then.

Our game, I think, was substantially influenced by those at the other courses. At one time we believed that the really good players in town were mostly at another public course, Meadowbrook. They did things like win the city championship all the time, which is something, incidentally, that neither Ben Hogan, Byron Nelson nor I could ever do. In our respective eras we each finished second in our best effort. So if anyone ever asks what Hogan, Nelson and Jenkins have in common, you now know.

And then there was Ridglea. Ridglea had players who might not have been as skilled as those at other courses, but they could sure outbet you. Legendary guys with names like Spec, Snapper and Simpo played at Ridglea, and while they weren't all that great from tee to green, they could talk you out of your savings account just by moaning. Occasionally you would get deluded by a 67 at wide-open Goat Hills and take your swing over to narrow Ridglea. You always came back busted, but at least you had been to the shrine where Titanic Thompson used to hang around.

Titanic Thompson was the adopted name of one Alvin C. Thomas of Rogers, Arkansas. During the 1920's and 1930's Titanic earned fame as the greatest golf hustler who ever lived. Right-handed or left-handed, Ti would bring you in crisp. Everyone had heard about the time at Ridglea long ago that Thompson beat Byron Nelson head-to-head, taking $1000 off Byron's backers.

At Ridglea you could sit around and listen to all of the good stories about Thompson, some of them maybe even true. People would tell how he got his name: from a guy called Snow Clark in a pool game in Joplin ("The way you're sinking everybody they ought to call you Titanic"), how he could throw a key into a keyhole, shoot a sparrow off a telephone wire, throw a watermelon over a hotel, bet it would rain in thirty

minutes—and win, outrun a jackrabbit, bet he could hit a
green with his driver from four hundred yards (he would walk
to the green and tap it with the club, you lose), how he could
sail fifty-two cards into a hat and beat anybody playing golf
if the price was right. And all the other tales. You would like
to have known Titanic Thompson more than any other man.

Since that was impossible the next best thing was just being
at Ridglea sometimes, back in those days before they turned it
into a country club for Jaycees. The fact that Thompson had
spent some time there left Ridglea with a tradition to uphold,
it seemed, and a lot of fellows worked hard to uphold it.

On one of the lazy afternoons I best remember, Raymond
Gafford, the pro, and a hell of a fine player, climbed up on a
wooden table in the old golf shop with a four-iron, put a ball
down on the table, addressed it and aimed it out the open
door toward the 1st green, a par five.

"I believe I can make a five from here," said Raymond.

"Five where?" asked Spec, a subtle, moon-faced man who
rarely begged off from any action. "From there to your pocket?"

"Oh, I think I could make five from here on the first hole,"
said Raymond, waggling the club.

"Well, I'll tell you one thing," said Spec, taking out a roll
of bills. "I ain't had nothin' this good lately."

"Can I get all that off you?" asked Raymond.

Spec grinned. "I'll guarantee you this man has *got* to
make me total rich some day, and there ain't nothin' I can do
about it."

"All I know is, I can make five," Gafford went on, waggling
the club, looking out the door.

"Well, I don't know a whole lot about it," said Spec, "but
I know a man can't make five on number one at Ridglea off
no tabletop."

"Just get it on," said Raymond.

"On?" said Spec. "On's here in my hand."

A few others got in, do or don't, and Raymond calmly
struck a nice four-iron right off the table top, out the front

door and a good ways down the fairway. It was obvious that he would have only a three-wood and another iron to reach the green and make his five.

"Piss on the fire and call in the dogs," said Spec. "The hunt's over."

And it was. Raymond made an easy five.

After this, we hit a lot of shots off the shingle roof at Goat Hills, and did a great deal of chipping off the hoods of our cars and, in fact, designed a very interesting hole that would start on top of the card table in the locker room, dogleg through the restaurant noted for its cold, greasy meatloaf, cut through the golf shop, bend around the putting green and conclude on the 1st green. Par was twenty-three.

It was, alas, in the last few years of Goat Hills, shortly before the city sold those sacred 106 acres to TCU so the school could build several more cream-brick buildings, that the games grew too big, too outrageously expensive for working men or students. Some guys got to where they couldn't pay what they lost and others didn't want to collect it. Nor was it any fun to play for scraps of paper. And then, of course, many of us were developing other interests—snooker, eight-ball, bridge, divorce. That sort of thing.

Looking back, our game might have dwindled out purely because of Moron Tom.

He had come to us as a likeable, muscular West Texan on a football scholarship at TCU, but he had quit football when he discovered he had to work out every day during the fall. Moron Tom hit a long ball in one direction or another, and he loved to bet. Anything. He would bet he could drive over anything, or under anything, shoot anything, not shoot anything or hold his breath longer than you could. He could drink a can of beer in four seconds—for money—by inhaling it. And when he was doing nothing else he kept you puzzled or aching from the fast code that he spoke. Moron Tom almost never spoke English. It was a wild kind of gibberish that you either had to learn and speak in or never know exactly what you were doing or how much you were losing.

Everything was usually "quadruple unreal" to Moron Tom, whether it was a good drive or a bad one, a lay-down gin hand or garbage, a good-looking girl or a dog. Things would also move Moron Tom to poetry. "Hit it fine, Por-ke-pine," he would say. Or, struggling over a difficult shot, "Lemme toil, Olive Oil."

There was a very special day in the history of Goat Hills— the day of the last truly big gambling game—that began with Moron Tom speaking his own language on the clubhouse porch.

"I'll take toops and threeps from Youngfut, Young-jun, Youngmut and Youngruss," he said.

Translated, that meant Moron Tom wanted two up and three up from young Foot, young John, young Matty and young Rush. He wanted other bets too.

"Ten and ten with Grease's men," he said. "Two and two with Dump-Magoo."

Everyone sort of drifted out to the first tee, making wagers, choosing partners, taking practice swings.

Moron Tom, who had a habit of aiming thirty yards to the right of every target and bringing a giant hook around and into the fairways or greens, stood up to his tee shot on No. 1 and aimed straight at the row of apartment houses on the right.

Before anyone had a chance to giggle or ask if Moron Tom could hook the ball that much he said, "Think I can't, Cary Grant?" And he smashed a big one that slowly came around and found the fairway.

"Cod Ee-rack Fockle-dim," he said. That was his pronunciation of Doc Cary Middlecoff spelled backwards and a compliment to the way he had hit the shot.

Somehow Magoo and I had wound up as partners against all other combinations and this was bad. Magoo was a strong player, but he, well, he was unlucky. Once in the Glen Garden Invitation in Fort Worth—that is the course where Hogan and Nelson caddied in their youth—he hit a splendid shot to a difficult green but lost the ball. After looking for about twenty minutes he found it in a man's mouth, being cleaned. Things like that happened to Magoo. It was also hard for him to play well when Moron Tom was in the game because he found himself continually laughing.

But this day Magoo and I were in good form. We teamed together awfully well, taking turns making birdies, and we had everybody screaming and bleeding half to death.

"Cod Eerack God damn Fockle-dim," Foot would say as Magoo drove repeatedly down the middle, just playing superbly.

Moron Tom's losses were mounting, but he remained good-natured as always. "Wod Daw-ret-sniff," he would say, hitting a shot. That was Dow Finsterwald spelled backwards, and it represented a cry of doom.

By the time we came off the 17th green, Magoo and I had birdied something like six holes in succession, and we began calculating that if we could only part the 18th, which was an easy par four, a birdie hole really, we would win so much money that we couldn't get it all home in a Grandma's Cookie truck.

"Ain't this somethin'?" said Foot on the 18th tee. "I ought to go somewhere and stand in line to give up."

"Ever day's a holiday and ever meal's a banquet," said Magoo. "Do I hear a young press?"

"Your ass is pressed on your backswing, your downswing and your follow-through," said John the Band-Aid.

Magoo smiled.

"My window's open," I said.

"Dump City," mused Foot. "I'm bein' took to Dump City by two clutch artists."

Easy Reid said, "Man, man. I don't want the cheese, I just want out of the trap."

Said John the Band-Aid, "I'm out, out, out, out, out, out, out and out. Press for fourteen million."

We finally figured up that we would win about $600 total with a par on the 18th, counting all of the get-even presses, and it was finally time to tee off.

The 18th at Goat Hills was slightly uphill. You teed off from a windy knoll with the south wind always helping and drove across a tiny creek and a couple of sycamore trees. A big drive would leave you only twenty or thirty yards short of the green, and many of us had, at times, driven right to the frog hair around the putting surface. Even a poor tee shot left you only one hundred yards from the green with a good chance at a birdie. It was almost impossible to make worse than four unless the green hadn't been mowed and you three-putted.

The only conceivable trouble was far, far to the right, across the 10th fairway, where Stadium Drive was out of bounds, but in all my years I never saw anyone slice that badly, or that far—only Magoo when Moron Tom spoke to him for that money.

At the height of Magoo's backswing, when he was coming out of his shoes to try and drive the green, Moron Tom quietly said, "Tissim, Oogam." Which was "Miss it, Magoo," spelled backwards.

Needles were commonplace in our game of course. Coughing, sneezing, dropping a full bag of clubs on a putt, yelling, burping, all such as that. It was something you expected when you were winning, and no one ever complained. Normally you just ignored it. But Magoo came apart with laughter at Moron Tom's remark and hit the drive like a two-ton Cecil the Parachute, almost falling down.

Everyone collapsed with laughter at the funny-looking drive, even Magoo and me, his partner, who had yet to tee off and who now would have the full weight of the $600 on his shoulders.

"Mighty fine, Por-ke-pine," said Moron Tom. "Oogam dewalb the Nepo," which was, "Magoo blowed the Open."

Magoo simply looked at his club after a spell and then at me and grinned, "If you don't make a four, I'm gonna stamp this Tommy Armour right on your young forehead."

Now, just on the other side of the creek down below us at the 18th, set upright into the embankment, there was a storm drain, roughly three feet in circumference. We used to pitch at it with old balls from the ladies' tee, but it was a remarkable thing if anyone ever hit it. From up on the men's tee, 100 yards or so back, it was an incredibly small target. In fact it never even entered my mind as I got set to drive the ball 300 yards to the green or know the reason why. I would get a birdie to make up for Magoo's misfortune, and that would be quadruple unreal.

But at the top of my swing Moron Tom whispered something else.

"Clutch, Mother Zilch," he said.

I didn't fall completely down coming through the shot, but almost. The clubhead hit about two inches behind the ball, and the shot snaphooked into the ground just in front of the ladies' tee, took a big hop to the right off of some rocks and— I swear to you—went straight into the storm drain.

It remains the only hole in one I ever made, and it is, of course, the shot which semi-retired me from golf forever.

Lockwrist and Cage Cases

Hitting a golf ball and putting have nothing in common. They're two different games. You work all your life to perfect a repeating swing that will get you to the greens, and then you have to try to do something that is totally unrelated. There shouldn't be any cups, just flag sticks. And then the man who hit the most fairways and greens and got closest to the pins would be the tournament winner.

—BEN HOGAN,
late in his career, after three-putting several greens

The devoted golfer is an anguished soul who has learned a lot about putting just as an avalanche victim has learned a lot about snow. He knows he has used putters with straight shafts, curved shafts, shiny shafts, dull shafts, glass shafts, oak shafts and Great-uncle Clyde's World War I saber, which he found in the attic. Attached to these shafts have been putter heads made of large lumps of lead ("weight makes the ball roll true," salesmen explain) and slivers of aluminum ("lightness makes the ball roll true," salesmen explain) as well as every other substance harder than a marshmallow. He knows he has tried forty-one different stances, inspired by everyone from the club pro to Fred Astaire in *Flying Down to Rio,* and just as many different strokes. Still, he knows he is hopelessly trapped. He can't putt, and he never will, and the only thing left for him to do is bury his head in the dirt and live the rest of his life like a radish.

If only, he thinks to himself, I had the confidence, the savoir faire, and the ability of those touring pros. They win those big checks every week—I see it on TV—and they wear those beltless slacks and those dinosaur-skin shoes. They stand up there before thousands of people, their bronzed faces expressionless, their mock turtle shirts unsweaty from not traipsing through the rough, their alpacas hanging just right, and they ram the ball straight into the cup, or near it. They must know how to putt, right?

Wrong. When it comes to putting, nobody—nobody—equals the pros for feelings of insecurity, inferiority, ineptitude and plain old fear. Despite anything you may pretend to have seen at tournaments, or on television, the pros are absolutely certain they can't putt any better than the Shaker Heights Kiwanians. Maybe worse, they claim, maybe worse. And if you heaped up all their theories on the subject of putting, you would have yourself a mountain big enough to ski the Arlberg-Kandahar on.

In an attempt to prove this, and to place the whole tormenting art of putting in some kind of perspective, a very famous golf writer who knew the pros reasonably well and was, himself, suffering a terminal case of the yips—ahem, me—decided to devote a few days on the PGA tour one time to observing the styles and listening to the agonies of the pros. Who could really putt, and who couldn't? Would Jack Burke, Jr., trade putting strokes with Arnold Palmer, for example? Would Gary Player simply allow God to line up the four-footers for him? Do you overlap, interlock, underlap, reverse overlap or just grip the putter like a snake and turn your head? Was there really an art to squatting down behind the ball? And what then did you look at, besides the protuberances on the redhead in the sweater across the green?

One should begin with Jackie Burke, it seemed, because at the time he was generally regarded as the very best putter in the game. He used an old wooden-shafted blade putter from a bygone era, but his touch with it was mystical. It was judged to be so delicate that tiny strands of bent grass had been seen to quiver with delight at his mere approach. He could glance at a putt and, rather uncannily, see a definite line to the hole, as if it were marked with chalk for only him to see. And he had this minor deity in the sky who would always whisper the speed to him. In fact, he sank so many putts during one stretch in 1952 that he won four tournaments in a row—a feat that had not been accomplished since Byron Nelson in 1945, and has not been equaled since. Burke would know all about putting.

"Who told you I was a good putter?" Jack asked. "Listen, I'm just an average putter. I've had streaks. We all have. But I'm no superputter, or I would have won more tournaments."

"But everybody says you're the best."

"Go tell everybody they're lighter than popcorn," said Burke.

Burke, obviously, could not hide the conviction that almost all of the big-time players had about their putting. It was average. It was streaky. And don't go placing him in the same category with whoever won a tournament the previous week. Whoever that was—Palmer, Julius Boros, Bill Casper—*he* was a great putter without question or doubt, and you could just ask anybody, anybody who lost.

All of which, right away, brought up one of the fascinating vagaries of golf. No pro ever wants to acknowledge that he is excellent on the putting surfaces, but he will refuse to admit mediocrity at playing from tee to green. After all, one calls for skill, but the other for luck. Slashing at a ball is manly, but tapping it is, well, womanly. Hitting a shot is muscle coordination, strength, timing, technique, balance, guts, *athletic* ability. Stroking a putt is something else. It is an unnatural leaning, bending or stooping. It is giving the ball a dainty caress and hearing it make a funny noise. Plink, kind of. Or foomp. In any case, it isn't stepping up to a drive and going crash, smack, splat and then hearing the crowd swoon as the ball soars away.

There is a pretty good reason the pros feel this way. They think of themselves, with some justification, as highly skilled athletes who have conquered the sophisticated timing of golf through hard labor and experiment. Their swings have become almost instinctive, so much so, in fact, that these swings never leave them, even under the most savage conditions, be it weather or intense pressure. A pro can shoot a 77, horrible for him, but it will be a good-looking 77 to the average golfer behind the gallery ropes. But the pro, because he has mastered the game, holds another conviction, not altogether logical. He believes that when a shot happens to veer off line and float into the rough—the trash, the garbage, Marlboro Country (he has a lot of terms for trouble)—he steadfastly believes that it can only be the result of cruel interference from that mysteriously evil force that goes around affecting the flight of golf balls.

"Everyone wants to be known as a great striker of the ball, for some reason," Gary Player said as he dropped five-footers by the dozen on the practice green. "Nobody wants to be called a lucky, one-putting s.o.b., and nobody thinks he is."

Indeed not. Some may remember Player walking off the 18th green after a televised match with Palmer in 1961 and complaining dismally. "From tee to green, I was never better. But I couldn't make a putt. And Arnold was knocking them in from everywhere." And I remember that Palmer came along five minutes later and said, "I don't understand it. Every time Gary reached for his putter the ball was in the hole."

The great strikers of the ball, it's true, are superb at describing shots they hit but never at describing putts that drop, or, better still, at admitting they drop. "I feathered a wedge in there and let it sit," one will say. Or: "I had a squirty lie, so I hammered a seven-iron." Or: "I really let that two-iron go at the thirteenth. I put the hands to it. Sometimes, when you've got to carry the water, you have a tendency to try to doghump it, but I let that one fly, boy." Gary Player has always been marvelous at this. Once he told the press, "It may have been the greatest four-wood anyone ever hit. It was so much on the flag that I had to lean sideways to follow the flight of the ball."

Terrific. But when did the press ever hear a pro ease into the interview chair, light a cigarette, settle back and say, "Now, you take that putt on the seventeenth. I had to have it, of course. Looking at the way the green sloped, I knew that a gentle rap would bring the ball down over the hill, about eight inches above the cup, and that the grain would catch it there and that it would have to pull slowly into the hole. I stroked it perfectly, as I always do. When you know how to read greens, of course, it shrinks those twenty-footers down to about three feet."

Not hardly. Rather, the man on the PGA tour who happens to be winning the most money in any given season usually carries along the unflattering distinction mentioned by Player: A one-putting s.o.b.

"Just go down the money list," Bob Goalby was saying in the 19th Hole. Goalby was a temperamental fellow who had tried out twenty-five different putters over the past two years. He'd give you a thought or two. "The guys who can putt are the guys who win money," Bob said. "There's nobody winning money who can't putt a little bit."

Gene Littler was with him, and the 1961 U.S. Open champion said he had to disagree with Goalby.

"Bob isn't a real good putter, and he wins his share," said Gene, a calm, pleasant gentleman with a fine, slow-motion swing. "I believe most of us divide up into two basic groups. There are the ones who are better players than they are putters, and those who are worse players than they are putters."

"And what is Gene Littler?"

"Oh, naturally, I'm a better player than I am a putter," Littler smiled.

To which Goalby said, "Gene's a great player, but, for Christ's sake, he's one of the all-time superputters."

Littler said, "You gotta be kidding."

Goalby said, "You can't putt, huh?"

"Not like we're talking about," said Gene.

And Goalby said, "Man, if you can't putt, then we all better pack it up."

Littler argued on. "There are only four superputters out here. Arnold Palmer, Bill Casper, Jerry Barber and Dow Finsterwald. Now, those guys can really putt."

"And Littler," said Goalby.

They were still threshing it out over their steak sandwiches when Jerry Barber came through the room. Barber could putt, all right. At Chicago's Olympia Fields during the 1961 PGA championship he holed putts of twenty, forty, and sixty feet, and practically in the dark at that, on the last three greens to tie Don January for the title. And he won the play-off with more of the same.

"Anyone who puts me on a list of great putters is drunk," said Barber, a studious little man, something of a health faddist. "There are three types of putters on the tour if you want the truth. Good, very good, and super. Nobody is awful, or he wouldn't be out here. I am very good, in the second division so to speak. I have to be. I've worked harder at it. Why? Because I can't drive the ball very far, and I can't play fairway woods. But I'll tell you. I'm no superputter like Arnold Palmer."

When Palmer was told what the verdict was about his putting he looked startled and hurt, as if Winnie had just asked him for a divorce. "Me?" he squeaked. "They must be crazy. Now I will have some good putting rounds, but I'll also have some bad ones—really bad. In 1960 I had some fantastic rounds, but I haven't putted that good since. When you talk about Barber, well, you can just put him way out there by himself. The rest of us are back here."

Arnold did confide, "Finsty's a good putter, day in and day

out. And Doug Ford. Follow Doug around for eighteen holes, and he'll show you something. Now I *will* say this. I don't think my good or bad streaks last as long as they do for most of the others. Casper is like that, too."

Billy Casper said he would modestly yield to Palmer as the game's greatest putter. Yes, yes, he knew he had been winning all of the awards as golf's best putter, the Putter of the Year, stuff like that, but that was wrong. That was a cliché. He was a fair putter, he said, but not brilliant. Palmer was brilliant. "I have my favorite distances and my favorite types of greens," Billy said, "but I go through periods lacking confidence. The reason Arnold is the best putter is because he makes more big ones that he *needs* than the rest of us. How else are you going to decide who's the best?"

By now one had to wonder about something. If the good putters weren't good putters, what and who were the truly bad putters? Several nominations came up among the pros for the worst putter: Tommy Bolt, Johnny Pott, Gardner Dickinson, Jay Hebert, Paul Harney and big George Bayer. Everyone agreed, pretty much, on this list. Right break, left break, no matter. These guys were just terrible on the greens. Pott would occasionally switch to a cross-handed style. Dickinson was in a state of spreading his legs far apart. Hebert and Harney were simply whip-dog, give up, no confidence. And poor Bayer, he knew he wasn't supposed to be able to putt because he was so big and so long off the tees—the Wilt Chamberlain of the tour. And then there was Bolt, that splendid shotmaker, the first and last angry man of golf.

With everyone Tommy ranked up there near Ben Hogan as a shotmaker, a guy who could "van Gogh it," as the pros say, off the fairways, but never, in any mangling of the imagination, was Bolt a decent putter. Worse than that, he continually blamed fate.

He would hit wonderful shots in wonderful streaks—as he surely did in 1958 at Tulsa's Southern Hills where he won the U.S. Open—but the outrage was always in him, ready to boil and explode. Tempestuous Tommy. Terrible-tempered Bolt. And nothing could make him explode like blowing a short putt. Once, the Bolt legend goes, he missed a short one that cost him a couple of thousand dollars and paused to talk it over with the Lord.

As the putt curled out of the hole Tommy wearily let the putter slide from his hands, grimaced severely and stared up at the sky. "Me again, huh?" he said. He stood there, squinting upward and boiling. And he spoke again. "Why don't you come down here and play *me!*" he said. "Come on, come on," Tom sighed. "You and your kid too. I'll give you two a side and play your low ball!"

Tommy, who often dressed as loudly as he swore, was pleased when told he had unofficially been voted one of the worst putters of the ages. "I'm glad they know *something,*" said Bolt. "Why do you think I'm using this kind of machine?" He displayed his putter, which was a lump of odd-shaped lead fastened to a shaft bending outward and down in a giant curve, like the stem of a maraschino cherry.

"That's so I can bend it when I get mad," Tommy winked. "They fine you a hundred, don't you see, if you break a club. This way I can just bend it a little."

"You're *not* a very good putter."

"If I could putt they could all go to the cabin," Bolt said. "All these little dudes out here runnin' around wearin' their Ben Hogan blues and grays, they could hang it right up if old Tom could putt a lick."

"That's right."

"You'd better believe *that,* pal," Tommy said.

"Of course, of course."

Bolt sauntered off a few paces, turned around and called back.

"Tell 'em how it is," he said. "And, hey. That list you got there of bad putters. You can take 'em all off there except me, old buddy."

I was standing around thinking about what great copy Bolt

always was when Gardner Dickinson came along. Poor Gardner. Wasn't he the one who had begun to putt with a wide, stiff-leg stance, looking something like a flamingo with arthritis? And wasn't that embarrassing for him?

Gardner said, "Hell, I'd putt sitting up in a coffin if I thought I could hole something."

Some players say you aren't that bad a putter, he was informed.

"Anybody who says I can putt is more of a cage case than I am," he said. "You better lock them straight up."

"It was Goalby, or somebody, who said you get stoop-shouldered sometimes taking the ball out of the cup."

Dickinson said, "Goalby? *Goalby?*"

"Uh, I think, yeah."

"Man, that's really something, that is," Dickinson said. "Well, you can put this down. There's *no way* I can putt as good as him, or a lot of others. My trouble is, I found out when I was fourteen years old that every putt doesn't have to go in the hole. Palmer and Goalby and some others haven't figured that out yet."

As for his weird stance, he went into theory. "You want to hit the ball square," Gardner said. "Get it rolling good toward the hole—and then pray. This wide stance looks like it might keep me honest. Keep me from moving on the putt. I'm looking for that immovable position that Palmer's got."

Hitting the ball square sounded good, but it only took a few moments to find a pro who said it was impossible and that Gardner Dickinson might as well go searching for the Dead Sea Scrolls.

"It's not humanly possible to hit the ball squarely every time," said Earl Stewart, Jr., who was more of a teaching pro now than a touring pro. "I think everybody takes it back a little differently every time—a little inside or a little outside. The thing you got to avoid is the old freeze. Lockwrist, we call it."

Lockwrist?

"You betcha," said Earl. "You don't want to take it back because you're afraid you'll miss it. That's lockwrist."

Golf is played by a bunch of *cage cases* trying to avoid *lockwrist*. Beautiful.

"It's mental," Stewart was saying. "But sometimes it's fatal. Why, it finally forced Byron Nelson off the tour when he was only thirty-four, when he probably had several good years left. He'll tell you that."

He did. "Putting affects the nerves more than anything," Byron said. "I would actually get nauseated over three-footers during my prime. And there were tournaments when I couldn't keep a meal down for four days. Missing a short putt is about the most humiliating thing in the world because you're supposed to make it."

Nelson remembered that Clayton Heafner, a big, burly man from North Carolina who was a tour name in the 1930's and 40's, so detested putting as part of golf that he used to tell his fellow pros of a great ambition. It was to come down to the final hole of the U.S. Open championship and have a one-foot putt—a gimme—to capture the biggest, most important prize in the sport. Heafner then wanted to take several moments, lining up the putt while the gallery stood frozen and hushed. Finally, he wanted to walk up to the ball, gaze down at it, then haul off and backhand it as hard as he could, knocking it off the green and into the stunned crowd, saying, "To hell with this crummy, rotten game."

Byron said that this golfing disease, lockwrist, could get to anyone, that it had finally got to Hogan, apparently, and that it would eventually get to Arnold Palmer, but it might take longer for him. Palmer's technique of staying motionless over a putt, solid as a statue, was envied by all. "You notice when he addresses the putt, pigeon-toed and knees pinched together, nothing moves but the hands and forearms," said Nelson. "That's the secret."

All good putters have something in common, Byron added.

They have a slow backstroke and they get a definite rap on the ball.

Jerry Barber said as much. "What you're doing when you putt is calling on all the years of experience and practice. You're concentrating and you're confident. When you hole a long one it's because you have a putter heavy enough to get the ball to the cup, you've stroked it nicely enough to give it good roll, you know the line—and you believe in the first place that you can make it," he said.

From any distance?

"Somewhere in there skill stops and luck takes over," Barber said. "The scoring range is probably from fifteen feet in. Anything outside that is plenty of luck."

Barber said, "We tend to get embarrassed, you know, if we hole very many putts of any length. There's so much talk about tee-to-green play, it's gotten to where you have to apologize for making a putt. I think that's silly." Barber noted that Arnold Palmer never apologized for making anything, the reason being that Arnold thinks he *deserves* everything that goes in. "He's *stared* the ball into the hole when he needed it a couple of times at the Masters," Jerry said.

For all of his confidence, it was well-known that Palmer spent hours every week in a golf shop, fooling with his putter—changing the grip, bending the shaft, weighting the head, unweighting the head, filing, chiseling, nailing—and doctoring the rest of his clubs as well. A lot of people wondered why. It did seem that Palmer changing his golf clubs was a little like Liz Taylor getting plastic surgery regularly, just for laughs. What are you doing in the pro shop with that club sticking in a vise, Arnold?

"When you putt poorly you think you ought to change putters," Arnold said. "But I can't find another one I like. So I do some work on the one I've got. I could possibly leave it alone and the stroke would come back, but all I'd do in the meantime is worry. At least working on the clubs keeps me busy and helps me think I'm doing something to correct the situation."

The Palmer putter, which up to this point in his career had won him three Masters championships, the U.S. Open, two British Opens, the U.S. Amateur and a caddy shed full of lesser tournaments, was an old Tommy Armour model, the one with the rear shaft and slight gooseneck. "The shaft is so weak I can actually bend it with my hands. I've got a nail driven through the head of it. It's been weighted and re-weighted a hundred times, I guess. I've tried a lot of others, but I always come back to this one," Arnold said.

Palmer isn't the first player to stay with one putter. Bobby Jones used Calamity Jane, so named by O. B. Keeler, the writer, a thin blade putter, throughout his career. It was a good weapon for the fast, slick greens Jones always found in the major championships. Ben Hogan also used the same putter to win all of his big titles. His was a handmade invention, a brass-headed, center-shafted relic, actually carved from a doorknob. Hogan got it from a fellow pro, Ky Laffoon, in his youthful days on the tour. I once asked Ben if he intended presenting the club to Golf House, the USGA museum, when he seriously retired, and he said, without sentiment, "I don't know where it is. It was stolen, I think."

Something else was stolen from Hogan by the years: his nerves. But only on the greens was it evident. As late as 1960, when he was forty-eight years old, Hogan still reached more greens in regulation than any competitor in the U.S. Open championship. He could still hit the shots, and still can, for that matter, but as fewer and fewer putts found the hole, Ben's attitude toward the game changed.

It was before the 1961 Open at Oakland Hills near De-troit—the Open Gene Littler won—that Hogan originated an interesting game for those who companioned him in practice rounds. Littler was among them. "You didn't count putts, or the score on a hole," said Gene. "You got a point for hitting a fairway, a point for hitting a green, and a point for getting closest to the pin. He won, of course."

The practice game was not the result of Hogan never being able to sink a putt. He had made some in his day; indeed, anyone who could win five U.S. Opens (counting an unofficial one during the war in 1942), two Masters, two PGA championships and the British Open—ten major championships in all—could, of course, putt. But now in these later years he couldn't, so he made up games and enjoyed holding court in the locker rooms with other players and with writers, discussing that abominable aspect of golf.

"Hitting a golf ball and putting have nothing in common," said Ben, after a round at Oakland Hills in '61. "They are two different games. You work all of your life to perfect a repeating swing that will get you to the greens, and then you have to try to do something that is totally unrelated. There shouldn't be any cups, just flag sticks. And then the man who hit the most fairways and green and got closest to the pins would be tournament winner."

Him.

Well, Hogan could have his intriguing games and theories. There were other cage cases on the tour who were far more desperate because of putting ills, it seemed to me.

Bob Shave, Jr., was one to consider. He was on and off the circuit, using a putter with a shaft adjoining the clubhead at the nose rather than in the center or at the heel. The grand design: force himself to strike the putt harder. Shave also liked to keep a portable radio playing near him when he practiced on the putting green. Soft music, smooth stroke. Bob Duden was another. Duden, in his never-ending quest for hitting the putt squarely, went to a croquet style, putting between his legs with a club that vaguely resembled an apple pie on a pogo stick. Freddie Haas was still gripping the club cross-handed and Johnny Pott was trying it. And Sam Snead, of all people, would occasionally separate his hands on the grip by as much as six or eight inches, or, at times, slip his right hand down the shaft to within about a foot of the clubhead, then bend way over and attempt to sort of sweep the short ones into the hole. And Doug Sanders, without resorting to any wild methods, was simply mumbling incessantly about the fact that if he could have sunk one more putt per week—of any distance—the previous year, it would have increased his bankroll by $20,000. Hogan was far from alone.

Men have always had trouble putting on the tour, of course. It was Joe Turnesa of the golfing Turnesas who once won a tournament on Long Island by throwing away his standard-size putter and using one with only a foot and a half shaft and stroking the ball from a low crouch. It was Leo Diegel who originated the style of pointing both elbows out in opposite directions and putting as if he were doing the Suzy-Q. Diegel, a fine putter, eventually wound up putting left-handed because he suffered slow-creeping lockwrist. And it was Ky Laffoon, an early-day Tommy Bolt in terms of temper, who used to open a moving car door and drag his putter along the road to punish it. Laffoon, in fact, who would begin to stutter in his anger, once grabbed his putter by the neck, raced to a water hazard, held it under and raved, "D-drown, y-you, d-dirty, b-bastard."

It is difficult to say whether Cary Middlecoff ever was afflicted by lockwrist or not—whether that was the reason he went into semi-retirement at so early an age. Cary, a splendid champion, was forever a slow player, refusing to strike the ball or a putt until he was absolutely ready. A joke on the tour used to be that Cary gave up dentistry because no patient could hold his mouth open that long.

"I never had any idea I was taking a long time," Middlecoff confessed. "You just don't realize it, especially when you're out there romancing with the high seventies. That's a struggle, believe me. I'm more and more convinced that putting is plain luck. You could take a machine that would stroke the ball exactly the same way every time, feed it ten balls to putt over the same line from about six feet away, and I'll guarantee you the machine would be lucky to make six of them. Too many things can happen to the ball after it leaves the clubhead. The tiniest thing, sun, wind, grass, anything, can move it off line. I've putted poorly and holed everything. And I've stroked it good and missed everything."

A few players share the opinion that putting is entirely mental and that, therefore, one should always think positively on the greens. Don January said it best. "A lot of guys are afraid to make a putt. By that I mean they're afraid to win a tournament, especially a big one. I try to tell myself all the time that I'm a good putter. I try to psych myself into believing I can make anything. But most of us, we like to bleed about putting badly and hope that a good streak will sneak up on us. It's all superstition, I suppose."

January went on, "Some fellows are afraid that if they talk about their putting the touch will go away. So they think the best thing is to moan about it even when they're putting good. One thing is very true. The better you putt, the bolder you play."

But doesn't that work in reverse as well?

"Of course," January said. "You putt bad, you get afraid to take chances. And you start worrying about your quota. You're apt to think: I've made two long ones already today. I know they won't give me another one, so I'd better lay up this time or I'll three-putt. This leads to other distractions. You start lining up putts and you find yourself staring at people across the green. Your concentration is gone."

When a pro starts watching fans in red shirts or ladies in short skirts or a passing jet overhead or the swallows going home to Capistrano his putter may be near the "crystallizing" point. Here is another tour expression. When a putter crystallizes it breaks in half. Hammering it against a tree trunk can speed up the process, needless to say.

Some players have almost crystallized their heads in anger over their putting. Such a man was Ivan Gantz, a man who never quite made it on the tour.

"The first time I ever saw Ivan," January said, "he was walking down a fairway parallel to mine. I hadn't been on the tour long, and when I saw Ivan I thought, 'Hold it, man, this is back in the cat games in Dallas.' Blood was streaming down his forehead over his nose. The man had hit himself in the head with his putter because he'd blown a short one."

January said he'd heard tales of Ivan Gantz leaping face first into a bunker because of a missed putt, of Ivan diving into creeks, of Ivan banging his head with a stone and of Ivan rolling and tossing in the grass. The pros laugh about Ivan Gantz, but they understand the fury that consumed him.

Nor is anger the only reaction to a case of lockwrist. Any pro can recite with warm relish the story of the man who had so much trouble putting he often visualized animals running across a green just as he got ready to tap the ball. One day he came down to the last hole with a chance to win a tournament. But as he prepared to putt a dog ran onto the green, the way a dog somehow always manages to run onto a football field at half time. The golfer just stood there, agonizing in fear, and presently he turned to his playing companion and asked, "Was that a real dog?"

For all of the pain that the pros seem to suffer on the putting surfaces, the good ones can still tell you how it's done, technically.

"Just get comfortable," said Billy Casper. "Then stroke the putt the best way you know how. Don't try to copy anyone else, unless of course you're doing something drastically wrong, like aiming a foot off line or something."

"Get a club that feels right to *you*," said Jack Burke. "Keep your head down, take the putter back slowly, and don't worry about where it's going after you stroke it."

"Stay down and don't move," Arnold Palmer said. "Get a

positive stance, a firm position, and be sure you're getting a good, solid rap on the ball."

"Just concentrate on the line and the speed and have confidence that it'll go in," said Jerry Barber.

And do all of these things work, all of them together, with a blade, a mallet, a centershaft, a gooseneck, with any putter you pick up? The club doesn't matter?

"I'll tell you what," said Bob Rosburg, a fast player and a good putter whose theory, mainly, is to hit the putt before it hits you. "You change clubs all you want, but you'll wind up like a guy I knew in Miami. There was a grab barrel in the pro shop. You threw your putter in if you didn't like it and took out another one, giving the pro five dollars. This guy kept doing it through eighteen putters and ninety dollars. He finally got his old one back."

Rosburg, a fairly cynical man, said, "I'll tell you why putts go in. Because the old National Open champion in the sky puts 'em in. How about this? Bud Holscher is paired with Bolt one day in Vegas, and he's been holing out from everywhere all day. Finally he comes to the last green, and he's got a two-footer. He stands there with his putter under his arm, tryin' to get in his pocket for a coin to mark his ball. He gets all tangled up, the club falls, hits the ball and knocks it right in."

"So if you're destined to make a putt, you're destined to make it, is that it?" I said.

"Pretty much," said Rosburg.

"And then from tee to green, does the old National Open champion in the sky ever hit any shots for you?"

Rosburg grinned, "Last I heard he was shanking."

Sam Snead
with Hair

Louise, we've got to hide this $600 before we hit the road. Since we're rich, we're bound to get robbed. But if we hide it, maybe they won't get it all.

—BYRON NELSON
to his wife after winning his first
big check in the Thirties

To the hordes of people who feel that Arnold Palmer invented golf on television around, oh, 1960, and who no doubt think the game is played over just four holes, from the 15th—where Jim McKay is—through the 18th—where Chris Schenkel is—the professional tour probably looks colorful today. Sure it does. After all, there goes Arnold again, streaking back to Latrobe for the evening in his twin-booster, partly deductible rocket ship *PGA One*. And there is Billy Casper eating baked buffalo tongue, or sea-lentil casserole, or whatever, for his diet and allergies. And there's Doug Sanders in his latest lemon-lime ensemble, a cluster of bell-bottomed lovelies foraging after him. And here comes Lionel Hebert on his way to the cocktail lounge to work his handicap down from eight to six on the trumpet. Jack Nicklaus isn't around this week, they say. He's off in Addis Ababa filming a TV series with the President of the United States, the Soviet Premier, the Sheik of Kuwait and eight former fraternity brothers from Ohio State. But all he does is win anyhow. This tour is splashed with color without him, boy. You look down that list of entries in our $500,000 Lucky Desert Cajun Festival and you'll see more excitement than the linoleum salesmen caused when the waiter brought the dinner check.

Well, perhaps not to some of us. The Sixties had their giddy moments, of course, give or take a Julius Finsteraaron. But there is another period in the history of golf that keeps coming back to haunt those who remember the cleek with a certain fondness. The Thirties. Maybe you have to be a little overaged for the discotheques to appreciate that decade. It would help if you could remember who Uncle Fletcher was on *Vic and Sade,* or if you could still set *One Man's Family* defensively: Paul's in the library, Clifford and Claudia are down on the seawall and Hank and Pinky are up at the Sky Ranch, right? If you can handle that and also identify a Russ Columbo, a Filipino Twirler, a black cow, a Ken Maynard, a sinking of the *Panay* and a Ky Laffoon—well, then. You certainly know that anyone who thinks the pro tour is fun now would have gone right out of his Spalding Dot in the Thirties.

For it was the Thirties that gave us Sam Snead with hair, right there on his head, parted on the left, and a brooding runt in a snapbrim hat and a wild hook: Ben Hogan. It was the Thirties that gave us Jimmy Demaret's pink shoes and polka-dot slacks—outfits that would make Doug Sanders look like a Bond's window today. It was the Thirties that gave us Lloyd Mangrum's mustache, Dutch Harrison's drawl, and Ky Laffoon anointing the greens with tobacco juice. It was the Thirties that gave us Byron Nelson throwing up between his dazzling rounds, Jug McSpaden's sun goggles, Horton Smith's ominous squint, Jimmy Thomson's booming tee shots, the sand wedge and steel shafts. It was an era in which Ruby Keeler and Dick Powell in their starched sailor suits couldn't do the Big Apple much better than Joan and Paul Runyon, or Emma and Harry Cooper, or Mabel and Frank Walsh. It was a decade with more individuals in professional golf than there were hominy wagons on the streets. And if the pro couldn't make the most of the spirit and hilarity of these struggling times, and if the fan couldn't enjoy them, then the pro could go back to raking cottonseed-hull greens, and the fan could go back to his radio serials.

One of the things that made it special is that golf, looking back on it, still belonged to the amateurs in the early Thirties, to aristocratic young men with hyphenated names, blonde sisters and portraits of whaling skippers over their fireplaces. A pro was anyone who had caddied beyond the age of fourteen, who knew how to run a mowing machine, who could wrap leather grips and who frequently had to take his meals in the kitchen of a country club. If he happened to be personable and didn't look *too* Italian, he might be very fortunate. He could give a few fifty-cent lessons each week to some kindly gentleman who owned a railroad or the state of New Jersey. Or if the pro looked like he could really play, a kindly gentleman might lend him $300 to go out and see what this tour was all about, what those chaps Tommy Hagen and Walter Armour were up to.

The exact date is not recorded when people first realized that a pro could make a niblick back up with more spin than an amateur, but it occurred somewhere in the Thirties. At about the same time Walter Hagen was finally about to convince everyone that you could let a pro in the front door of your club and he wouldn't steal the crystal. Hagen had been working at it for a long time—outdressing, outspending and out-traveling the rich. These two circumstances began to combine in the years of the Depression, and this is what actually led America into today's age of the alligator shoe. This was the beginning of the big-money tour that has put Conni Venturi in Balenciagas, made Dave Marr a bon vivant along 52nd Street, transformed Arnold Palmer into a permanent, floating, corporate crap game and made a worldly, theorizing, hard-cover author out of every ex-caddy who can chip from sand.

One of the more obvious results of this progress is that going on the tour now is as easy as getting into the University

of Houston if you can shoot 65. You birdie four holes in a
row at Bending Wedge Country Club and some automobile
dealer with a coat of arms on his blazer will step up and hand
you $12,000, plus an air travel card. A day later, you're
standing on a putting green near Bert Yancey. You're on the
tour. To say it was somewhat more of an adventure in the
Thirties would be like saying Valerie Hogan has seen a clubhouse veranda or two.

You could get to the tour, all right, by hitchhiking or
riding a freight if necessary. But to *stay* there, that was the
challenge. To put enough chuckburgers down your neck to
fend off the hunger from Flagstaff to West Palm. If you shot
a 74 in the first round somewhere, forget it. Fifteenth place
was the last pay spot in any tournament, and of the thirty to
forty regulars who were out there trying to beat you Ben Hogan
was the least known. "We used to figure $160 a week was the
break-even figure," Byron Nelson remembers. So if you shot
74 you loaded it and yourself into somebody's Graham-Paige
or Essex and drove until the connecting rod made a double
bogey. Air travel? That was fantasy, something you saw in
the movies for a dime. Air travel was for Noah Beery, Jr., up
there flying the mail in the sleet without any de-icers, while
Jean Rogers wept softly in the control tower.

The tour began in Los Angeles, just as it does today, but
little else is similar. There was none of this three hundred
guys teeing off on both nines of a public course, everybody
trying to finish a nervy twenty-ninth. The L.A. Open was
held at the class clubs, Riviera, L.A., Lakeside. Nor were the
players scattered everywhere from the Polo Lounge at the Beverly Hills to the cheapest motel in Santa Monica. Everyone
piled into the Hollywood Plaza for a dollar a day, single, or
five dollars a day for a suite, the hotel providing a whole private
floor for the competitors. And at night the established stars
congregated at Musso Franks, or the Brown Derby, or Clara
Bow's It Cafe, to drink with Richard Arlen, Clark Gable,
Randolph Scott, the serious golfers of Hollywood who also

entered the tournament. There, they contemplated the happy fact that L.A. offered the biggest purse on the tour. First place was worth $3500, and that, for example, was five pay windows higher than the U.S. Open.

L.A. also lured the largest galleries of the year, crowds sparkling with movie celebrities and rising starlets. There were so many one year, in fact, that Dick Metz had to park two miles from the course before the second round and buy a ticket to get in. This would not have been so embarrassing for the sponsors if Metz hadn't been leading the tournament at the time.

"We knew everybody in Hollywood," says Jimmy Demaret. "It was pretty impressive to be hanging around Bing Crosby and folks like that all the time. And there were an awful lot of dandy little old gals around. We didn't know who they were. They had different names then. But we realized later that they were Susan Hayward and that kind of thing."

The tour might stay on the Coast for a month. It would go from L.A. to a Riverside Open, where the players would stuff their golf bags with fruit from the citrus trees in the rough, or it might go to a Pasadena Open, where they scooped niblicks around the Rose Bowl. It might go to an Agua Caliente Open. And one they certainly didn't miss was the Bing Crosby Pro-Am at Rancho Santa Fe, which was only thirty-six holes. It would also head north to a weird thing called the San Francisco Match Play championship. The pros would get into the Sir Francis Drake Hotel, dine at Vanessi's and Nujoe's with a wealthy host and work up the pairings in the locker room. "You figured out who you thought you could beat and challenged him," Demaret says. "And you hoped you didn't get Leonard Dodson because he'd pay a guy to follow you around with a camera and click it on your backswing."

After the flamboyant times on the Coast, fan belts permitting, the tour moved lazily through the Southwest, the South, the

East and the Midwest, until, quite sensibly, it came to a dawdling end as football season began. It embraced a variety of tournaments, many of which sounded as if they ought to be on a billiard circuit, namely, the Miami-Biltmore Four-Ball, the Goodall Round Robin, the Westchester 108-Hole Open, the Dapper Dan and the Vancouver Jubilee.

It was not always easy getting from one place to another. Hogan and Nelson would be more intent on reaching a destination than some of the others because they wanted to practice. They would form a mini-motorcade, Byron and Louise following Ben and Valerie, and dart for shortcuts like Bonnie and Clyde. "Ben wanted to get there and start hittin' golf balls," Demaret says, with a slight trace of bewilderment. "Nobody ever practiced. First guy I ever saw do it was Bobby Cruickshank, about 1932. I didn't know what he was up to. But Ben *really* practiced. I'm sure he invented this business of spending two and three hours hitting balls."

Demaret, of course, would be late because he would still be throwing a party from the previous week. And Lloyd Mangrum, with Buck White or Leonard Dodson, would have found a card game—seven-card low, pitch, auction bridge, casino—while Sam Snead would have to sit around and wait for them in the car. Johnny Bulla's car. "For a while, we traveled in Bulla's Ford sedan. Can you imagine anyone loaning Lloyd Mangrum, Sam Snead and Buck White his car?" Mangrum says. Some cars made the next stop easily, like Walter Hagen's front-wheel drive Cord, or Denny Shute's Graham-Paige. But others didn't. Johnny Revolta has vivid memories of a fan belt going out somewhere in the infinity of a Texas horizon. His companion at the time, Henry Picard, sat in the car and held his head while Revolta hiked twelve miles, got rescued by a Mexican family, finally found a belt to fit and, six hours later, returned.

This would have been on the way to San Antonio for the Texas Open, the oldest of the winter events (1922). The tournament was distinctive for a number of reasons, not the least of which was that it was usually played among the willows and pecans of Brackenridge Park, a short, tight little public course featuring rubber mats for teeing areas. It was on this course that the most headlined practice round of the era was played one year. In a group with Hogan, Nelson and Paul Runyan, the easy-going Jug McSpaden, wearing sun goggles as always and putting with a mallethead, shot a stunning 59. The round was accented by the fact that Nelson had a 63, Hogan a 66 and Runyan a 71. And it was also at Brackenridge Park one year that Wild Bill Melhorn, who made most of his expenses at the bridge tables, finished with a seventy-two-hole score that looked as if it might win, provided Bobby Cruickshank didn't par the last hole. Melhorn climbed a live oak and tried to heckle Cruickshank into a three-putt on the 18th, but when Bobby survived, Melhorn toppled off the branch and into the crowd, without backspin.

From San Antonio, the tour normally frolicked onward to New Orleans, which was both a good and bad town for a riverboat gambler like Lloyd Mangrum. He once arrived on Mardi Gras Eve with the town so crowded—and himself so busted—that he joyfully bunked in the city jail for two days. "The only hard part was going without cigarettes," says Mangrum. "Try that course sometime."

Mangrum went on the tour with a $250 stake he got from John Boles, the singer. Cards kept him on it when his golf didn't. "I never won as much as everybody thought at the card tables," he says. "But the first time I ever got enough money to afford it, I bought me a big LaSalle with a couple of four-foot chrome horns on the front fenders, and folks thought I was rich." Stories would spread on him. And grow. When he won $4000 at gin rummy in Arizona it would be $25,000 by the time it reached Toots Shor's in New York. "The public thought you got thousands from the club companies," he says. "But all I know is I thought it was a big lick to get $300 and some clubs and balls out of MacGregor."

There was usually a way to get something out of somebody.

If Mangrum couldn't do it with cards, Leonard Dodson would think of something else. "We're in Niagara Falls, I think it was," says Lloyd, "and I've got about $1.35 and Dodson's got $1.25. Together we can't buy enough gas to get half-way where we're going. So Dodson scares up this Canadian millionaire and bets him $500 he can outrun his automobile at 100 yards. Now we can't get $500 up if we rob everybody on the tour, and I don't think Dodson can outrun me if I got a heart attack. But Leonard takes the guy out in the country to an old dusty farm road where the tires can't get any traction in the deep soft sand, and damned if Leonard doesn't win the race on his start."

The tour had its elegant stopovers where the foolishness gave way to a more formal atmosphere. Pinehurst was one, the North and South Open was held. You had to have a tux and your wife needed a gown for dinner or it was off to a roadhouse for pork and beans. The same was true at the Masters when everyone stayed at the old Bon Air Hotel and went to millionaire Bill Wallace's ante-bellum mansion for ham cooked in wine, biscuits, barbecue and corn whiskey in a pitcher. There was also the fanciness of Palm Beach—golf amid the lockjaw accents—a place where Paul Runyan had a fascinating partner in the Seminole Pro-Am one winter.

"He drove three hundred and ten yards off the first tee and hit his approach about eighteen inches of the flag," says Runyan. "Now, I'm thinking to myself, we've got this thing all wrapped up. Nobody told me this guy could play like that." But then Runyan's partner took out the putter and tapped his gimme roughly eighteen feet past the hole with all of the gifted feel of a coal miner. His name: Gene Tunney.

It was in Florida that the pros first began to suspicion that they might be semi-celebrities—and all because of the Miami-Biltmore Four-Ball. This was a partnership tournament sponsored by a hotel, which guessed correctly that a lot of sports-page stories with the word Biltmore in them could give ideas to tourists. The Four-Ball tournament also invented "appearance money," for it paid the current U.S. Open and National PGA champions $1000 each to show up, as if they had somewhere else to go. Promoters were everywhere. Each birdie scored won a bottle of White Horse Scotch for a player plus a tin of Lucky Strikes. Daily, for those willing, players and wives were hoisted by autogyros over to Miami Beach for a swim. Occasionally, when the sponsors grew lax at providing entertainment, some of the players would take over. Such as the evening that Walter Hagen and Joe Kirkwood came back from fishing in the Everglades and dumped their entire catch in the hotel lobby, including an alligator.

Early in the Thirties not much was made of the identity between a pro and the club where he spent at least part of his summer or winter teaching. Ben Hogan would later make this a profitable thing through his connection with the Hershey Country Club in Pennsylvania. But before that only a few of the stars were closely associated with certain clubs—Vic Ghezzi with Deal, New Jersey, Craig Wood at Winged Foot, Tommy Armour at Medinah and Sam Snead at Greenbrier, to list a few. Being dragged to his first promotional breakfast by the tour manager, Fred Corcoran, back in '37, Snead told Corcoran, who became Sam's manager as well, "Would you mention that I'm from Greenbrier? Those folks pay me a nice $45 a month to say so."

The Miami Four-Ball, being publicity-conscious, helped promote the clubs to which many of the pros were attached, and it also helped to convey the idea, through its partnership format, that there were certain cliques and friendships on the tour. Hogan and Demaret were nearly always partners, for instance, as were Nelson and McSpaden, Snead and Ralph Guldahl, Horton Smith and Paul Runyan, Johnny Revolta and Henry Picard. The teams, few realized at the time, were mostly formed by the club manufacturers.

As the tour moved through the South the players would note from time to time the emergence of a strange, squealing species that came to be known—Denny Shute is credited with the name—as "Sammy's Lambies." These were the crowds that traipsed after Snead, a pre-war Arnie's Army, so to speak. The South was quail and wild turkey country as well, and part of the fun of the Thomasville, Georgia, Open was being permitted to shoot as much game in the fields and thickets as you could between rounds, no limit.

Trying to cook quail and turkey gave the wives something to do besides compare verandas. Hettie and Denny Shute liked to think that the wives broke up into three categories, and they named them: ramblers, setters and shadows. The ramblers walked about the course, chose vantage points, and viewed the tournament distantly, sunning, gossiping and getting exercise. The setters were generally older and clung to the porches or lawns with their embroidery or played cards or pondered the possibility of getting a permanent wave like Carole Lombard's. The shadows never left their husbands. They tied bandannas on their heads and did the full eighteen holes, shot for shot.

Potential sponsors for all of these tournaments were mostly where Fred Corcoran could find them, and they came in all shapes and sizes and bankrolls. A sponsor was usually the first to leap in front of a camera, putting his arm around a Snead, a Hogan or a Nelson, buddy-buddy. But not all of them were like that in Corcoran's day. There was this one gentleman, quite amiable, who put up a good portion of cash for the 108-hole Westchester Classic in 1938. Except no photographs, please. Corcoran himself had to present Snead with the victory check so the sponsor could hide from the press. Four years later everyone discovered why. The gentleman was convicted of printing bogus whiskey labels. And no one has yet, to anyone's knowledge, tracked down one of the sponsors of the Indianapolis Open of 1935. It took Al Espinosa, the winner, three years to get his thousand dollars prize money from the PGA because the Indianapolis fellow skipped town with the purse.

In all there were no more than twenty-five tournaments

a year, compared to forty-five today. If the total prize money added up to $150,000, that was sensational. It looked as good as the $5.5 million of 1968. And a player in the Thirties knew that if he could reach most of those tournaments, if he could attach the clubheads, which were made in Scotland, to the shafts, that were made in Tennessee, if he could assemble a set he liked, and if he could survive the card games and the parties and the fan belts, he could bank as much as $6000 for the year and rate as high as fifth on the money list.

Of course if he *practiced*—that odd ritual Ben Hogan originated—hitting old balls into a vacant lot for Stepin Fetchit to pick up, there was no saying how affluent he could become. It could lead to victories, which could lead to exhibitions, which could lead to club affiliations and on and on, conceivably into movie contracts. A man might become good enough to make some of those marvelously plotted instructional shorts, like Bobby Jones did with W. C. Fields or Buddy Rogers. ("Say, Bobby, since my car seems to have broken down right here by the golf course, how about a tip on playing the mashie-niblick?") It might even help a man get one of those incredible deals that Johnny Farrell had: smiling and holding a pack of cigarettes on the back cover of a magazine. Farrell got $1000 for that, somebody said.

Sam Snead saw the ad one day and took it to Fred Corcoran, his agent.

"What they call that there?" Sam asked.

"That's an endorsement," said Fred.

"How come you don't git me some of those?" Sam said.

"You don't smoke," Corcoran explained.

Snead thought for a moment and said, "Reckon them folks know that?"

Winning had been outrageously simple for Snead. His big, graceful, natural swing and his hillbilly personality made him an instant star, and Corcoran sold him well. Almost oversold him, in fact. Snead had no sooner begun to earn money on the tour when reporters were phoning Corcoran long distance to ask if this West Virginia guy was real. "He has the finest swing since Jones," Fred would reply. And a few days later Corcoran would see a headline proclaiming: SNEAD PICKED TO WIN US OPEN. That, of course, was something Snead never did, although he gained a negative fame for coming close.

While it was never a problem for Snead, winning that first pro tournament is still, even today, one of the most difficult things for a young player, regardless of how talented he may be. Byron Nelson's baptism in the hazards of near victory makes one of golf's better horror stories. Unknown and unsure, thin, young, broke, nervous, married, armed only with a good, quick, upright swing, Nelson learned the hard way. He was playing along in the General Brock Open at Niagara Falls when, suddenly, at the end of the third round he was the leader.

On Sunday morning it took Nelson a while to adjust to the headlines in the papers. That was Byron Nelson they were talking about. Guy from Fort Worth. Then he looked closer at the stories, at the pairings for the last round. Good God. He was paired with Walter Hagen. He turned to his wife, Louise, and in something akin to a death rattle, he broke the news.

"I, uh, I have to play with, uh, Hagen today," he said, as if to apologize for the 88 he was bound to shoot and the no-money they would leave with.

Now in a situation like that a pro got to the course early, and Nelson did. He chipped awhile, putted awhile and worried awhile. He blushed a lot and hung his head and hid and kept checking to see if his trousers were buttoned. Finally it was time to tee off, but Walter Hagen, naturally, had not arrived yet. "Looks like Mr. Hagen is late again," sighed the starter, unconcerned.

"Late?" Nelson said. Of course. Late was part of it then, what a real pro did to a rookie without penalty or disqualification; in fact, what Hagen usually did to everybody. Didn't he once send to the clubhouse for a folding chair so that Gene Sarazen, the man who introduced the sand iron and steel shafts, could sit down and rest while he, that cunning Hagen, studied a simple chip shot? Wasn't it Hagen who liked to psych guys out by strolling over to their bags, peeking in at their clubs, shaking his head mournfully and walking away? Others, like Horton Smith, just squinted peculiarly at the rookies until the sad young men worked themselves into incurable hooks. And still others, like Dutch Harrison, would sweet-talk a rookie out of his game. "Man, can you massage that ball," Dutch would say. "I ain't seen a swing that good since Mac Smith." But prince of the Slow Plays, that was Hagen.

And so it went for Nelson, the starter telling him, "Go ahead and tee off with Willie Goggin, Byron, or with Ed Dudley. We'll pair Mr. Hagen with someone else when he arrives."

"But Walter Hagen's my idol. I've wanted to play golf with him all my life," Byron said, torn between high privilege and dire necessity.

"Well, we're very sorry."

"But I'm leading the tournament," Nelson said.

"Yes, we know."

Nelson practiced some more and paced and sat and paced and putted, his slacks ballooning in the Niagara breeze like the Graf Zeppelin, his wide-bottomed tie whipping past the curled-up collar tips of his dollar-nineteen shirt and on around his neck.

Fidget, pace, putt, stroll, throw up went Nelson until, thanks a million, two hours later along came Hagen in his white-on-white silk shirt, his gold cuff links and more oil on his hair than they were pumping out of the East Texas fields.

"Hi, boy," he said.

"It's—it's a real big honor," said Nelson in a trance, a

trance he did not recover from until forty-two strokes later on the front nine holes.

The disaster was not total. Nelson somehow rallied himself, shot a 35 on the back for a 77 and salvaged second place in the tournament. He won $600, which was almost as much money as Andrew Mellon had, he thought.

"Louise, we've got to hide this $600 before we hit the road. Since we're rich, we're bound to get robbed. And if we hide it, maybe they won't get it all," Byron told his wife. She agreed. So $50 went in the glove compartment, $100 in the suitcases, some more in the purse, some in the pockets, a little more under the seats, until it was neatly put away where the Dillinger mob would never find it. As a matter of fact, it took the Nelson mob a couple of hours to find it all when they reached a motel down the road.

If Jimmy Demaret had won the money he would have been 8 to 5 to leave it in a bar or blow it on a handmade pair of orange and purple saddle oxfords. The man who singlehandedly led golfers out of neckties and into knit shirts had little trouble getting rid of money. On the contrary, Demaret's problem was that he destroyed it with the same ease of the wealthy people he loafed with.

When Demaret left his native Houston to become a tour rookie in 1935 he had a set of clubs, a car and $600 loaned to him by Sam Maceo, a Galveston nightclub operator, D. B. McDaniel, an oilman, and Ben Bernie, the bandleader. He also had the fervent hope that he could drive through Juarez without stopping. But no such luck. All it took to nearly ruin him during what he hoped would be a brief stopover was for a man to ask him a question.

"Hey, señor, you want to shoot a leetle pool?" the man asked.

Demaret lost the car the first day, the clubs the second and the $600 the third. The only reason he didn't lose the River Oaks Country Club of Houston was because nobody in Juarez would take an IOU for it. The only thing he did right was save the pawn slip for the clubs so his brother, Milton, could retrieve them and ship them to the West Coast where Demaret hoped to wind up on the freight train he boarded.

Jimmy got there, and he did squirm through the first couple of weeks on a diet of sandwiches and muscatel. But as destiny often ordains for free spirits, especially if they can fade a high two-iron, he cashed in for a few hundred the third week, and Demaret has been throwing a party ever since.

From almost the instant he arrived Demaret's quipping nature, his friendliness and his passion for clothes that screamed made him golf's unofficial publicity agent. If the sports pages ever nurtured a grander cliché than "Navy won the toss and elected to receive," it was "colorful Jimmy Demaret, golf's goodwill ambassador."

Demaret wore lavender, gold, pink, orange, red and aqua slacks; yellow, emerald, maroon, plaid, checked, striped and polka-dot coats; and more than five hundred hats—berets, Tyroleans, straws—importing all of it from Europe. He paid $250 for the coats as soon as he could and $125 for the slacks in an era when that kind of money could avert a bonus march. He ordered ladies' pastel fabrics from abroad and had them tailored in the U.S. His idea about shoes was to give a factory swatches from his slacks and have matching saddle oxfords made.

Not only did Demaret have a color for every occasion, he also had a quip. Some of the more classic were these:

To an L.A. radio announcer who asked him which player on the tour had the most even disposition: "Clayton Heafner. He's mad *all* the time."

To a sportswriter who asked him if Ben Hogan had said much to him while they were winning the Inverness Four-Ball: "Once I think he said, 'You're away.'"

To Robert Trent Jones, the golf architect with a reputation for building monster courses: "Saw a course you'd really like,

Trent. On the first tee you drop the ball over your left shoulder."

To Roberto De Vicenzo at the Masters: "Play good, Roberto. I'm betting on you to be low Mexican."

When the Thirties didn't have Demaret for comic relief, they had Ky Laffoon. He was a portly, balding part-Indian who got his start by caddying for Titanic Thompson, the famed hustler who liked to bet on this and that and usually won. Titanic liked to say to an opponent, "Hell, my caddy could beat you," and Ky Laffoon could.

Except on the tour. Laffoon never won as much as he probably should have, and his temper was largely responsible. It wasn't a legendary temper, the kind which caused earth tremors or broke up a party. It was more of a lovable temper, they say. Almost. Kind of.

Laffoon would wander off into the rough and discreetly, or not so discreetly, flog all of the leaves off of a small tree. He would miss a short putt and spurt tobacco juice into the cup, enough so that a man putting next would reach for his ball rather gingerly. And he would sometimes curse so audibly around a gallery that his wife, embarrassed, would stalk to the clubhouse and call a lawyer.

Once Laffoon had three putts from five feet to win the Cleveland Open. He missed the first, missed the second and thereupon became so violent that he slammed the putter down on top of the ball, not caring whether he finished first or eighth. But the ball ricocheted up in the air and—truly, truly—plopped right into the cup. Seeing it in the newsreel later, Laffoon is said to have let out a screech that cleared three rows.

Lloyd Mangrum remembers being paired with Ky when the Indian threw away one club per hole, finishing with Mangrum's clubs from the 15th in. Paul Runyan was with him one day when he broke the head off of his putter out of anger, but stepped up to putt again with the jagged shaft. When he realized what he was doing Laffoon, who had a tendency to stutter when he grew mad, said, "W-what the h-hell h-happened here?"

To appease his wife during a rare period of resolution, Laffoon decided he would play through a whole tournament without cursing. Surprisingly enough he scored fairly well in the first round and succeeded in doing it. He then started decently the second day, but he soon played himself into the lead and things got touchy. He held back for a while. But when an approach shot soared over a green on the back nine and landed in a bed of honeysuckle, that did it.

A jungle guerrilla with a machete could not have attacked the ball more furiously. One swing. Two. Three. And out came a torrent of get-even words that had spectators blushing as far away as the parking lot, which was precisely where his wife headed. Ky chased after her, caught up and began a panting, futile plea.

"I-I w-wasn't cussing," he said. "N-no k-kidding, d-darlin'. It w-wasn't a-anything to d-do w-with the g-golf. I just don't like honeysuckle."

The group to which Ky Laffoon felt the most philosophical kinship was a self-confessed pack of wolves acutely aware that prize money was not the only means of supporting oneself on the golf course.

Dutch Harrison, the Arkansas Traveler, eventually became a consistent money-winner, but he spent his first six years without earning a single penny of official cash. He lived off the fat of other men's golfing egos. In this respect he was much like Leonard Dodson, or better still, the brilliant trickshot artist, Joe Ezar, from Waco, Texas, who could make a golf ball sit up and speak. Ezar would stow away on freighters to Europe and hustle his way back on the *Queen Mary* balancing golf balls on top of each other on a bet. He could balance one ball on top of another—Lord knows how—hit the bottom ball onto a green and catch the other in his hand before it reached the ground. For money. Ezar would turn up at a tournament armed only with a derby hat, an overcoat and a pair of street shoes. "Loan me the equipment, and I'll pay you back double," he would say, and do it.

Dutch was never greedy. All he and his pal, Bob Hamilton, wanted was a couple of "nine-dollar pigeons" a day, enough to make expenses. Harrison had that splendid talent of being able to name his score. If his opponent shot 71, Dutch shot 70. If his opponent shot 80, Dutch squeezed out a 79 and convinced the guy how unlucky he was.

One afternoon on the Coast in 1937, as Dutch and Hamilton negotiated on the first tee for a game, a stranger asked if he could play along. He had a raw swing and a country voice, like Dutch, which meant he couldn't be all bad.

Hamilton, ever eager with loot in sight, said something subtle like, "How much you want to play for?"

"Well, I don't know much about betting," the man said.

"You come along with us," said Hamilton.

No more than a few holes had been played before Dutch and Hamilton were distracted from their game with the nine-dollar pigeons. For every good shot they hit, the stranger hit one better.

"My, my, son, you sure got yourself a pretty swing there," Dutch said. "That old hook grip don't bother you none at all, does it?"

Birdie, birdie went the innocent fellow.

Presently, Harrison lashed a spoon shot into a green—a career shot—and he thought to himself, "Now we see who the men are."

To which the stranger put a two-iron inside of him.

"Bob," Harrison said to Hamilton. "We done got ourselves a-hold of something here."

Later on, after Dutch and Hamilton had paid off, the young stranger said, "Sure do thank you fellers. Say, what time you gonna be here tomorrow?"

"Son," Harrison said, "you work your side of the road, and we'll work ours."

"That," Dutch says today, "is how I met Sam Snead."

The tour had no sooner become acquainted with Sam than along came another newcomer who would help fill the glamorous void that had been created by Bobby Jones's retirement. Fellow named Hogan. He was a loner and a brooder, weighing in at one hundred thirty pounds with an uncontrollable hook off the tees. No one thought he would ever make it. And he warmed up to only a few of his contemporaries—Demaret, whose humor he admired, and Henry Picard, a gracious and helpful veteran who loaned money and advice, and Harrison, whose ability to survive he found intriguing.

Harrison discovered one evening when he was rooming with Hogan just how determined the Texan was. As Dutch tried to sleep, Ben gently beat his fists against the bedposts in their hotel quarters.

"You done gone crazy?" Dutch said.

"I'm strengthening my wrists," said Hogan.

The thumping continued until the manager arrived, having been summoned by an annoyed guest next door.

"I'm through," Hogan explained, contentedly. "I just figured out what's wrong with my grip."

He almost had. Hogan struggled through the Thirties by settling for such stunning successes as third place in the North American Long Driving Contest behind Jimmy Thomson and Porky Oliver at Niagara Falls. He would get a check here and a check there. It wasn't until 1940 at Pinehurst that he finally won a tournament, the North and South. He found it so much to his liking that he quickly won two more, at Greensboro and Asheville—three in a row. And for the next twenty years there never lived a better golfer.

Throughout the Thirties only one player came on the tour in absolute comfort, unfettered by financial worries. That was Lawson Little, golf's first bonus baby. He was a handsome, husky, carefree Californian with a square face, curly hair and white duck trousers. He had been the greatest amateur since Jones, winning both the U.S. and British Amateur championships in 1934 and again in 1935—a feat that sportswriters called, rather clumsily, the Double Little Slam.

Little's decision to become a touring pro was final proof that amateur golf was minor league. And when he signed up with Spalding for $10,000 and all expenses to play golf and be a public relations man, it was the most amazing thing the pros had heard of since beltless slacks. Not until twenty-five years later, when Jack Nicklaus made a deal twenty times as big, did amateur golf produce so dazzling a celebrity.

Once Little was in the Spalding stable a group was formed that became known as the "trained seals." They were Little, Horton Smith, Thomson and Harry Cooper, and they were a popular exhibition team. They traveled together, mostly by luxurious train, and staged their own pre-tournament matches and clinics. "Can you fellows really balance golf balls on your nose?" Demaret would ask them.

Horton Smith was the boss and the bookkeeper. At the clinics he demonstrated the short game, Thomson hit the woods, Cooper, a nervous man who had a habit of jingling coins in his pocket, especially when someone stood over a putt, displayed the mid-irons and Lawson Little hit the long irons, the strength of his game.

Gallery ropes were nonexistent in the Thirties. Spectators literally formed a barricade around their favorite players; a golfer hardly had room to take a backswing. Self-appointed officials would stand in the middle of the fairways, puff on their pipes and say, "You're away, Byron." During one match Harry Cooper, who carried up to twenty-six clubs in his bag before the fourteen-club limit was set in 1936, kept finding a spectator's shadow over his ball when he addressed it. "Very unethical," Cooper would mumble and hit a fine shot. It happened all the way around the course until about the 16th hole when the shadow disappeared. Cooper then hit a ball roughly ten feet. "You bum," he called out. "Why'd you step on those leaves just as I was swinging?"

There were occasions when the fans were permitted to be

so indelicately close to the players that a championship could be settled by them. Very nearly. A spectator almost cost Little the U.S. Open. The Californian never became the big winner that everyone expected, possibly because he was so well-fixed, but he did achieve a week of glory at Canterbury during the Open of 1940. He tied with Gene Sarazen for the championship, and they played off over eighteen holes the next day. It was a duel of different personalities. Little was friendly, outgoing, a fine socializer, particularly when he had Jimmy Thomson to drink with. Sarazen was grim, independent. When the pros switched to knickers, Gene introduced slacks. When they switched to slacks, he went back to knickers.

Little took an early lead in the play-off, but even as he led Sarazen he public-related. At the 5th hole a fan came up to him and wanted to ask a question. Sure, said Little.

"What I want to know is whether you inhale or exhale on your backswing?"

"Are you serious?" Little said.

"Quite," said the fan. "As for myself, I think I inhale, but I'm not sure."

Little duck-hooked his next series of shots, trying to figure out if he inhaled or exhaled. He managed to recover, however, and shoot a 70 to defeat Sarazen by three strokes. He was the U.S. Open champion, regardless of how he breathed, and the Spalding Dot was once again guaranteed to give you extra distance.

But that was 1940. The Thirties were gone—sunk slowly in the background like the wooden shaft. A wonderfully unpredictable and rather remarkable era of golf had passed, but the legacies it left were many. Among others it left us the fond memory that somewhere around every dogleg there lurked an individual—a Snead, a Hogan, a Nelson, a Demaret. A Laffoon, a Harrison, a Little, a Mangrum. And all of the others. Individuals is what they had to be, really, to last it out.

And what none of them would ever have guessed at the time is that out there on the tour in the Sixties a pro could hardly scrape by at all without an agent, a manager, a copilot, a secretary, a valet, a tax consultant and a corporate jet.

Lights...
Camera...
Double Bogey

The thing I've noticed most is that celebrities aren't celebrities on the golf course. They're more relaxed. They don't have to play a role.

—MAC HUNTER,
head professional at Riviera Country Club

I guess you missed the item, although it was in all of the trades—right there with the news about George Plimpton's scheme to impersonate an airline captain for his next book, *Paper Mountain,* which has been pre-sold to Epic Pictures. The item explained how I decided to take a plunge into self-involvement journalism myself by challenging some show business personalities like James Garner and Glen Campbell and Vic Damone to a game of golf, a sport to which Hollywood has always been devoted. The item further told how I brought them to their knees one day at Riviera—or rather how my bronchial asthma did—and how Epic is interested in making an epic out of the experience. The tentative title is *The Ugly, the Bad and the Unplayable,* but I think it will be changed to something a bit more commercial, like, for instance, *Midnight Caddy.* At any rate, the studio hopes to get Raquel Welch to star as two hills above Mandeville Canyon and four bearded dropouts from a Berkeley die-in to portray my wood covers. The item told how Epic is eager to begin production as soon

as it finishes shooting *Paper Russia,* a film based on the week
George Plimpton spent as President of the United States.

The story went on to say that the studio is still considering
the possibility of turning the film into a big musical if it can
decide that enough spunky tunes could be written about stan-
dardizing handicaps, the care and management of Hybrid Bermuda and post-flood silt removal. Personally, I am not all that
ecstatic about this idea, knowing Hollywood's track record on
musicals. I can envision Joe Day having to learn the banjo just
to portray himself, Arnold Palmer in the role of Charlie Coody,
Charlie Coody in the role of Orville Moody, and Tom and
Jeanne Weiskopf tapdancing down a globe-lighted stairwell
of broken putters in the big production number while the
blue-and-white-clad ladies of the Colonial National Invitation
motor pool sing a chorus of "My kind of town, Fort Worth
is." In any case, Epic Studio, I understand, is going to conduct
a nationwide search of municipal courses to find an unknown
to play me; someone, the story went on to say, who coughed
incessantly from smoking and possessed the wraithlike ability
to shank a two-inch putt.

I suppose that, like me, you are a little distrustful of what
you read in the trades. I know I didn't for a second buy the
rumor that Jim Murray, the columnist, had the title role in
the remake of *Arthur Daley Discovers Horton Smith.* And I don't
believe the gossip that Billy Casper has the lead in *Jesus Played
a Onesome,* which they say will be filmed on actual location at
La Scala. I do, however, think you can trust the item about
me. Epic is very excited. Only a moment or so ago the head
of the studio, Zeth Dorian-Baker, phoned from the candy store
during a see-through contest to say that everything looked
plenty all right from where he sat.

By now, I expect, you are anxious to hear the full story
behind the film and something about a lot of the Hollywood
celebrities who play golf these days when they aren't digging
their homes out of mud slides. Why else would your Guccis
be tapping so restlessly on the pegged floor of our Mixed Four-

some Room? Well, I will tell you. But first, I think you ought to know something about the history of golf in Hollywood as it has been recorded on napkins at the Polo Lounge.

This background is vitally important, not just because it will give you a deeper insight into my film, but because it relates to something bigger than all of us—the pro golf tour. Surely you realize that the PGA tour, Arnold Palmer and all that, might never have become what it is today without Hollywood's support or perhaps even its consent. The fact is, pro golf sort of grew up with Hollywood the way the bosom grew up with acting. "To know more about Hollywood is to know more about the backswing," said an old philosopher. Forget the name. Bruce Cabot, maybe.

At any rate, it could be argued that the tour might have staggered through its early days of the 1930's on its own. I mean, Jimmy Demaret might have pulled it through by the laces of his pink-and-gold saddle oxfords. But I can look back and see that it certainly did not hurt anything that the tour chose to begin each new season (and still does) out in that strange, almost mystical boomland of southern California. It did not hurt anything in the beginning for the pros to be able to socialize with the Clark Gables, Richard Arlens and Randolph Scotts. It did not hurt anything that the Los Angeles Open often had such stalwarts as those playing in it, with swarms of other celebrities in the galleries. And what a glorious thing, the world took note. Going to a golf tournament on the Coast could be a giddier thrill than attending some world premiere and seeing a million dollars worth of feet, hands, legs and noses being pressed gently into Chinese cement.

What has since made Hollywood's role in professional golf even more meaningful, of course, is the fact that many of these old friendships have endured, and just as many fresh ones have blossomed. I have learned that a celebrity today who is not chummy with at least one touring pro is either a lousy softball player on Sundays or a motorcycle freak who drops acid. After

all, the giants of the industry have lent their names to tournaments. Bing Crosby. Bob Hope. Dean Martin. Andy Williams. Frank Sinatra for a while. And as one looked at the tour
in the 1970's it was noticeable that no fewer than seven championships were played up and down the coast, from L.A. to
Carmel, from San Francisco to La Costa, with more Clint
Eastwoods around than you could shake a Raymond Floyd at.

What it has all come down to, I decided, is a happier,
gaudier, more glamorous scene than any pro or entertainer
could ever have guessed at long ago. There they all are in their
insular bedazzlement, speedy swings matched against speedier
quips, a snappy time for the sport. Bronzed pros in violet knit
and hair-sprayed stars in tight little trousers, all thrust against
the glittering backdrop of palms and mountains and sea, not
to forget the arrangements of raven-haired, orange-haired,
golden-haired, moon-haired starlets in their sideless, backless,
frontless fashions.

For a few weeks out of every year, at least, pro golf was a
happening. And who among us was strong enough that he
could resist being near it, or a part of it, if the opportunity
presented itself. Not me, boy.

But first I had to learn more about the fascinating history
of golf in Hollywood, which I shall finally unveil. It all begins
with a popular misconception: that the game was actually
invented by Bing Crosby and Bob Hope. That, of course, is
wrong. Golf, as a matter of fact, was invented by Maurie
Luxford, a friend of theirs, about 1925 at the Lakeside Country
Club. Lakeside is located in the valley area near Warner Brothers, roughly two or three wife-swapping bars from Beverly
Hills. Luxford dreamed up the game at Lakeside to provide a
healthy, recreational activity for men like Howard Hughes,
Guy Kibbee, Adolph Menjou, Richard Arlen and Oliver
Hardy. Some people have argued that over in Palm Beach
about the same time Chris Dunphy invented golf for Wall
Street vacationers and cosmetic executives. Chances are they

both invented the game; Maurie Luxford simply got more publicity, Hollywood being second only to Washington, D.C., in the number of press releases that are mimeographed daily.

I once asked Maurie Luxford if it were true that he invented golf.

"No two people have done more for the game than Bing and Bob," he said.

Luxford was a pleasant, friendly, gray-thatched gentleman who had remained very much involved in golf through the years. He had organized and officiated at hundreds of pro-celebrity tournaments up and down the West Coast, and he had held up well under the immense pressure of having to turn down requests of heavy industry presidents to play in the Bing Crosby National Pro-Am.

Now, then, shortly after Maurie Luxford originated golf the sport became very popular with scads of Hollywood celebrities. Among other things it gave them something to devote themselves to other than swinging from balcony to balcony rescuing Myrna Loy, and Lakeside gave them a place to hide from the public. All the public ever saw, the public being mainly back in Des Moines then, were photos in movie magazines of these tanned handsome figures in white shirts and slacks with polka-dot scarves addressing two-foot putts, sometimes a bit too awkwardly to convince anyone they played to a strong six.

There were some good players and, according to Maurie Luxford, fascinating characters during the early days, however. Well, heck, there was George Von Elm, who won the 1926 U.S. Amateur and lost a play-off (over seventy-two holes, the longest on record) to Billie Burke for the 1931 U.S. Open. There were a couple of other strong amateurs, Johnny Dawson and Bruce McCormick, who made the Walker Cup team. And there was the mysterious John Montague, the trick-shot king, who beat Oliver Hardy one day using only a baseball bat, a shovel and a rake. All of these, together with low-handicap celebrities like Bing Crosby, Randolph Scott, Richard Arlen, Buddy Rogers, Douglas Fairbanks and Howard Hughes, inspired Grantland Rice once to write that no golf club in the country could defeat a team from Lakeside.

Gossip columnists of the era also wrote about the huge gambling games at Lakeside, but Maurie Luxford rarely saw more than $5000 lost in a foursome, that foursome usually consisting of Howard Hughes, George Von Elm, Scotty Armstrong and Duke Hinnau. Another group that would bet it up, Luxford remembered, was comprised of Adolph Menjou, Guy Kibbee, Frank Craven and Oliver Hardy. And still another, in later years, was Bing Crosby, using shafts three inches longer than normal and addressing the ball two inches below the spot where it was teed, and Randolph Scott, Dennis O'Keefe and a newcomer, Dean Martin.

"The world knew that Bing liked golf," said Maurie Luxford. "But only the members around Lakeside knew how well he could play in his younger days. He was very accurate and a fierce competitor. After all, he won the club championship five times against some pretty fine golfers."

For a time Howard Hughes, an impoverished lad from Texas who played golf in sneakers because he couldn't afford saddle oxfords, was a 1-handicapper at Lakeside, as strong a player as any in the film colony. But Hughes wanted to be better than that. And one day he asked his close friend, George Von Elm, what would happen if he really worked at golf. Could he, Hughes, get to be good enough to capture, say, the National Amateur? Von Elm said probably not. So Hughes quit the game altogether. He did return on a later occasion, it should be noted, to crash-land a private plane on the course at Bel-Air one day, and the legend is that Howard Hughes, having given up the game, refused to replace his divot.

This about covers the early history of golf in Hollywood, at Lakeside, the "home of the stars." If anything other than the intriguing gossip filtering out of Lakeside served to focus more attention on the fact that the celluloid heroes had adopted golf as their very own game, it was the tournament Bing Crosby started with his brother Larry in 1937—the now famous Pro-Am. It was first staged in Rancho Santa Fe, where it rained, and subsequently was moved to the Monterey Peninsula, where it snowed. It was first played over thirty-six holes, then was stretched to fifty-four and finally to seventy-two, and Bing's tournament has ultimately become a total must for corporation executives around the land as well as for celebrities and touring professionals.

For a week every winter, the only place for a self-respecting golfer to be is either in the Del Monte Lodge or the Pine Inn of Carmel or in a palatial rented home along the 17-Mile Drive. There one should be having cocktails with Bing or Arnie or Jack or perhaps Clint Eastwood, Jack Lemmon or Jim Garner or the board chairman of Pacific Mobile Homes or Eastern Chemical or some such thing. It has become so much of a status symbol to be invited to the Crosby—only three hundred or so amateurs out of nine thousand applicants are admitted, after all—that businessmen who do *not* make it suddenly find their lives growing dreary if not desperate. They may arrive at their offices to discover their doors locked and their secretaries thumbing through the classifieds. Or they may go to their country clubs and find the locker attendants sullen and unfriendly. Until he has played in the Crosby a business tycoon simply cannot say that he knows anything about life, love, Palmer's hip trouble, Doug Sander's clothes or whatever happened to Rhonda Fleming.

Conversations between certain happy Crosby invitees often tell you more about the tournament—indeed more about Hollywood golf—than anything else. I happened to have overheard one a winter or so ago in the Del Monte Lodge between two gentlemen I shall calls Sims of Nuclear Plumbing and Thurman of Southern Mail Fraud. It went like this:

SIMS: Hi, Thurmo. How'd you play?

THURMAN: We were paired with Jack Lemmon. How about you?

SIMS: We had Phil Harris.

THURMAN: How'd you do Thursday?

SIMS: Jim Garner. Yourself?

THURMAN: Not bad. Dick Shawn.

SIMS: Last year I got Dean Martin.

THURMAN: I've had Bob Hope.

SIMS: I've had Andy Williams.

THURMAN: So have I.

SIMS: How'd it go Friday?

THURMAN: Terrific. Danny Thomas.

SIMS: Yes, I've had Danny at the Springs. Ever been around Indian Wells with Desi?

THURMAN: Well, no. Down there I usually play Eldorado.

SIMS: Not a bad layout, but Frank talked me into joining Tamarisk.

THURMAN: Frank Buck?

SIMS: Sinatra.

THURMAN: Oh, sure. Say, next time you see Frank, ask him about the time I took him to Merion.

SIMS: Fine course, Merion. Gave up the membership though when I joined Pine Valley. Say, ask old Garner about the day I took him to Pine Valley.

THURMAN: I will. Ask Hope about the day I took him to the Augusta National.

SIMS: Was that before or after we built the cottage for Ike?

THURMAN: Well, I'm certain it was before because I remember telling Bobby and Cliff where they ought to put it.

SIMS: Get back there much?

THURMAN: Not really. Somehow I can't get away from Seminole when I go South.

SIMS: Know what you mean. Ever since Joe got me in the R&A I've found it difficult even to play in this country.

THURMAN: Joe *Day*, you mean.

SIMS: Yes.

THURMAN: Quite a fellow. He offered to do the same for me one day at Locust Valley, but I had to tell him that the Brigadier had already handled my case.

SIMS: Nothing like St. Andrews, of course. Ask Dino about the time we ripped up The Old Course.

THURMAN: Sure will. Ask Andy about the day we tore up Muirfield.

SIMS: Glad to. Well, gotta run. Coming over to Bing's for a drink after a while?

THURMAN: I suppose so—if Arnie wants to.

SIMS: Good. The Duke and I will see you there.

THURMAN: Duke Wayne? Is Duke here?

SIMS: Of Windsor.

THURMAN: Oh, naturally. Say, ask him about the day I talked him into abdicating so we could take a pop at Sunningdale.

It would be impossible to assess the impact that Bing Crosby and his friend Bob Hope have had on golf. Hope, of course, also sponsors a tournament for corporate executives, celebrities and pros—the Bob Hope Desert Classic in Palm Springs, or rather near Palm Springs, most of the five courses that are used being located in towns like Indio and Cathedral City and Palm Desert. The sun beams down on Hope's tournament—whereas Bing's has been called The Four Seasons; the players crawl along on electric carts and a lot of orange-haired ladies loiter in the galleries. At night everyone goes to Ruby's Dunes for dinner in the hope that Frank Sinatra will come in. The food is good if, as somebody once said, you like steak and Jade East.

For all of this, however, it may be established one day that the greatest contribution Hope and Crosby made to the game was the creation of the Golf Joke. They have been telling them since they used to take putters along to their radio broadcasts. Crosby would talk about Hope's game for Kraft Foods, and Hope would talk about Crosby's game for Pepsodent. And the world would laugh whether it played golf or not.

"Bob Hope's swing?" Crosby would say. "I've seen better swings on a condemned playground."

"They're making a movie of Crosby's round yesterday," Hope would say. "It stars Bela Lugosi."

According to Crosby, Hope invented the nonbody turn, the interlocking grip on a money clip, the fast backswing and a good short game—off the tee. According to Hope, Crosby invented the pipe, the shirt worn outside the pants, the cocked hat, the impression he was so rich even his caddies subscribed to *Fortune*.

And all of those lines.

But so much for the background of golf in Hollywood. So much for what history there is. So much for all of the noble pioneers. What of today? Where must an autograph seeker go now that no one is left at Lakeside except an occasional Frankie Avalon, a Gordon MacRae, a Guy Madison and a Don Knotts? I put the question to my main contact man with the stars, a public relations consultant from Chicago named Bill Martin. As far as I could tell, Bill Martin, over the years, had been in Las Vegas, Palm Springs, the Polo Lounge and the men's grill at Bel-Air a lot more than he had ever been in Chicago, although I had never been at Binyon's without running into him.

This time, I had found him at Binyon's with Vic Damone discussing a way for Vic to sing through cigarette machines and entice the buyer into a certain brand.

"You know I've always had the big lights—the baby juniors—in my eyes," I said. "I want to play golf with the stars."

"That's a good story," said Vic. "I'd rather have someone write about my golf game than my voice any day."

"Who you want?" asked Martin. "You want Vic? You got him. You want Crosby . . . Hope . . . Dean? What do you have in mind?"

"I want the really serious players today, like Jack Ging, whom I know. Pretty good athletes. I don't want to listen to a pile of Buddy Hackett jokes," I said. "Where does anybody play?"

Bill Martin explained how it was. There was the Bel-Air crowd: Dean Martin with his group of toy manufacturers and auto dealers, and Dick Martin, Bob Sterling, Richard Crenna, Howard Keel, Bob Wagner and loads of others. There was the Hillcrest crowd: Jack Benny, Danny Kaye, Milton Berle, Danny Thomas, a gaggle of top bananas throughout the dining room. There was the Brentwood crowd: Jack Lemmon, Gary Morton, Buddy Hackett, Joey Bishop, Jerry Lewis, Jan Murray—a panel show. There was the Los Angeles Country Club: nobody. Nobody? Yep. Bing Crosby lived near the 14th green of the great North Course for years but could only play at L.A. as a guest. No show biz types allowed. Sooner the Viet Cong should be members. Somebody said Randolph Scott finally got in after he swore that he would never have anything to do with Hollywood again, or maybe it was because the membership decided that, after all, he was never an actor. Anyhow, finally, there was the Riviera crowd: Jim Garner, Jack Ging, Vic Damone, Donald O'Connor, Lindsay Crosby, Bob Wilke, the badman, Jim Backus—the good, serious golfers with a few Robert Stacks and Gregory Pecks thrown in.

"Riviera's quite a course," I said.

"And they go to the back tees there, my man," said Bill Martin.

"A team of show business personalities from Riviera could beat a team from any other club in the area," Damone said. "Call when you're on the Coast and I'll arrange a game."

"Just tell me who you want," said Martin. "Andy? Frank? Duke?"

I told Martin I wanted Jill St. John, Jacqueline Bisset and Raquel Welch and thought no more about it.

A short time later I happened to be at the Crosby tournament listening to my good friends Sims and Thurman in the Del Monte Lodge when I ran into Jack Ging, who had come to win the Pro-Am with Pro Bob Dickson. And did.

"Come on over to Clint's and we'll talk about a game at Riviera," he said.

"Has Murchison got a house here?" I said.

"Eastwood," he said.

"Oh," I said.

Ging is a curly-haired, grinning, ingratiating little man whom I had known better as a halfback for the University of Oklahoma than as the quiet psychiatrist, Dr. Phillip Graham, of the TV series *The Eleventh Hour*.

Jack Ging had apparently become the best golfer in the Hollywood community since his days at Norman. One heard he was a strong 3-handicapper from the back tees at Riviera, which is a mere 7022 yards of bunkers and eucalyptus trees, the course where Ben Hogan won the 1948 U.S. Open. He had been winning a number of member-guest and pro-celebrity tournaments regularly, the kind that Bob Sterling and Bob Wilke used to win. And if there had been any question about Ging's claim to being Hollywood's best it was surely erased after this Crosby. He not only played extremely well as Dickson's partner through rain and mud, he actually hit the stroke that won the Pro-Am for them—an eight-foot birdie on the final green at Pebble Beach—before a big gallery and a national TV audience.

"Isn't this great," said Ging then. "This is greater than winning an Academy Award."

A little later on he said, "You know how I made that putt? Bob Goalby made it. He walked over to me on the green and said, 'I know you're nervous. We all get nervous. But you deserve to win this, and you're a good putter. It breaks a little left. Just give it a smooth stroke and it'll drop.' Boy, Bob Goalby's great. Isn't he a great guy?"

Ging said he would get with Vic Damone the following week and they would round up a lot of great guys and we would have a Sports Illustrated Open Invitation for celebrities at Riviera so I could see how the stars play golf. He said he would get Jim and Glen and Don and Lindsay and Bob and maybe his Malibu neighbor Jack Warden from *Twelve Angry Men* and *The Bachelor Party* and all my favorite movies for a forecaddy, and I said I would get a photographer, Marty Mills, who was married to Edie Adams, and he said Marty was really a great guy and we would have a great time.

I barely managed to get out of the Daisy, The Candy Store and Ging's own night spot, Cisco's, in Manhattan Beach in time to transport my headache to Riviera when the day came. The clubhouse at Riviera, which is in Pacific Palisades, can best be described as early Morro Castle, and I rattled around in it for a while before I found anyone. Mac Hunter, then the pro, came along and said I had better warm up my three-wood for the back tees, and he asked what was first prize worth in this tournament Ging and Damone were having.

"The winner gets a tour of the sumptuous Hollywood homes," I said.

Mac and I had a cup of coffee, and the pro talked about some of the stars and their golf games.

"Ging's a hell of a competitor," he said. "It stems from his football days. He has a real winning attitude that I suppose Bud Wilkinson instilled in him. His swing is a neat package— short and compact. He's very consistent and straight."

Mac said, "Bob Wilke used to be head and shoulders better than any of the actors and personalities. And he's still very good. A solid four-handicap, but his putting is deteriorating. Wilke must have won more celebrity tournaments than you can count.

"Bob Sterling is a fine player, of course, a graceful swinger. And Randolph Scott they tell me was terrific several years ago.

But I think Wilke must have been better, day in, day out, and now I think Ging is better than Wilke."

I asked, "What about Garner and Damone and some others?"

"Well, nobody loves golf more than Vic. He'll play from dawn till dark," said Mac. "Garner could be one of the best but he doesn't work at it. He's got his racing cars, and of course he's frequently working on a movie."

Mac said, "The thing I've noticed most is that celebrities aren't celebrities on the golf course. They're more relaxed. They don't have to play a role. Around here they're cheerful, easy-going. They'll play golf with anyone at all who enjoys the game as much as they do. I think this is truer at Riviera than at the other clubs. You've got to like golf a lot to get on this monster. So this is another reason why you'll see the Bob Stacks and the Robert Mitchums out there with just plain folks, playing golf. They don't have to *be* anybody around here."

Until he walked in I wasn't sure I would know Bob Wilke, one of the durable Western villains, a man who had been gunned down by everyone from Wild Bill Elliot to Grace Kelly. But I remembered. Cold, steely eyes, drawling, solemn expression, a slow, cocky, gun-slinger's grin. Tall and evil.

"Didn't Grace Kelly get you in *High Noon?*" I asked.

"Right in the back," Wilke smiled.

"Who else?" I said. "I may want to refresh my readers who aren't that familiar with your name."

Well, said Wilke, Jimmy Stewart had shot him in the belly in *Night Passage,* and Gary Cooper had shot him in the chest in *Man of the West,* and Jim Coburn had stabbed him in *The Magnificent Seven,* and he'd been blown up in James Mason's submarine in *20,000 Leagues Under the Sea,* and he probably had died four hundred other times in films since the mid 1930's.

"Jack Ging killed me yesterday at Riviera," he said.

Presently all of the other players showed up, Glen Campbell,

Damone, Ging, Donald O'Connor, Lindsay Crosby and James Garner. So did Jack Warden, who said he had just come out to watch and see what Hollywood types were really like.

"This is all pretty dazzling for me," he said, looking around at the table of coffee drinkers.

Warden shook hands with Damone and squinted at him and pointed his finger at him and said, "Aren't you that, uh, that fellow that, uh, sings a lot—that, uh, Jack Jones?"

Everyone teased Glen Campbell about being the hottest thing in town and suddenly rich. And didn't it beat backing up Perry Como records on the guitar or playing one-night dates with the rhythm pickers at truck stops?

"You know what they say," said Campbell. "It takes about ten years to become an overnight success. I thought Johnny Hartford never *would* write 'Gentle On My Mind.'"

James Garner addressed me and said, "You're Time, Inc., right?"

"Sort of," I said.

"Did you *read* what they said about my car at Daytona? They referred to it as 'the *implausible* Lotus of Jim Garner.' I know what implausible means. I looked it up."

"Wait till you read what I say about your golf game," I said.

"Oh, wonderful," said Garner. "Ging. Hey, Ging. Where'd you get this one, Sweets?"

Garner had grown a black mass of a beard for a role he was about to play. There were a lot of cracks about it. Marty Mills, the photographer, asked him where he had left the two boards he was nailed to.

And Ging said: "Hey, did you hear what Dino said to Jim at the Crosby when he saw his beard? He said, 'Say, man, when you bite into one of those, you're supposed to turn loose.'"

Everyone traded Dean Martin stories for a while. Funny man, everyone said. Fun-nee. There was this time he was on the 1st tee at Bel-Air with two of his golfing pals, Fletcher

Jones and Art Anderson or somebody, and Buddy Hackett came jogging up, hoping to join them. "Sorry, Buddy," said Dean. "We've already got three." And there was this time that Bob Newhart or somebody almost fell down hitting a shot and Dean said, "If you step on my suedes one more time I'll . . ." And there was this time Sinatra hired a guy to dress up in a grizzly bear costume and dash out of the woods to scare Dean, but when the man did he tripped and fell, and all Dean said was, "Look fellows, I think the poor thing's hurt."

After a while we were all out on the 1st tee at Riviera, taking warm-up swings, preparing for the first, only and last Sports Illustrated Open Invitation Hollywood Celebrity-Celebrity Minus One.

A couple of mildly curious members stood by. One of them wore a pair of red, white and blue golf shoes. I made some comment to Marty Mills about the shoes, quietly I thought. Something about how much Ronald Reagan would like them, but Vic Damone heard me.

"Don't joke," said Damone. "I've got a pair like that."

Marty Mills said, "I've got a flag like that."

A few bets were made. Ging announced that it was "Get Wilke Day," and Wilke announced that it was "Get Ging Day." Garner asked for a couple of ups, and Ging offered one or two.

"Oh, please button your shirt before your heart falls out," said Jim.

"Aren't we gonna play seriously?" Damone asked.

"You bet your sweet bippy," Garner said.

"How *is* your bippy?" said Vic.

"Him dust so thweet," Garner said, gripping the driver.

I guess I would put Garner up against most anybody at imitating, let us say, an interior decorator on a golf tee. He wiggled his hips, touched at his hair, as if it had just been rinsed and set, put a finger to his lips and glanced down at the ground.

"Let's thee," he said. "Thith is a club and thith is a ball and that muth be the green down there. Oooo, it's tho far."

Garner has the swing of a good, natural athlete, which he was when he was Jim Bumgardner back in Oklahoma, like Ging, a guy who had played football, been in the service and was laying carpet when somebody made him an actor by accident. And a good one.

Garner had a fine drive off the 1st tee and swaggered over to the side with his left hand on his hip. With the right he took the driver by the clubhead and slid the shaft down through the left hand, like a cavalry officer placing his saber back in the casing on his leg.

Glen Campbell stepped up next in tight-fitting, stitched, tailored blue denims, pink shirt and a somewhat incongruous yellow hat with a brim, a reminder, it seemed to me, that he had come from Delight, Arkansas. He took a wide stance and I knew he would unleash a big, fast, powerful swing and that the shot would soar away for a mile in one direction or another.

Standing over the ball Campbell said, grinning, "Kill . . . destroy . . . ravage . . . plunder . . ."

Campbell's drive was a big one, and as he retrieved his tee he sang a note or two in his country-style voice.

"Oh, the lace time I seen Paris," he sang. Then he said, "Hear about the hippie who took LSD but didn't take a trip— he went home?"

Donald O'Connor and Lindsay Crosby teed off quietly and nicely. They were to remain quiet, pleasant and concentrating for most of the day. There would be no missing Lindsay for a Crosby either in looks or voice. Had he broken into a chorus of *The Old Ox Road*, ba-ba-ba-boo, it would not have astonished me.

Ging, Wilke and Damone got off the first tee very businesslike. They were intense, it seemed, eager to get at it, and I struck some sort of drive into the rough, and we were away, an eightsome, ten counting Jack Warden and Marty Mills. As we bounded down the hill of the 1st hole, a 508-yard par five, Warden came over to me and nodded toward all of the celebrities up ahead.

"I, uh, I just can't describe to you what a thrill this is for me," he said. "When I go home and tell my wife that I was with Jack Jones and Andy Griffith, well—"

It didn't take long for me to discover that Hollywood has some pretty good golfers. Ging and Campbell birdied the first hole, and Damone, Garner, O'Connor and Crosby parred it. Ging also birdied the 2nd hole, a 526-yard par five, and so did Damone and Crosby, while everyone else made par— except me. Granted, these are probably the two easiest holes at Riviera, but I skillfully managed to play them in 6–7.

By the time you reach the 5th hole at Riviera, the course has started, the real golf course, which is nothing but drives and spoons, particularly on a heavy day as this one was. But Jack Ging was still one under, and the others were only one or two over, and Jack Warden, my favorite actor, was still strolling along beside me, throwing out lines.

"This fellow with the beard," he said. "He looks familiar. Don't he work in the movin' pitchers?"

"Yes," I said. "That's Cary Grant."

Warden said, "That's it. I knew I had something in common with one of them stars."

"Oh?" I said.

"Yeah," he said. "That, uh, Cary Grant over there. The thing is, I used to ball his maid."

The 5th hole is one of the great holes at Riviera, a long par four with out of bounds on the right, a row of trees on the left and a slightly sunken green which hides to the left of a mound.

When Garner sliced his tee shot out of bounds he instantly blamed it on Marty Mills's camera. I remembered that I had heard Garner had a temper at times. I guess I expected him to explode, but he didn't. "Thank you, James Wong Howe," he said.

"Sorry," said Marty.

"Forget it," said Jim. "It's just a double bogey."

"I'm really sorry," Marty said.

"No problem," said Garner. "I'm not picky. I'll take a six, seven, anything. It doesn't matter."

Whereupon Garner walked over and beat his driver against a tee marker.

As the round progressed Ging, Campbell and Garner, all of them being native country boys, developed a rapport that seemed to amuse everyone. When Campbell hit a bad shot he would holler, "Glen Travis Campbell, you come in this house!"

When Ging had a shot go astray, he would shout, "Jackie Lee Ging, get down off that roof!"

And, in turn, Garner, roaming in the rough, would call out, "Jimmy Jack Garner, you're gonna get your ass wore out."

Glen Campbell, a very natural and likable sort, hardly the hairspray king of his television show, eventually fell into the throes of an incurable darting hook, but he kept singing and dropping gems of rural humor.

Once he said, "That sumbitch right there dropped like a bell from a tall cow's neck."

Hitting a good shot he would say, "Oh, Glen Travis, son, you daince so purty."

Before the day was over Riviera nearly wrecked everybody's game, of course. It was not a very clever or energetic eightsome that limped up the 18th, a 443-yard par four known as "cardiac hill." Donald O'Connor was headed for an atrocious 96, his worst score in years, and I was struggling in with 91, my worst since the day before. Vic Damone's loose swing and sort of pale fade had worked him around to 88, far from his best, and Jim Garner, his back aching, was gaining on an 85, hardly worthy of him. Lindsay Crosby was rounding out an 81, which surprised me, since I felt he stood up to the ball better than anyone except Bob Wilke. As for the villain, he'd played a 79 that looked lower and would have been had some putts curled in. Wilke and Ging had both gone out in 39, but Jack had nailed him on the back side with a dazzling even par 36 and a fine three-over 75. Jack Ging, thus, was our winner.

There had been one more intriguing moment on the last green. I stroked a fifty-footer that never came close to the cup, but along the way as the ball curved over two or three breaks it hit a tree that someone had used to mark his ball with and then it skipped again over an unrepaired divot, and as it bounced and wiggled over its path Jim Garner started to laugh. Then he said: "This putt will self-destruct within ten seconds."

Later on we gathered around a huge table in the bar to trade golf stories and show biz stories and figure out that Ging had won about $150 and to try and settle on where we'd go to dinner.

Everyone decided that he was a better golfer than he had shown out on the course and that if you eliminated a couple of triple and double bogeys his score wasn't so bad. I quite agreed.

Donald O'Connor told a story about hitting a golf ball into somebody's kitchen, I think, and settled back for a long evening of storytelling with Wilke and Lindsay Crosby. They weren't going anywhere, they said. Vic Damone invited everyone up to his office on top of the Playboy Building on The Strip. Plenty of booze, he said, a great view and a sound system. Ging wanted the group to drive out to his joint, Cisco's, where he had a rock band and nine million stewardi. "I need that like I need a hole in my git-ar," said Campbell, adding that he was going home to watch Wilke get killed on television. Garner also excused himself, saying he was going home to put his feet up. "Him tired?" asked Campbell. "Him's little bippy is three down and two to go," said Garner.

All good guys, I thought. Really regular. Gee. And what a movie it will make. No sham. No phony pretentions. No tinsel. Who says this town has a popcorn machine for a heart? Script by Neil Simon. Songs by Jimmy Webb. Direction by

Mike Nichols. Realism. Integrity. Only one minor change, I shoot 74 and beat Ging. Jenke Birdie Flick Boffo.

My thoughts were interrupted by Jack Warden who put it all back in perspective. He stared across the table at Jack Ging, put down his drink, snapped his fingers and said:

"Excuse me, sir, but I've been looking at you all day. Aren't you that, uh, that funny guy I seen so much in the flicks . . . that, uh, yeah! Ain't you Peggy Ann Garner?"

America's Guest

Give me a millionaire with a bad backswing and I can have a very pleasant afternoon.

—GEORGE LOW,
on the subject of survival in golf

In professional tournament golf the clubhouse veranda can often be a noteworthy blend of rumble seat, wax museum, promenade deck, theater wings and courthouse steps. As the tour moves from one Crystal Rancho Happy Avocado Creek Country Club to another, the verandas undergo some severe botanical changes—a palm will beget a pine, or a eucalyptus will beget an oak—but the human plantlife will remain practically changeless. Except for the occasional intrusion of a spectator fully equipped with binoculars, periscope, chair seat, transistor, program, pairing sheet, camera and hot dog, and the almost invariable presence of at least one young female in form-fitting slacks, huge dark glasses and a straw bonnet, the regular veranda standers comprise a remarkably homogeneous and identifiable part of golf. They are the hanging-in, cooling-it, businessmen of the game. And as they spread across the lawn, gazing toward the nearest leader board while a tournament progresses, they are not unlike a cluster of military commanders observing the glow of shell-fire from a distant valley.

To almost anyone in the 1960's who knew the difference between a Ben Hogan driver and a shooting stick the faces of these fringe personalities looked as familiar as casual water, but only the true insider was able to identify them by name. There was the stocky, pink-faced man in the dark blazer, his hands usually folded behind him, the one ready with a Sam Snead anecdote or a story about the 1937 Ryder Cup team. That was Fred Corcoran, Snead's lifelong agent and the tournament director of the International Golf Association. There was the tall, blond fellow in the white shoes, a briefcase in one hand and Winnie Palmer's arm in the other. That was Mark McCormack, a Cleveland lawyer and manager of Palmer, Gary Player and most of the ships at sea. And there were several others, forming a part sort of corporate blur, spaced equidistantly among the umbrellas: J. Edwin Carter of the World Series of Golf, Jack Tuthill, the PGA tournament supervisor, Bob Rickey, a Brunswick-MacGregor vice-president, Ernie Sabayrac, an equipment distributor, Bob Drum, a hulking writer, Joe Wolfe, the Wilson clubmaker, Darrell Brown, Palmer's pilot, Doc Giffin, Palmer's personal secretary, Malcolm Hemion, a TV director for ABC, and, finally, the most familiar figure of all, that of a man called Bubble Head, a man who was always there, never doing anything.

On or off the verandas, Bubble Head, or George Low, was (and still is) the stand-around champion of three decades. He is, all at once, America's guest, underground comedian, consultant, inventor of the overlapping grip for a beer can, and, more importantly, a man who has conquered the two hardest things in life—how to putt better than anyone ever, and how to live lavishly without an income.

For thirty years George Low has been the vaguest, most mysterious man in all of golf. Outwardly solemn and immobile, he stands like an urban renewal project on the verandas in a plaid jacket and an open-collared shirt, deeply tanned, granting interviews only to bookmakers and forcing grins only toward those who might seem inclined to buy him lunch or a cocktail. It has been said that if George Low is not on your veranda the tournament simply hasn't started yet. When the

Western Open was held at the Field Club in Pittsburgh in 1959, for example, George did not reveal his two hundred forty pounds until the final round, whereupon a friend on the committee scolded him for being tardy and nearly giving the event a bad name.

"Well, you got to understand that a man who don't have to be back to his office for thirty years is sometimes gonna be lax," said George.

The only office that George Low has ever had is the trunk of someone's automobile, preferably a Cadillac, which, if he borrowed it for long began to look like a rummage sale of golf clubs, clothes and photo albums. George has no age. His lungs are one hundred, his stomach is one fifty, and his soul is two thousand, says he. The body has been fifty-four or so for a while. For most of these years, at any rate, George's home has been a car seat, a convertible couch in someone's living room, a roll-away bed in a friend's hotel room, or, when he's going good, the vacant wing of a friend's mansion. But always these places have been where the sunshine is—either on or near the PGA tour. He is also very comfortable in Palm Springs, Scottsdale or Miami Beach, whether the tour is in the vicinity or not, or at Saratoga, Santa Anita or Gulfstream.

"I go where some rich guy's got a bed and a kind heart," George says. "Most guys are if-come in this world, but there's a few that ain't phony, and they like having me around. They understand that I got to be where it's warm 'cause I can't afford no overcoat."

To the person who is "strung out," as George puts it, which means he has a steady, respectable job, it may seem that Low's existence is mostly a matter of survival. But George has never thought of it quite that way. On the contrary, George Low has usually lived comfortably, and often far better than the strung-out fellow who rides a commuter train or drives the freeways to work, who is paying off a divan and a Frigidaire and who has to purchase a daily ticket to a golf tournament, not admissible to the clubhouse.

The main reason why George Low has been able to survive in reasonable splendor is that he has one of those personalities that appeal to gentlemen of means. He has a rare sense of humor that makes him one of the superb put-down artists of his time, an unobtrusive manner for being around and not bothering anyone and a crashing honesty, all of which can add up to good company. Aside from these things George knows as much about golf as anyone, and a lot of gentlemen of means like to play golf, apparently while being put down unobtrusively, honestly and without being unduly bothered.

If he *does* have to work he does that on a putting green in Palm Springs or Miami Beach, mainly, where he is apt to putt with a wedge or with his shoe against a wagerer using a putter, and come out all right.

"Put me on a putting green in Miami for a week," says George, "and I'll kill more tourists than the Fontainebleau."

Among the celebrities who have demonstrated that they enjoy George's company and have, therefore, been his happy hosts, are, just to touch on four different sports, Jimmy Demaret, Willie Shoemaker, Horace Stoneham and Del Miller—a golfer, a jockey, a baseball owner and a harness racing mogul, respectively. George has visited with Stoneham in Phoenix during November, he has spent Christmas with Demaret in Houston and he has devoted a lot of weekday drop-ins to Shoemaker in Los Angeles and Miller in Pennsylvania. It was Paul Grossinger of the resort by that name in the Catskills who once labeled George "America's guest."

"After which he come up with a freebie," says George.

Another associate, Bob Johnson, once the president of Roosevelt Raceway outside New York City, may have summed up George perfectly—at least it delights George—for all of his hosts one evening as Low kept badgering Johnson for another hundred dollars to buy drinks for everyone at a Palm Springs party.

"Just loafing with George is better than having a Dun & Bradstreet rating," said Johnson.

All of this helps make absolutely clear George's uncompli-
cated philosophy of life, or rather his blueprint for leading a
life of ease.

"There ain't no use hanging around a broke 'cause nothing
falls off," he says. "The only time I pick up a check is to hand
it to somebody."

This, for George, sharply divides the world into two
distinct categories of people—those who "come up," or pay,
and those who "plead the fifth," or don't pay, when a tab
appears.

Since most everyone who knows George knows him well
enough to keep his pocketbook either handy or hidden, there
are never any surprises or embarrassing situations. If George
strolls by you prepare to pay or you prepare to leave. "It's an
honor to pick up my check," he says. "How many true celebrities do you know? Anyhow, if you plead the fifth I'll go
find a live one somewheres."

Low has a carefully thought out term for the man with a
reputation for being something less than a wild spender. A
very cautious student of the dollar, George calls him. Like
Sam Snead.

"When I dine with Mr. Snead he always suggests that I
order as if I was expecting to pay for it myself," says George.
"I have known many great destroyers of money, but Mr. Snead
is not among them."

Anyone who might happen to stand near George on a veranda at a tournament is likely to be treated to a comic routine.
It oozes out naturally from his husky voice and always with a
cynical tone. Most of the competitors have learned to feed
George straight lines just for the pleasure of picking up a new
expression.

Al Besselink came by one day at Pensacola and said, "Loan
me fifty, Bubble."

Staring straight ahead at a sheltering palm Low said, "Loaning you money is like sending lettuce by rabbit."

Another time, as George rested himself against the trunk

of an elm at Colonial, Billy Maxwell good-naturedly said, "Wish I had your energy, George."

"I wish I had a rock in each hand," said Low.

When Mark McCormack began packaging and selling Arnold Palmer, a close friend of Low's, in ways that no one had ever thought of before and practically printing money in the process, it gave George a lot of ammunition for his veranda standing. If someone were to ask Low if he had seen McCormack lately George would reply, "Yeah, he was sticking up a supermarket about an hour ago."

Mark learned to approach Low delicately, but it would never do any good. George would only tell McCormack, "Driving your getaway car is the best job in golf."

Bing Crosby once told George, who had insinuated he needed a room during Bing's tournament, that he could probably fix him up at the Del Monte Lodge and probably for a good rate.

"Thanks a lot," said George. "Can I loan you a dime to mark your ball?"

The Crosby has never been famed for drawing large crowds to the Monterey Peninsula for two reasons: it is inconveniently located on a 17-mile drive from Earth, and the weather is nearly always deplorable. When Crosby seemed rather excited one year by what appeared to him to be a better than average turnout Low remarked, "I seen more people on the back of a motorcycle."

Though George might frequently have a hangover gaze about him, his mind remains quick. Roasting in the Las Vegas sun one afternoon during the Tournament of Champions, when it was still being held at the Desert Inn course and when Wilbur Clarke was still alive, George noticed something unusual going up on the scoreboard. Arnold Palmer had just posted a nine, a seven and a five, in that order. Turning quietly to Clarke, Low said, "That's twenty-one. Pay him."

One of the better verandas to stand around on is that of the Augusta National Golf Club during the Masters. It has two

big shade trees, some crawling wisteria, a scattering of umbrellas and tables and, always, George Low. He will move
from a table to a bench to a tree trunk to a slope in the sun
and back again, covering his steps, mumbling comments about
the wretched state of the world and how many brokes there
are in it. One year George arrived fresh from having spent a
weekend sharing a hotel room with a friend, Bob Drum, who
was then a writer for the *Pittsburgh Press*.

"How do you like rooming with Drum?" George was asked.

"It's okay," he said. "If you don't mind taking a shower
with your money in your hand."

And there was the time at Augusta that George was hearing
about Oscar Fraley, a former columnist for UPI, getting into
a minor argument in a bar and causing some mild excitement.
As the tale was being related by someone who had witnessed
it, Fraley happened to stroll by. George interrupted the story
and called to Oscar. "I hear you didn't start no fight last night
for a change," he said. "Where'd you stay? In a room full of
nuns?"

George Low may not have been born bourbon-faced or angry,
but he was certainly born "energetically lazy," to use his words.
"He was born retired," is the way Jimmy Demaret has put it.
The event of George's birth occurred before World War I,
that much is known, and not three hundred yards, a stout
Nicklaus tee shot, from the pro shop at Baltusrol Golf Club
in Springfield, New Jersey.

"I like to say I was born in the 19th Hole—the only one
I ever parred," Low says.

He was the son of a rather famed Scot, George Low, Sr.,
who was runner-up for the U.S. Open championship in 1899
and who became the resident professional at Baltusrol. As one
of those Scots who came to America to teach the game to an
intrigued continent, George, Senior, numbered among his
pupils a couple of renowned White House slicers, William
Taft and Warren G. Harding.

"There were poor guys like that all around Baltusrol,"

George remembers. "The Toppings and then kind of charity cases."

Despite the fact that George grew up near the 1st tee of a golf course, he did not try to learn the game until he was fifteen. And this after his father had retired and taken his son back to Scotland. George *had* to play golf in Scotland, he felt. "What else is there to do over there? Wear a skirt?"

Try as he did to avoid playing golf, two things came naturally to George. A good swing and a deep, nagging feeling about the game. These attributes combined—conspired, more probably—to bring him back to the U.S. in the early 1930's. But in those days George returned as more than just an assistant pro at a variety of clubs in the upstate area of New York. For instance, there was one summer when he was working at a club in the Catskills when he was struck with a get-rich scheme. He found a friend who owned a Ford Tri-Motor airplane and together they dreamed up the idea of shuttling newspapers from the cities to resort areas.

Soon they decided they could make their business even more profitable by shuttling more than papers. Like booze, this being during Prohibition. And at the same time, on weekends, they staged what could only be described as the world's worst air show featuring George Low parachuting out of the Tri-Motor.

"I didn't exactly jump," he says. "I'd open the door of the plane, and then I'd open the chute and let it pull me out. Who the hell wants to jump if he don't know if the chute's gonna open?"

All of this came to an end one cold evening during a shuttle flight when the plane somehow drifted into a small mountain.

"Me and the pilot got out safe, but the booze died," George says.

It was also during these early, formative years that George developed a special fondness for Saratoga and thoroughbred racing itself. In August during the Saratoga meeting, he got acquainted with the sport by becoming a runner, one of those

guys who found out what the swells in the box seats wanted
to wager on a race and then ran to the betting tables to get
it down for them.

"I knew all the rich guys," he says. "Most of 'em were
empty suits."

To this day, George has a knack for going to the tracks in
style. One recent summer George was back at Saratoga, quite
comfortable in the home of Harry M. Stevens III, a young
Stevens of the family that invented the hot dog, the straw,
the paper cup and now caters no fewer than forty-one tracks
and stadiums around the country. Sitting on young Harry's
porch one evening, George was asked by his host if he wanted
to pitch coins at a line for cash.

"Now what would I do with a catering business?" said
George.

But let's retreat back to those 1930's again, to the days
when Low honestly felt he could make it all the way from his
assistant pro jobs into a handsome living on what had become
a burgeoning PGA tour.

George started out on the tour determined to make his way
as a champion, but, well, it was too much fun in those days.
Card games all through the nights—pitch and bridge, that
kind of thing. And there were all of these characters to pal
around with—Demaret, Jimmy Thomson, Leo Diegel, Craig
Wood. "And that Indian," he says. Which was Ky Laffoon.

"Laffoon is the only man who ever beat me outa something
on the putting green," says George. "At the old North and
South Open at Pinehurst we got into a game that lasted day
and night. I should have known I was in trouble when we
putted at night. Laffoon was an Indian and Indians can see at
night. I didn't get in that jackpot no more."

Low made an attempt which might generously be described
as feeble to win the British Open of 1939. The idea of returning
to semi-native soil gripped him, one reason being that he
might be able to redeem himself for the last round he had
played in Scotland. A long time before, in the British Boys'

championship at Edinburgh, George had been beaten 8–7 by
a cross-handed Scot, and he was so disgusted about it he heaved
his clubs out of a train window. So George and Johnny Bulla
sailed on the *Transylvania* in the summer of '39 for England.

The trip abroad took too long for George. Struggling to
occupy his time on board ship, he got into a high-stakes game
of shuffleboard with a gentleman of nobility, and he lost so
much money that he was forced to delay his arrival for the
British Open. Instead of going straight to St. Andrews he
went with the earl or count or whatever he was to Perthshire.
There they would bowl on the green.

"My bankroll looked like an elephant slept on it when I
got off the ship," George explains. "Took me three weeks
bowling on the green to get it back."

Low finally got to St. Andrews but not in time for a practice
round. And he isn't altogether clear on how well he played.
"I think I missed the cut—if I teed off at all," he says. "I
forget. In those days, me and Clayton Heafner had a bad habit
of being withdrew."

Where are the characters on today's tour? That's one thing
George would like to know. Where are the fun-lovers, the
withdrews? "All you got out there is a bunch of authors and
haberdashers," he says.

"All you got to do to write a book is win one tournament.
All of a sudden you're telling everybody where the V's ought
to point. And them that don't win, they're haberdashers. They
sell sweaters and slacks and call themselves pros."

Says George, "There ain't many of 'em knows how to repair
a club in a shop. They can bend 'em, but they can't work on
'em until they know what's right. Most of 'em couldn't win
consistently if they had Dick Tracy for a partner. I do a little
club work for a few of 'em, but there's not too many who'd
give the ducks a drink if they owned Lake Mead. They'll pop
for a handshake, but those I got plenty of."

One of George's last flings as an active tour player came in
1945, and history confirms that he went out beautifully.

Among the more remarkable facts of golf is that George Low helped end the fantastic winning streak of Byron Nelson. It happened in the Memphis Open that summer. Nelson, the Mechanical Man, had won eleven straight tournaments when he got to Memphis to try for the twelfth. Nelson finished third at Memphis behind Amateur Freddie Haas, who shot 270, and none other than George Low, who shot 276.

"Haas win the tournament, but I win the front money," says George. "I was the first pro to beat Nelson. Look it up."

Very shortly after that Low retired to the putting greens forever.

So many legends and half-truths have been written, spoken and whispered about George Low's putting ability, he ought to be a folk song. There are wild tales of George putting with a rake, a shovel, a pool cue and a broom handle and defeating others using a legitimate putter. There are stories of George kicking the ball with his foot and acing five out of nine holes in one round on the putting green. Other stories say that George has given putting "secrets" to Arnold Palmer, Bing Crosby, Willie Mays, all sorts of celebrities who turn up in his photo albums with their arms around his bulky shoulders. And there are stories that in the old days George took so much money away from tour winners on the putting greens that he should have been given a speeding ticket.

Low only forces a sly grin when the stories are put to him.

"They get started because I live good," he says. "I spend $50,000 a year of somebody else's money, that's all."

Oh, there are a few things George could talk about if he wanted to get himself in some kind of jackpot, as he says, but it isn't worth it. Sure, he can kick the ball with his foot and get it down in two from almost anywhere. For example, at Las Vegas a few years ago he was walking around in a practice session with Bo Wininger when Bo plopped a ball down on the 16th green at the Desert Inn and said, "Three cases of beer to two you can't get it down in two from here." The putt was seventy-five feet long. George called it, put his shoe to the ball and rolled it up within two inches of the cup. And George *can* beat you putting, even if he uses a wedge. "Don't ever try him," Byron Nelson has warned.

"I shall have to admit, in all modesty, that I'm probably the greatest putter who ever lived," says George. "At least I'll try anyone for a nominal fee."

There is a simple reason why George Low is the greatest putter who ever lived. "I've done more of it than anybody else," he says. "Back in Scotland, in Carnoustie, there was a thirty-six-hole putting green right outside our house. I putted for three or four years, eight, ten, twelve hours a day, before I ever started playing golf. I've always been able to do things with my hands anyhow. Build things. I have feel in them. So I putted and putted before I ever played golf, and then I've done nothing but putt since I quit. I can beat anyone on the tour because they have to worry about getting to the green. I'm already there."

George is not keen about giving away his putting secrets— not for free, at least. But he can offer a little advice.

"Everybody has a different problem putting," he says. "The best thing you can have is a quick left wrist. That makes you take the clubhead back on the inside. Most of your weight ought to be on the left foot for good balance. Another important thing is to keep both thumbs squarely on the top of the grip for the right feel."

He goes on, "The feel of the club may be the most important thing of all. When you reach in your pocket for a coin the last thing that touches the coin is your thumb. You use it to roll out the coin. It's the most sensitive finger. That's why you grip the putter with both thumbs on top of the handle."

And on, "After you get the feel of the club the thing to do is be sure you get a good, solid rap on the ball when you hit it. And there's only one way to be sure of doing that. Take the club back on the inside, like opening a door, and then bring it forward. When you open a door you take it back slow.

When you close the door, that's the way the putter should meet the ball."

And on, "The worst way for the beginner to putt is to jab at the ball. You'll see some of the pros jab at it, but it's their own method they've worked out, which they think is good for all of the bad greens they putt on. There are a couple of 'em that jab the putt on any kind of green. Billy Casper, for instance, and Bob Rosburg. They're pretty good putters, but there are exceptions to everything. Besides, they jab the same way every time, which is the real key to good putting. Consistency."

And finally, "That's why I'm gonna beat everybody. I'm gonna hit the ball the same way every time, and you're not. And if we putt long enough for the luck to scare off, I got to be the winner."

George Low might be a more mysterious figure than he is if it had not been for Arnold Palmer. When Palmer won his second Masters in 1960, Low's name burst into print as some sort of weird genius of the greens—and all because of a remark Arnold made to the press. That year Palmer sank dramatic putts for birdies on the last two greens to win, not only before the thousands in Augusta, but before millions more watching television. And later on, in an interview, when asked about those heroics, Palmer said, "The only thing I did on those putts was keep thinking what my old friend George Low always says: 'Keep your head down and don't move.'"

A short time after this Low's small but impressive notoriety resulted in an autograph-model putter, the George Low putter, a mallethead type with a marketing slogan that went "the putter with the built-in touch." It was made by a company called the Sportsman's Golf Corporation of Chicago. A few of the pros began using the Low putter, mainly Gary Player. And exactly one year later, back in Augusta again, Player, using the Low putter, won the Masters and George Low got even more publicity.

"But I was lucky," says George. "The putter started selling
so well I got fired. It was a relief. With a lot of money in
your pocket, it takes away the torment of where you're gonna
sleep."

Along about this time another change took place in Low's
career. A motel chain, Ramada Inn, hired him as a goodwill
ambassador. His job was to follow the tour and guide as many
pros as possible into Ramada Inns across the land. They gave
him a Cadillac to drive—"the only Cadillac in the press lot"—
and let him have free rooms in all of the Ramada Inns he could
locate.

"It didn't feel right," he says. "I knew it wouldn't last.
Something was missing. The daily challenge that I'd grown
used to. The challenge of whether I'd be able to borrow Frank
Stranahan's car and lose it to somebody in a coin flip or something. It got so bad for a while I almost bought a pair of shoes
on my own."

That wouldn't have been right. George hadn't bought a
pair of shoes in thirty years. He'd got them all from Foot Joy.
"I been a test pilot for Foot Joy forever. I test their sixty-five-
dollar alligator models to see if standing in them for long
periods of time in a bar brings them any serious harm. What
effect spilling beer has on them."

Rarely is George anything in appearance but the portrait of
prosperity. Foot Joy shoes, a handsome plaid jacket that he
got from Joe Jemsek, a golf course owner from the Chicago
area ("he wears my size") and a Western-tooled, monogrammed
leather chair stool, courtesy of Bob Goldwater, Barry's brother.

"No if-come about him," says George. "Bob stands up."

There have been, sad to relate, times when George Low has
insisted on paying up himself. Not often, but some. And only
in these latter, more prosperous years. One such occasion was
in Augusta in 1965 in a place called the Bull Bat Lounge,
just off the lobby of the Town House Hotel. George was sitting
with a few journalist friends he could trust, drinking beer and
getting ready to go search for a cafeteria. He prefers cafeterias

to elegant restaurants because they have a lot of vegetables. Anyhow, George was in the middle of an anecdote when an old friend appeared.

"Good to see you, Bubble," the voice said, the voice belonging to a Tampa car salesman named Madman Morris. "Where you been? I been all over. Pensacola. Miami. Everywhere. How come I didn't see you?"

"Madman," said George. "Either shut up or sit down and assume the financial obligation. I got my own lies to tell."

"Sure good to see you, Georgie," said Madman. "I know this guy thirty years. . . ."

"Are you gonna sit down and buy something, Madman, or just stand there looking like a buried lie in a bunker?" George said.

"I been all over, Bubble. Jacksonville. Pensacola. Miami. How come you wasn't anywhere?" Madman said.

"There's a rule in this joint that any guy stands around has to *buy* something," said Low. "Why don't you take your shag bag somewhere else and hit your shanks?"

"Whatta guy," said Madman Morris. "Same old George. I'd see this guy everywhere. Palm Beach. Orlando. Pensacola. Miami . . ."

"I can't get in no jackpot with an unplayable lie like this," said George, excusing himself, sliding out of the booth in the Bull Bat Lounge, paying the check and leaving to go look for vegetables.

There are also occasions when George Low can be persuaded to play a round of golf. Actually play. Naturally, the type of golfing companion George prefers is someone with money and questionable talent, an ego-inspired handicap, perhaps. "Give me a millionaire with a bad backswing and I can have a very pleasant afternoon," George says.

An afternoon like this occurred not so many winters ago at the posh Seminole Golf Club in Palm Beach. George got into a game with the Duke of Windsor and the late Robert R. Young, the railroad magnate. An earl or a duke or a count could always entice George into a game of something. George's putter was good to him this day as it usually is when more than laughs are involved. The other shots he could hit well enough from memory. George came out in good shape, don't worry. Except that when the round was finished Low didn't notice the Duke straining to get in his pocket.

They were all sort of strolling toward the clubhouse—to the veranda, of course—slowly, amid a rather awkward silence. George cleared his throat a couple of times. They stopped and chatted about the nice day, how lovely the course looked this time of year. George shifted his weight from one Foot Joy to another and cleared his throat again.

Finally, Robert Young discreetly took George aside and whispered something to him.

"Oh, by the way, George. I should have mentioned that His Royal Highness never pays money," said Young.

"He don't do *what?*" said Low.

"His Royal Highness never pays. It's custom with him. It's rather a privilege, you see, to play golf in his company."

"Mr. Young," said George Low, the only George Low there ever was or ever will be in golf. "You take care of your railroads and I'll take care of my dukes."

Down South

You'd think I'd never done anything else but hit that shot. In the Orient for a while I became known as Mr. Double Eagle, which nongolfers probably took to mean that I was an Indian chief.

—GENE SARAZEN,
reflecting on the shot that made the Masters

It is commonly known among a select group of Masters goers that many of the best shots of the tournament are served in tall paper cups on the upstairs porch of the Augusta National Golf Club. The truly great moments occur out on the course, to be sure, but you have to wait for those, and the porch outside the upper Grill Room is a very pleasant place to wait. There, one can sit where corporate insurgents sit and mill where double eagle makers mill. There too a man can listen to the Masters, not only from the logy, anecdotal mumbling around him, but from the mighty braying of the crowds in the valley below. Off on the fragrant horizon there stands a big, faintly readable leader board reacting to the roars, and near the white porchrail is a contemplative wisteria, and down on the umbrella-dotted veranda there is an ever-present cluster of Jeanne Weiskopfs and Barbara Nicklauses to holler at. In the whole Renoir of the Masters there is really no better place to await the premonition that Gene Sarazen will hole out a four-wood, or that Billy Joe Patton will slice a spoon into a creek, or that Roberto De Vicenzo will shank his scorecard.

Augusta premonitions come in several different forms of course. It can be a whoop from up around the 8th green, where, according to one's watch, Arnold Palmer's gallery ought to be. It can be ominous wailing from down near the 10th, where, perhaps Jack Nicklaus is. It can be a series of red numbers going up on the leader board for someone who was out of it—say, Bert Yancey—but who now, suddenly, is back in it. Or it can sometimes merely be an intelligence report. A sunburned soul will hike up the stairs to pant and puff the news that W-Wadkins . . . has . . . b-birdied four holes . . . in a r-row. J-jay and B-bee . . . and water, please . . . t-tall . . . ice . . . t-twist . . . aaaaaiiiii, whew.

In all of its years since the beginning in 1934, the Masters has been a tournament of premonitions closely followed by explosions. One simply knows that every afternoon something cinemascopically dramatic is going to happen, as in no other championship, for the Augusta course is laid out to make things happen, to entice the field into grandiose delusions. These explosions can be of the mild kind that only make the ice cubes swirl, but they can also be violent enough to rattle the porch and send everyone scrambling out onto the course like Hollywood-style Spitfire pilots darting toward their planes.

Bobby Jones, who started the Masters, must have had a premonition himself as long ago as 1935, the year of his second tournament. He had played in the event (Jones played in the Masters until 1948) and he was in the clubhouse with most everyone else, toasting Craig Wood as the probable winner, when he decided to wander out on the back nine. He wanted to watch his old friends, Gene Sarazen and Walter Hagen, who comprised the last twosome. Jones reached the 15th green just as they were nearing, Sarazen holding a remote mathematical chance to tie Wood if he could manage three birdies out of the last four holes. Some chance.

Sarazen, as he recalls, was not really thinking about making a double eagle as he stood out there in the fairway of the 15th, waggling a club, his plus-fours fluttering in the spring breeze. All he wanted to do was clear the pond in front of the green, get on in two, and score an easy birdie. Nobody ever thinks about making a double eagle except fourteen-year-old junior champions.

Sarazen lashed at the four-wood from the right side of the fairway, and the ball took off in a high, drawing arc, slightly right of the flag. He might have hit more club, a spoon or brassie, to be certain of clearing the pond, but it would not have done him much good for the shot to wind up in Savannah. The trick was to reach the green and hold it.

"There was a pause and then I heard some yells," Sarazen recalls. "I walked a few yards before I realized it had gone in and wasn't just close for an eagle. Frankly I'm tired of discussing it. You'd think I had never done anything else but hit that shot. In the Orient for a while I became known as Mr. Double Eagle, which nongolfers probably took to mean that I was an Indian chief. To me the most interesting thing about the shot is that both Jones and Hagen saw it."

Sarazen's remarkable shot did not alone win him that Masters of course. He had to par the last three holes to tie, and then defeat Craig Wood the next day in a thirty-six-hole play-off. The fact remains, however, that the double eagle has done more to publicize Augusta than all of the growing of azaleas and pruning of junipers have since. Rudy Vallee had Sarazen recreate the shot the following year for a network radio show, for example, and many a newsreel cameraman has had him trudge back to the scene. And once, in 1955, the tournament committee commemorated the event by staging a double eagle contest on Wednesday instead of a clinic (or the par-three tournament it now holds). Each member in the field took three whacks from where Gene hit the four-wood. Freddie Haas, Jr., was the winner with a shot four feet from the pin.

Few men, including Sarazen, have won the Masters under more desperate conditions than Byron Nelson did—twice. His sub-par barrages on both occasions, in 1937 and 1942, were nearly spectacular enough to make everyone forget all about double eagles. They were, in fact, memorable enough for the green-jacketed sponsors to erect a bridge in honor of his deeds at the 12th hole, a bridge similar to the one they built for Sarazen at the 15th.

The Byron Nelson of '37 was barely twenty-five years old, tall, slender, nervous and usually outfitted in starched dress shirts with the cuffs turned up twice on the order of a pharmacist. But he opened that championship with a 66, the lowest round Jones and his friends had seen in the tournament. Nelson's lead slowly dribbled away to a more experienced Ralph Guldahl, and on the last day, with nine holes to play, Byron trailed by three strokes.

Guldahl was playing one hole ahead of Nelson, who was paired with Wiffy Cox, and when Byron reached his drive down the 10th fairway it was just in time to see Guldahl take a birdie putt out of the cup. "If I don't get a birdie here, I'm four behind with only eight to go," Nelson thought to himself. "I wonder what second money is?"

Without thinking much more about his predicament than that, Nelson hit a good shot into the 10th green and saw it spin up close for a short birdie putt. He made it, and Wiffy Cox said to him, "Kid, I think that's the one we need. It'll show Ralph he can't shake you, and there are plenty of holes left."

Both men got par fours at the long, dangerous 11th, but when Nelson reached the 12th tee, the crowd, he noticed, was scurrying over to him in mad droves, jamming around him. And he thought he heard someone talking about Guldahl taking a double-bogey five on that dandy little water-logged par three.

"My adrenalin really got going," Nelson says. "I suddenly realized I'd been playing negative golf for two days." Nelson, somehow was seized by aggressiveness. He splintered the flag with a six-iron at the 12th and dropped the ten-footer for a birdie two. Wiffy Cox did a little dance.

Now, up ahead on the par five 13th, Guldahl, reeling from Nelson's pursuit, gambled on a second shot to the green, plopped it into Rae's Creek and took a bogey 6. Then Nelson, almost in a dead run, whomped a spoon over the creek and off the left edge of the green, whereupon he took a three-iron and gently chipped in a fifty-foot eagle three.

In just two holes Nelson had gone 2–3 to Guldahl's 5–6, and it was all over.

"I really didn't realize the importance of it at the time," Nelson says. "It was quite a while before I remembered I'd played the first four holes of the back nine four under. In those days, the money was the main thing, the *only* thing I played for. Titles were something to grow old with."

Five years later the Masters saw a different Nelson, this one more sophisticated, confident, popular, established, secure, already, at thirty, the holder of three major championships, those being the Masters, the 1939 U.S. Open and the 1940 PGA. He was Lord Byron, the Mechanical Man, a man obviously reaching his peak ahead of Ben Hogan and Sam Snead, who were among his contemporaries. And a handy thing it was, for only this kind of player could have defeated Hogan, another rising star from Texas, in a classic Masters.

Nelson began that tournament as if he intended to turn Augusta into a Roanoke chicken ranch, shooting 68–67— 135, tying the thirty-six-hole record. He played ahead to 280 and what seemed like victory, but Hogan, burning inside for his first major title, made up eight strokes over the last two rounds and gained a tie. So it was Nelson vs. Hogan, a couple of old Texas pals, from the same caddy pens in fact, in a play-off. It was a Fort Worth city championship—on the road.

"Still the most vivid thing to me is that many of the players stayed over on Monday to follow us around," Nelson says.

Byron did not begin the play-off like any sort of mechanical man. He double bogeyed the 1st hole, and then bogeyed the 4th, and Hogan stepped onto the 6th tee with a three-stroke lead. But it was from this point on, through the next eleven holes, that Nelson, by his own admission, played the finest golf of his life. All he did was birdie the 6th, eagle the 8th, birdie the 11th, 12th and 13th, and play the next three holes in par. The harsh fact was that Hogan played those same eleven holes in one under par—and lost five shots, not to mention the Masters.

"The round was a little on the cool side," says Byron, who shot 69 to Hogan's 70. "I don't know that Ben and I exchanged many words. It was a big deal for both of us, naturally. The Masters was very much entrenched then as a major championship, more or so than in the previous years."

As just about everyone knows who doesn't use rented clubs or tee off in sneakers, Hogan's best years were still ahead of him. He would win the Masters twice (among ten major titles in all), would finish second three more times and would post a record of never finishing worse than tenth in fourteen straight Augusta appearances. For all of this, however, Ben's finest moment came many springtimes after his prime, and it was a very moving moment for the Masters. Where were you on April 8, 1967, the day Hogan almost turned Augusta into a soap opera? If you were in warm, sunny Georgia that Saturday you must have been in Hogan's gallery on much of the last nine holes when he shot a record-equaling 30 and completed the round in 66, the lowest of the week.

Quite possibly Hogan's last nine was the most elegant shot-making ever in a major tournament. It was certainly an amazing performance for a man only four months shy of his fifty-fifth birthday. Hogan played the nine in six birdies and three pars, without a single error in judgment or technique, without a single fairway miss or a putt of more than twenty feet in length, including the two par fives.

Soft music, please, and build that applause while the graying man in the old-fashioned white, billed cap and the pleated trousers plays it again. Let's see. There was a seven-iron into the 10th for a six-foot birdie, a six-iron into the 11th only one foot from the cup for a birdie, a six-iron onto the 12th for a ten-foot bird, a four-wood onto the 13th in two for a two-putt birdie, a five-iron onto the 14th for a par from eighteen feet, a four-wood onto the 15th for another two-putt birdie, a seven-iron onto the 16th for a par from twenty feet, a seven-iron onto the 17th for par from twenty feet and a five-iron onto the 18th for the last birdie that curled downhill and in from thirteen feet.

Ben had trudged up the last fairway to the building roar of thousands, and when the final putt dropped, the burst of joy from the great crowd must have awakened every tired body in the parking lot. It was followed by endless applause, like a marathon curtain call, and one had the feeling that even on the blasé clubhouse porch there surely couldn't be a dry eye.

For sustained whoops and hollers, and all-record-breaking in Spectator Hop, Step and Jump, no Masters has ever equaled that of 1954, in which a younger Hogan was intimately involved along with Sam Snead and a crazy, chattering North Carolina amateur, Billy Joe Patton. Those were the days when Tournament Chairman Clifford Roberts did not edit the crowds at Augusta. They were larger in the mid and late 1950's, the biggest, trompingest galleries golf has ever known. Mary Queen of Scots doing her naked dance of the rut iron (or whatever she did to get some credit for inventing the game) could not have lured more people into Augusta than the masters had in 1954 for the Ballad of Billy Joe.

Well, it wasn't so much a ballad as it was a slapstick whodunit. Billy Joe Patton, known only around Morganton, North Carolina, tied for the first round lead, which was unreal in itself, but then he led all alone after thirty-six, and he hung in there five behind Hogan and two behind Snead, in third place, after Saturday. Bareheaded, bespectacled, grinning, with a faster swing than a kitchen blender, Billy Joe kept the bulk of the throng enslaved with his scrambling tactics and his comments. "I may go for it, and I may not," he would drawl, addressing a shot. "It all depends on what I elect to do on my backswing."

Sundays are always psychotic at the Masters, but this one more closely resembled a South American revolution than most. Hogan and Snead, playing one hole apart, had every reason to think they were going to have their own private little tournament on Sunday but Billy Joe, two holes ahead of them, got back in it shortly after everyone had teed off. At the 6th hole he hit a seven-iron right into the cup for the loudest hole in one in the history of Morganton, North Carolina, or Augusta, Georgia.

And all anyone could hear from the galleries during the next hour or so as Patton, Hogan and Snead began to shift the lead around, was "Billy Joe gonna do it. He gonna *do* it."

Everybody did it down around Amen Corner, the nickname for a cruel and scenic bend of the 11th, 12th and 13th holes. Snead three-putted himself to a 72 and 289, the highest total that ever looked like it might win. Hogan uncharacteristically hit an approach shot into the water at the eleventh for a double-bogey six and a 75 to tie Snead at 289. But while all this was happening and the hordes were running around like children at recess, Billy Joe threw the Masters so high in the air only the azalea goddesses knew where it would land. At a point when judicious play would have won it for him easily—laying up at 13 and 15 or sure pars in other words—Patton went for the greens on his second shots and landed in the water both times. To the complete horror of his followers he made a seven and a six on those holes for a 71 and missed tying by a stroke. Pars there would have given him 68 and a two-stroke victory.

The 13th hole provided the more important and dramatic incident, for Patton knew he was leading then, that Hogan had just made six at the 11th. He could see too, one presumed, that he had a nasty sidehill lie for his shot to the green with a three-wood. He studied the shot momentarily while the crowd shouted for him to be cautious. Then he looked over at those near him, taking a wood from the bag.

"I didn't get where I am playin' safe," he said, promptly hitting the ball right into the creek bottom bordering the green.

For a moment or two there was still a glimmer of hope for Billy Joe. Walking toward the ditch Patton heard a few frantic calls and saw some members of the gallery pointing down into the high grass below the green. They were telling him the ball had not submerged quite as deep as Conrad Veidt usually took his U-boats, that perhaps it was playable. Soggy and weed-covered but playable.

Patton removed his shoes and socks, rolled up his trousers, grabbed a wedge and climbed down into the ditch. He got set once or twice for a slash at it but finally decided, amid some nervous giggles in the crowd, that it was too risky. He could take fourteen or fifteen slashes at the ball once he got going. So he took a penalty stroke, laid out, pitched up poorly, pitched again and required two putts for his calamitous seven.

The ballad of Billy Joe ended with him sharing a cart with Clifford Roberts the next day to follow Snead's narrow play-off victory over Hogan.

"I wouldn't play it any differently," says Patton. "I was elated to play as well as I did. Going into those last nine holes I knew I had to take a pop at it. What if I'd played safe and lost? That wouldn't have answered anything. I didn't feel I had any lead at all with Hogan behind me. I'm talkin' about the Hogan of *then*. If I'd played it safe I'd always have wondered how good I really was. I'm almost delighted I lost, in fact. I might have turned pro."

The remainder of the 1950's at Augusta were not what you would term unexciting. Certainly the victories achieved by Cary Middlecoff, Jack Burke, Doug Ford, a new fellow named Arnold Palmer and Art Wall, in that order, were not without suspense and splendid play. But the Masters, like pro golf itself, was suffering a disease we might call the In-betweens. It was mourning the gradual but obvious exit of Hogan and Snead and waiting for the real Arnold Palmer.

The love affair between Palmer and Augusta actually began in 1958 when he won the first of his four Masters. He won it with his pants too long, his shirttail out and no one sure at that time whether Latrobe was in Pennsylvania or Poland. Specifically, he won it on the last day with a free lift from an imbedded lie on the 12th hole, an eagle on the 13th and some unfortunate three-putting by Ken Venturi. The affair simmered the next year, Wall's year, when it was Palmer who *lost* the tournament in the last round on the same hole, the 12th, where he had won it with the free lift. With a two-stroke lead he splashed a seven-iron into the creek and about two dozen guys up front, led by Art Wall, regarded the news so jubilantly they birdied every cup in sight, including a few paper ones.

Now, with this buildup, Palmer and the Augusta crowds were ready in 1960 to embrace one another, Swedish film style. He quickly mobilized his now famous Army with a first-round 67 and continued to lead the tournament all the way until the last thirty minutes. The charge of the Winnie brigade was on. At this point, however, Ken Venturi was in the clubhouse caressing a 283, believing he had redeemed himself for collapsing twice before when he had been close. Poor Ken Venturi. He was forced to watch a TV set while Palmer rammed in a thirty-foot birdie on the 71st and then an eight-foot birdie on the 72nd to beat him by a shot.

"I'm sitting there with the press, all pleased and comfortable," Venturi would describe it later, "and when Arnie holes the thirty-footer they leave me like I got the pox."

By 1961, of course, there was only one player in the Masters—Arnie. The championship was his to win or lose as he saw fit. That Gary Player would have the audacity to share the lead with him at thirty-six and then to open up a four-shot bulge through fifty-four was practically unspeakable. Cries of "Get him, Arnie" echoed through the pines on Monday (Sunday's round was washed out) as Palmer set chase. There was one particularly frustrating moment for Gary as he doggedly tried to hold his lead with Arnold slowly creeping up. Bouncing down the 11th fairway, Gary looked at the big leader board and saw that the scorekeepers had posted a huge impromptu sign on it. It said GO ARNIE.

Player got home with a 74 for 280, but Arnold, working

on a 69, had struggled to a one-stroke lead and when he crushed a drive up the center of the last fairway, leaving himself no more than a seven-iron to the green, the Army was ecstatic. The war had been won and they, as much as he, had won it. There were slaps on the back and long, giddy choruses of whooha, Arnie.

The Army had forgotten one thing though. Palmer could go to sleep at times like these, the challenge over, the hard work done. And sleep he did on the seven-iron, which plinked off into a right-hand bunker. Well, that was all right, the Army felt. He would either get it up and down in two or take a bogey, in which case he would simply win it in a play-off the next day with a 63 to Player's 97. And then, right there, before all of those worshipping thousands and before all of the millions watching television, before Winnie and Mark Mc-Cormack and everybody, he hit a Joe Zilch out of the bunker. A Sam Sausage.

"He Dick Smithed it," a man quietly said to himself in the stunned gallery. Guy named Dick Smith.

The ball squirted across the green and sped down a far slope into so difficult an angle that no mortal could have chipped back to rescue the bogey. Palmer made six and lost another Masters.

"I guess I was in too big of a hurry to win it," Arnold said later. "Or something. Hell, I don't know what I was up to."

Palmer very nearly suffered a worse humiliation in 1962 when the Masters was all his again in tone, mood and suspense. He grabbed the lead the second afternoon with a blazing 66, tacked a 69 onto that, and although Player and Dow Finsterwald were hovering near enough to the top to cause trouble, most of the porch talk Sunday morning was all about Palmer breaking Ben Hogan's seventy-two-hole record of 274. Why not? All he needed was a piddling 68, which he could surely shoot if he had enough cigarettes with him.

Arnold didn't shoot the 68, but he came close to a 78. In one of the most curious rounds he ever played Palmer frittered away stroke after stroke until he eventually arrived at the 16th hole to find himself two shots behind Finsterwald and Player with par in for a fat 77 and with some of his Army sacrilegiously mixed into Dow's Dragoons.

Then it was like this: Ah, good, says Palmer. Are the TV cameras in focus? Swell. Flick the cigarette. Hitch the pants. And there goes a sixty-foot chip, uphill, downhill and in for a birdie deuce. On to 17. Flick. Hitch. Hitch again. And down goes a six-foot birdie putt. Play-off. Which, of course, he wins, largely with the jolt of a gimme birdie at the 12th hole, good old breezy, bitchy No. 12, Amen Corner, where he had splattered and splashed and won and lost before.

Palmer won the Masters again in 1964, but this one was more or less of a, well, porch-sitter some called it. He led all the way and finished six strokes ahead of the field. And he may win it some more. Harry Vardon, after all, won six British Opens, so there is no law against a man building up his own stockpile of particular major championships. Never again, however, will he dominate the atmosphere of Augusta as thoroughly as he did over those five consecutive years from '58 through '62. Nor does it seem likely that anyone ever can again.

If winning alone could do it Jack Nicklaus would already be there. Think about Jack for a moment. Over the past 15 years as an amateur and professional he has not only taken four Masters but 14 major championships in all, which is more than anyone. Along the way one of his modest projects at Augusta in 1965, was to fire a 64, equaling a twenty-five-year-old course record, and wind up with a total of 271, seventeen under par, which broke Hogan's record by three strokes. Jack also has wavy blond hair, drives a roadster and is considered well-liked around the frat house. But what he needs for a future birthday is warmth.

Jack's problems are that he has had too much talent and maturity for his age. After all, no one can identify with a beefy rich kid who hits the ball across the state line and goes around beating Arnold Palmer all the time. The warmth is there to those who know him well, but it only rarely transfers to the crowd.

What Nicklaus *could* do some year to evoke sympathy perhaps is approve a Masters scorecard with a mistake on it and blow a championship. Had it been Jack who did what Roberto De Vicenzo did in 1968, he would have a whole new image, the Rules of Golf would still be under siege and the tournament committee would be hiding out in Pueblo, Colorado.

The 1968 Masters should have been filed away as one of the most dazzling ever played. Just about anyone in town who owned a set of clubs was in the thick of it all four days. Starting the final round, for instance, no fewer than eleven men were all within three strokes of one another, and going into the last nine holes at least six players were seriously in contention. When the day appeared to be over the following results had been produced: twenty-two players had broken par and twenty-one had finished under the par of 288 for the championship, nine more than ever before. There had been so many red numbers (for under par) on the leader boards it looked as if the place had been bombed with Bloody Marys.

Hottest of all were two men who had been, possibly, the least considered as potential Masters winners: Roberto De Vicenzo, a carefree, if elderly, Latin, and Bob Goalby, a plodding veteran of the PGA tour whose often brilliant golf was becoming less frequent. Roberto pitched in a wedge at the 1st hole for an eagle two and birdied the next two holes, getting off to the kind of start municipal hustlers enjoy when they're betting the trailer rent. Ever smiling and looking at times quite astonished, he birdied the 8th as well and came through the first nine in 31. Goalby stayed close with a 33.

Roberto kept it up on the back side. He birdied the 12th and then the 15th, but Goalby birdied the 13th and 14th, playing two holes behind him, and by now it had come down to just these two. Then as Roberto stood over a short birdie putt at the 17th, Goalby addressed a fifteen-footer for an eagle at the 15th. If both putts dropped they were tied. Both did, as one was privileged to see on television's split screen, an utterly delicious moment for the electronic journalists involved. Roberto now needed par on 18 for 64 and 276, and Goalby needed pars on the last three holes for 65 and the same total.

For the next few moments, both men seemed determined to avoid a play-off. Roberto played a sick three-iron into the 18th, bunkered it and wound up with a bogey five and 277. Goalby, meanwhile, having parred 16 three-putted the 17th for a bogey. They were, alas, still in a deadlock—if Goalby could manage a par on the last hole. And he did so with a career two-iron from a hook lie that soared 220 yards, fading perfectly onto the green for an easy two putts.

What no one knew at the time except the Masters officials and De Vicenzo was that even as Goalby played his stirring 18th hole, Roberto had lost a stroke through bookkeeping. Tommy Aaron, his playing companion for the day, had accidentally marked down a 4 instead of a 3 at the 17th hole on his scorecard, a 35 instead of a 34 for the last nine and a 66 instead of a 65 for the round. And Roberto had hastily approved the card. The Rules of Golf state that a player's card stands as he approves it. If it is too many, that's what he gets. If it is too few, he's disqualified.

Most of the Rules of Golf, of course, were written for the days when men played in heavy tweed suits, smoked pipes on their downswings and were galleried mostly by sheepherders. But there was nothing anyone could do about it, least of all De Vicenzo, who would only say, "What a stupid I am," or poor Bob Goalby, who became a Masters champion in the most unlikely of ways since Gene Sarazen's double eagle knocked everyone off the clubhouse porch.

Each year that the Masters reemerges as such a scented and luxuriant success, it strengthens the notion that God must have been a 2-handicapper from Georgia. At least it encourages the legend of how it all seems to get started every spring: Clifford Roberts goes outside the Augusta National clubhouse upon a certain divine morning in April, does a *verónica* with one of those green blazers and, all at once, wonders occur. Grandiloquent pines rise up. Acres of emerald turf appear. Obedient servants begin stirring around. And suddenly great swarms of happy people are encircling Arnold Palmer, who happens to be threshing about in a million or so fresh-blooming dogwoods.

But the Masters does not happen quite like this. It evolved painstakingly, building its traditions and its distinctions. It was caressed, loved, patted and prodded into shape until it finally became the most glorious scene that golf has to offer. Because it grew slowly and mellowed quietly, there is much to the Masters—and Augusta National—that goes unseen by the swarming galleries and even unappreciated by the players, who are the people this particular tournament was made for.

The town of Augusta itself is more than two hundred years old, and for most of those years it squatted in a state of semi-decay on the red clay banks of the Savannah River. It wasn't even important enough for Uncle Billy Sherman to burn down on his march toward Atlanta. And in the early days of the Masters it got to be known as a place where Georgia got even for the Civil War. Hotel accommodations were once as scarce as clean sheets. Jim Murray, the columnist, looked around his hotel room one year and wrote: "I am staying in the house on Tobacco Road that Jeeter Lester moved out of." Dining out, even today, is still the sort of treat that would put Craig Claiborne in the insurance business. Florida killed Augusta as a winter resort, which it was for a time, and nearby Fort Gordon, where the Normandy invasion troops were trained, almost killed it as anything more than the annual meeting place for the Southern Baptist Congregation of Hookers. But despite all of this it is a beautiful town, and it has endured, and for one exciting week every spring it becomes the only place in the whole world to be—to smell and enjoy the visible Masters and to feel that all around you there is another one going on.

Subtle sounds and sudden glimpses help reveal this hidden Masters. It might be the clinking of ice in a cocktail glass as a green-jacketed member moves through the white portals and multicolored umbrellas on the terrace, or a quick look toward a row of cottages along the 10th fairway, with the knowledge that one of them was built for a President. It might be the way the sun drifts through the dark row of magnolias on the avenue leading up to the clubhouse entrance, or Valerie Hogan sitting on the lawn with a handful of cables and letters of congratulation for Ben. It could be a gathering of caddies, lounging in a fenced-off yard, weary from trudging over the course's valleys and too tired to play pool at the table provided for them in the caddie house, or the clacking of typewriters from inside the massive Quonset hut that serves the press. It might be nothing more than the glow of the club at night during a private dinner of the past champions, or something as remarkably simple as a hand-lettered sign on a swinging door leading from the kitchen into a dining area called the Trophy Room where Jones's clubs are displayed on a wall, a sign that advises the waiters: PLEASE TALK JUST A LITTLE LOUDER THAN A WHISPER. Perhaps, most of all, it is a devastating orderliness and a Southern loyalty that almost hurls you back to the veranda at Twelve Oaks where the Tarleton twins are giggling with Scarlett O'Hara.

A behind-the-scenes look at the Masters can well begin with the man who put up the sign to the kitchen help, Bowman Milligan, the club steward. Bowman is a big fellow with a smudge of gray at his temples and a baritonish voice, who has probably heard his name called out more than anyone in the history of Augusta National. But unrattled and dutiful, he maintains the carriage and aplomb of one who has spent a lifetime catering to millionaires. Primarily, Bowman is in charge of hiring and overseeing the Negro employees at the club—the waiters, bartenders, chauffeurs, maids and others. But if during Masters week Claude Harmon cannot get a glass of iced tea fast enough, or if Ben Hogan does not like the look of the lettuce on his sandwich, a holler of "Bowman!" is heard, and somehow Bowman is always nearby. "I work from can't to can't," he says of Masters week. "I try to rise to the occasion. My main job is remembering—trying to remember everything there is to be done."

Bowman, whose father was a groundkeeper on the Harry Payne Whitney estate in Aiken, South Carolina, which is just across the river, came to Augusta National in 1930, before the golf course was built on some nursery land Jones had discovered. He cooked, washed dishes and shined shoes for Roberts and Jones and began to learn the things that have to be remembered for a Masters. At one point Bowman even earned himself some personal prestige by managing Beau Jack, an Augusta National shoeshine boy who fought his way to the world lightweight championship. In the old days, it is said, battle royals were staged in the ballrooms of the Bon Air Hotel for Augusta National people, affairs in which five boxers were in the ring at once, and there Bowman's Beau Jack reportedly won many a fight that does not show on his record.

Today Bowman gets into the spotlight, too, but in a different way. He is official custodian of *the* green coat, that cherished piece of either gabardine or Palm Beach fabric (the player gets his choice) that goes to the Masters champion. Those who have witnessed a prizegiving at the putting green after a Masters may have wondered about the identity of the Negro gentleman in the dark suit, the one who marched, almost to an imaginary drum roll, from the clubhouse out to the course, carrying the green jacket and handing it to the past champion who, in ceremonial turn, slipped it on the new champion. It is Bowman Milligan who carries the coat.

Augusta National did not invent the idea of wearing blazers, even green ones, but it did start the custom of presenting one to its champion, a ceremony that some other tournaments since have copied. However, in the case of the Masters, the champion may leave town, but the green coat rarely does. All the green coats are stored in lockers. There is an unwritten rule that the coats of the past champions and those of members are to be worn only at the club. No one knows exactly what would happen if a man walked into Mike Manuche's wearing his Masters coat and Cliff Roberts were there, but one hates to guess.

The green coat and the winner's check for $20,000 or so are the most publicized of Augusta's rewards to the golfers, but there are many, many others. The champion receives a sterling silver replica mounted on pine of the permanent Masters trophy. The permanent trophy is just that, permanent, principally because no one could lift it. Made in England of nine hundred separate pieces of sterling, it weights some one hundred twenty-five pounds. The winner also gets a gold medal, a silver cigarette box and, finally, a year later at the dinner for the champions, a gold locket (Cartier) made like a book, with the club symbol—a map of the U.S. with a flagpin where Augusta might be—on the front and a photo of Bobby Jones on the inside of the back cover.

Augusta National gives away almost as many prizes as it serves thin steak sandwiches on toast, a basic part of the club menu that Jimmy Demaret once described as "the back nine of Bowman's cuisine." The pro runner-up gets a medal, the low amateur and runner-up get medals, each day's low scorer gets a Steuben crystal vase, the maker of a hole in one gets a Steuben vase, the maker of an eagle gets a Steuben highball glass, the winner of the Wednesday par-three tournament gets a silver tea service (Reed and Barton, Hampton Court design) or twelve Wedgwood bone china plates decorated with an etching of the clubhouse, the par-three runner-up gets one piece of a tea service or two plates, the third-place finisher gets two plates, and anyone who scores a hole in one in the par-three event gets six plates. There is one other prize for the competitors, which may be tougher to win than the championship, a giant Steuben bowl given for scoring a double eagle. There have been only two—Gene Sarazen's back in 1935 at the 15th hole and Bruce Devlin's in 1967 at the 8th hole.

In addition to all of the above, the Masters gives away to hundreds of officials, volunteer workers, players' wives and members of the press some different kind of remembrance each year. Almost every idea for a gift has been exhausted, but Cliff Roberts always hopes to better an ashtray, a billfold, a card case, a tool kit or whatever. It must be something green— Masters green—and monogrammed. Those are the only requirements.

One of the reasons why the Masters comes off so beautifully, no doubt, is the presence of all of the volunteer workers, who labor for a green billfold under a total of twenty-two committee chairmen. The personnel on these committees rarely changes. For instance, though it takes one hundred forty men to operate the scoreboards and bulletin boards there is rarely a turnover of more than five people. Of the one hundred twenty-five men signed up by the Gallery Guards Committee, there will be only ten or so working next year who were not working last year. The waiting list for such jobs is formidable. The volunteers are rarely Augusta National members—indeed most of them will never even get to play the course—but their loyalty and affection for the Masters seems limitless.

In a quite different way, one Augusta National member made a considerable contribution to the Masters. That was Dwight D. Eisenhower. The late President gave the tournament a lift that would be impossible to overestimate and prestige it could not otherwise have achieved. For example, several cottages seemed to have been sitting over in the woods by the 10th hole for years, but not until 1952 when some anonymous members built one for Eisenhower, which they first named "Mamie's Cabin," did cottage row become a tourist attraction for Masters spectators. It is an attraction seen only from the outside, needless to say.

There are seven cottages in all. Besides Eisenhower's and

Jones's, there is Tennessee, built by a group of members from Tennessee; Firestone, which was certainly not built by Goodyear; Peek, built by a late member named Burton Peek and now owned in part by John Hay Whitney; one called Butler, the latest, built by member Thomas Butler and three friends; and one unexcitingly named Duplex, which consists of four compact, identical apartments that were originally used by the club to house guests when clubhouse space was full.

The cabins all appear to be small as one gazes at them from, say, the 10th tee, which is about as close as non-residents ever get. Inside they are large, however, for they tumble off down a hill in the rear. Butler, the new one, has eight bedrooms on three levels, each with a bath. No one would ever really want to sneak into Butler cottage for a look around. It is, naturally, the Eisenhower cottage that attracts the gallery's attention. It is golf's equivalent of the LBJ Ranch or Bebe Rebozo's yacht.

Eisenhower's cottage is three-storied. On the main floor is Mamie's all-pink bedroom, a dressing room and bath suite, a living room with card tables, a spare suite just like Mamie's, a screened-in porch and a butler's pantry. Over a fireplace hangs a painting by Ike of the 16th hole. Eisenhower's bedroom is on the second floor along with a small office, a large paneled sitting room with more card tables and another bedroom suite. The walls are adorned with photographs of Mamie (dated from 1911 to 1928), pictures of houses the Eisenhowers have lived in at various army posts, five Remington prints and an oil by Ike of his grandson David. Naturally, David is in a golfing stance.

One of the most interesting things about the cottages is that ownership did not mean exclusive use, even by Eisenhower before he died. Any of the club's accommodations are available to any member and his wife. This includes the cottages and five suites in the clubhouse. During Masters week another group is also eligible to live at the club: *amateur* participants in the tournament.

The amateur's felicity at Augusta, which certainly harkens

back to Bobby Jones, is shown in another way. The week of the tournament three dinners are given for competitors. There is the one for the previous champions, which is held on Tuesday night, and one for the foreign golfers in the field on Wednesday night. But first of all, on Monday night, is a dinner given by the club for the amateurs.

Of these occasions, and, indeed, of all the things from Ike's cottage to Bowman's omniscience, nothing typifies the hidden Masters any better than the dinner for past winners, a tradition started in 1952 by Ben Hogan. No gathering in golf can rival it. On Tuesday night of Masters Week they meet in the Lower Grill Room at Augusta National—Hogan, Snead, Sarazen, Nelson, Palmer, Nicklaus and all the rest, along with Bobby Jones and Clifford Roberts, but nobody else. Absolutely nobody. This is, after all, how the Masters started, a little get-together for Bobby and his friends. A fine wine will be selected—usually a 1945 or '47 Château Lafite-Rothschild. The defending champion, who as host must also pick up the tab, will be responsible for the menu, and like as not out will come the strip steak again, hash browns and those peaches that Cliff Roberts likes. "I think Roberts owns a lot of peach orchards instead of Wall Street," Jack Burke, who won in 1956, once said.

The evening will begin with cocktails and reunions, for some of the oldtimers will just have arrived, and a thirty-minute business meeting of the Masters Club, during which a group photograph is taken, a process that shortens some tempers. Then comes the very carefully seated dinner; Hogan always in the same chair, a few others, for various reasons, always a safe distance apart. Everybody will discuss everybody's health and current activities, the defender will speak briefly and with consummate modesty about how he happened to win last year and no one has ever been able to prevent Sam Snead from telling a few hillbilly stories. Ultimately, the group will enter into a somewhat sacrilegious discussion of how the course and the tournament can still be improved. This bunker will have to go, one will say, that fairway will have to be narrowed, another will point out, this tee is too low, that one is too elevated—all of the talk being somewhat colored by personal experiences with the bunker, or what have you, involved. At some point it will certainly be mentioned, while Gary Player busily looks the other way, that there are too many foreign players in the field. It will be said that there seem to be too many amateurs. Contemplating the size of the dinner check, the defender may even decide that there are too many Masters winners.

Slowly the opinionated discussion will subside, the last bite of Nectar peach will be eaten with the last piece of Brie cheese and the group will move to the Upper Locker Room where the defender gets his money's worth, because everybody watches a movie that shows him winning the Masters last year.

By ten P.M. the bar is closing, the retired champions, with their thoughts of the past, are headed to the homes that they have rented for the week, and the younger champions with some real work ahead of them—Nicklaus, Palmer, Player— are off to reflect on their private tensions, for tee-off time is near. The Augusta National clubhouse is now strangely quiet. Only Bowman and his people are moving through it—talking, of course, just above a whisper.

The Big
Window

Mechanically everything worked fine, including the jaws of the commentators. Cut your talk in half. You're not saying anything interesting, anyhow.

—FRANK CHIRKINIAN,
at a television production meeting
during the Masters

Except, possibly, for a handful of seminomadic quinine hunters somewhere in Sumatra, just about everybody in the world has come to realize what American television's basic dedications are. The three networks are very strong for the elimination of cavities among the kids, dirt among T-shirts, sweating at high school dances, frowsy wives who can't cook, malnourished pets and freestyle burping. They are also very strong for the advancement of better mileage, scented breath, guava-colored jetliners, staying skinny and tourism to places where everyone looks like Jane Fonda. This is all terrific for the guys in the industry who play a lot of paddle tennis and throw around terms like "thirty-six mill" and "eighty-four thou" as if these were towns near Old Greenwich. The time salesmen know the viewers will swing in there with whatever comes up in the big window, be it *Secret Squirrel* or another Bette Davis smoke-a-thon. Anyhow, they ask, what do the viewers know about love, which is money? Don't they all have eyes like fusilli with meat sauce, suffer from chronic neck-aches and want Walter Cronkite for President? Don't worry about the programming,

Joe Bob. Anything sells. Let's all just phase into "21" for the day and do a total face-down in the salad.

Fortunately for at least some of the country's nearly two hundred million dial twisters, the industry is not always so insensitive. There are instances when its thinkers will drive a root canal through the great bicuspid of Madison Avenue and put something live and in color up there in the big window— a political follies, a space shot, or, more often than those, a sports event. When it happens, and when it is done well, TV becomes the electronic pleasure pill that it should be.

One such happy occasion came about in the spring of 1966 in Augusta, at that essential American quiltspread, the Masters golf tournament. Few annual events, sporting or otherwise, lend themselves to television quite as well as the Masters. For one thing, it is the first major outdoor sports event of the year if you agree that post-season football games really belong to another calendar. And it literally reeks with live action furnished by a pretty well-established cast: Poor Arnie, Big Jack, Black Gary, Darling Doug, Buffalo Billy. It is also accustomed to mixing in some old eagles—gray ones like Hogan and bald ones like Snead—and a variety of Chen Ching-Po's for international flavor, all of this amid the set decoration of dogwood and azaleas. The whole scene is awash with color, Augusta-CBS color, which, of course, is better than the less vivid hues of God, though perhaps not as good as NBC's.

The Masters has continually presented television with a perfect opportunity to be a newsy, gorgeous, creative showoff, to further enhance the good images left it by, well, Edward R. Murrow's cigarette, Sid Caesar's parodies and Paddy Chayefsky's old dramas. It is, indeed, one of the prestige presentations that CBS has worked hard to keep over the years, like NFL football. Networks have an awful time establishing their identity with the viewer at home, and this kind of show helps. If you ask the average viewer, for example, to tell you the differences among the three networks, he could be hard pressed to explain that NBC is the one with Johnny Carson, and a lot of funerals, that ABC is the one with the Olympics interspersed by demolition derbies, and that CBS has Cronkite, politics, the NFL and the Masters.

Doing the Masters or any other tournament right is never easy, and not at all what the viewer might imagine—a lone cameraman bounding along a fairway with the equipment on his back and a commentator looking more tanned than usual in the giddy social whirl of the 18th green. To come out with the splendid show CBS did in 1966 required ten years of bungling, worry, argument, mechanical refinement, thought and invention. To be specific, it took months of planning, 150 men, 15 cameras, a bastion of giant trailer trucks, 60,000 feet of underground cable and $600,000.

What this produced was a record four and a half hours of live color coverage that began with Saturday's third round of play and did not end until late Monday evening when Jack Nicklaus won his play-off victory. It is well that this television effort was closely observed, for it has not been equaled since, artistically or journalistically, where electronic golf coverage is concerned.

Backstage at that Masters was a sort of athletic event of its own, a week of flickering madness in the control truck when the show was beaming out to millions, and of bizarre hilarity practically everywhere else, and all of it rotating around a producer-director named Frank Chirkinian, who will slowly emerge as the hero of this story.

The week started, as most weeks do for TV, with a lot of worry—terrible, grave worry. Let's pick up our CBS executives now on the veranda of the Augusta National clubhouse where they are worrying. There they are, all dressed in their dark blue blazers with crests, looking something like a haggard group of AAU officials trying to figure out why amateur athletes take cash under the table. They are concerned about the opening of their show, the fact that it is being written and rewritten, approved and unapproved, and criticized by everyone in town. They are also uneasy about the man who will do the opening on tape.

Their situation takes some clearing up. CBS has agreed to a request by Tournament Chairman Clifford Roberts that each day's telecast would begin with a solemn opening. They had also agreed that the introduction would not only set a prestigious mood, but it would state the fact that there would be a reduced number of commercials in tribute to the importance of the event. Clifford Roberts, of course, is a lifelong friend of Bobby Jones and the man who runs the Masters like Napoleon ran France. Reducing the number of commercials was his idea. No one ever ignored a Clifford Roberts idea, least of all CBS.

When Roberts had first asked the show's sponsors, Travelers Insurance and Arrow Shirts, for fewer commercials, an agency man in New York had said, "What does he think the Masters is, a moon shot?"

The answer was no. Clifford Roberts thought the Masters was infinitely more important than that.

Roberts did manage to get five commercials sliced from the scheduled two days of telecasting—a feat, some said, that was comparable to Bobby Jones winning the Grand Slam. But the tournament chairman also felt that this fact should be announced before and after each show by someone outside the realm of sport. A Walter Cronkite, perhaps. Or a Dwight D. Eisenhower.

For a while, no one involved could think of a satisfactory person. Cronkite and Eisenhower were unavailable. So were George Washington, Abraham Lincoln and Thomas Jefferson. Finally someone in New York decided on a different tack and suggested Ed Sullivan to Clifford Roberts.

"Ed Sullivan!" Roberts reportedly bellowed. "If we wanted anybody from show business, we could get Randolph Scott."

The man finally suggested by CBS and approved by Roberts was a fellow named Jim Jensen from the WCBS-TV news staff in New York. Roberts had seen him and liked him on the screen in New York. Jensen had a convincing manner and sincere tone and he was handsome in a dignified way. Ah, but the opening. Somehow, in the editing by Roberts and his assassins and by ad agency writers and CBS writers, Jensen wound up identifying himself on the tape as a "news correspondent."

Now that may seem accurate enough to outsiders, but in television there is an important distinction between a correspondent and ordinary Earth people. A correspondent is most properly a man over in Vietnam eyewitnessing assaults on poppy fields, or, at the very least, a familiar face famed for discoursing on vital events. Jensen, whether Masters officials realized it—and CBS was afraid to ask—was a *local* news announcer. This meant that the peak of his journalistic success might involve a description of traffic problems on the Long Island Expressway during a blizzard.

Now, back on the Masters veranda, one could naturally understand the genuine distress among CBS executives. If they asked to edit the word "correspondent" from Jensen's opening by having him retape it, Roberts might get the idea that Jensen wasn't big enough to be doing it, and he might ask to edit five more commercials. On the other hand, with Jensen, through no fault of his own, falsely identifying himself, the phone would be sure to ring at Masters control, and it would be Jack Schneider wanting to know what was going on. Bill MacPhail, the vice-president in charge of sports, would have to take the call, and he didn't really *need* a call like that from Schneider, who is the boss of everyone at CBS except William Paley and Dr. Frank Stanton.

Finally, as they all stood around, Frank Chirkinian said, "Bill, just tell Schneider that Cliff Roberts promoted Jensen."

Chirkinian was not overly worried about the Jensen dilemma. Jensen could introduce himself as Nancy Dickerson and it would be all right with Frank. The producer-director was far more concerned with the camera angles, the audio, and the velvet words that would fill the tense hours of live coverage when the show went on the air.

Bill MacPhail, a gentleman at all times, finally sighed and said, "This is serious and I think worthy of a cocktail."

CBS Sports Director Jack Dolph, who was sort of a self-appointed vice-chairman to MacPhail in charge of Augusta Worry, agreed. So did others. Chirkinian said, "Go ahead. If I wanted a drink, I'd go get Randolph Scott."

Chirkinian, who had long been acknowledged as the best golf director in television, one who had been responsible for all kinds of innovations, proceeded to stroll away, doing one of his favorite things. He sang a parody.

> *You take Lionel, and I'll take Jay.*
> *You take Marty—and I'll take Ed.*
> *Hebert, Hebert.*
> *Furgol, Furgol.*
> *Let's call the Masters off.*

That evening the problem of the program opening and other assorted worries were temporarily put aside, and the elite guard of CBS turned to something of a more pressing nature—its annual, underground Calcutta pool on the tournament. It was held in one of the six sumptuous homes in Augusta that the network rents during Masters week. It was staged in the house Chirkinian lived in with his close associates and commentators.

The evening began with all of Chirkinian's invited guests mixing several dozen drinks for themselves and tearing into a large ham on the drainboard in the kitchen and then collapsing on the living room carpet, in sofas and chairs and against the wall paneling. Chirkinian and MacPhail decided to take turns auctioneering—selling the players—and Bill Brendle, CBS's publicity director, would do his best to keep the books.

"It might be a little hard for Brendle to write with a drink in each hand," said Chirkinian.

Frank kept up a steady stream of comedy as he sold the top contenders individually.

"What am I bid for Arnold Palmer?" he would say. "I understand he's divorcing Winnie and smoking pot now. What am I bid?"

When Palmer sold for about $500, Chirkinian said, "He's a good buy. I spoke to him today in the hospital. He doesn't think that fall he took off the twelfth tee will bother his swing at all."

As the players were sold, one by one, there would be occasional shouts from the floor.

"Fifteen hundred for Conni Venturi," somebody said.

"That's too much for Ken," said Frank.

"I don't want Ken. I want Conni," the voice said.

Fields were available to the buyers. You could purchase a dozen Dudley Wysongs, say, with a Terry Dill thrown in, for only five dollars. A couple of visitors, being somewhat less than golf-wise, refused to believe that there were any golfers named Cobie LaGrange or Ed Tutwiler in the field.

In the end MacPhail and Jack Dolph were the most active bidders, and later on they had the foggy recollection that they had managed to buy almost everyone, including, they feared, Randolph Scott.

Thursday, the day of the tournament's first round, was important to CBS for two reasons. First, there was to be a complete dress rehearsal, "full fax," they call it, which in television means complete dress rehearsal. Secondly, MacPhail and Dolph had to go to the airport to greet an assortment of brass from New York which included Jack Schneider, John Reynolds, then the president of CBS-TV, and a sales vice-president, Ted O'Connell. The brass had to be taken to the club and impressed by the fact that the veranda was literally teeming with hosts of corporate celebrities.

After the rehearsal Frank Chirkinian held a massive production meeting in a downstairs room of one of the clubhouse cottages to remind everyone that they weren't getting ready to do *Supermarket Sweep* come Saturday. He had not especially liked the rehearsal.

"Mechanically, everything worked fine," he said, "including the jaws of the commentators. Cut your talk in half. You're not saying anything interesting anyhow."

The crew of commentators included Jack Whitaker, CBS's most knowledgeable and presentable talent, at the 18th green, Jack Drees and Byron Nelson at the 17th, Henry Longhurst, the noted British writer, at the 16th, John Derr at the 15th, Cary Middlecoff down in a clubhouse basement. Middlecoff's job down there was to deliver expertise while staring at hole diagrams, stop-action, or the tournament in progress through a contraption called the TNT Eidophor, a special projection device that provides a screen within the screen and can be clearly explained only by the Swiss scientist who invented it.

When Chirkinian concluded what he called his "harpoon-the-commentators" meeting, he asked if there were any problems or questions anyone cared to bring up.

"No, I don't think so," said Jack Whitaker. "Now that my morale is destroyed, I'll just leave. If you'll excuse me, I'm taking Dr. Zhivago's calls tonight."

Jack Dolph said he did not want to frighten the crew unnecessarily, but he had received word that the Scotch tape, rubber bands and paper clips had been lost.

"You jest," said Chirkinian.

"I jest not," Dolph said. "You ready? They were shipped to Nevada."

Chirkinian dropped his head and then spoke quietly to the room.

"Gentlemen, for the first time in the history of this network, we're going to do a show *without* Scotch tape, rubber bands and paper clips."

Thursday evening was devoted to that fine old American pastime of tension-relieving. The directors, commentators and brass split in all directions, making the rounds of the private parties that are a feature of Masters Week. A few dropped by a house that had been rented by Bedford Wynne, one of the owners of the Dallas Cowboys and found Wynne cooking steaks in the backyard for a small group of one hundred. Just down the street others went to a similar party being given by the Atlanta Falcons. Most people went to both, doing some fancy hedge-hopping with their drinks.

"I thought this was a golf tournament, not an NFL convention," said Ted O'Connell.

Before the night was over, several of the group wound up at what passed for the late, late show in Augusta that spring. It was a place called the Key Club. A members-only cocktail lounge—you joined by walking in—it offered a number of treats, namely a combo that could play guitar louder than the siege of Vicksburg, an incredibly lucky blackjack dealer, enough noncoms from nearby Fort Gordon to invade Normandy again, and scads of painted, gum-chewing ladies barely out of their teens.

Someone had insisted on taking Jack Schneider there. It was part of the flavor of the town he ought to see, this being his first trip to the Masters. Having just recently recovered from the unflattering publicity that accompanied Fred Friendly's resignation as head of CBS News, Schneider gazed around the room and said, "Well, here I am. Where's the *Daily News* reporter?"

Friday's dress rehearsal went well, considering the hangovers, and Chirkinian's production meeting afterward reflected this. Frank strolled in good-humoredly, working up a new parody to the Roger Miller tune "Engine, Engine Number Nine." He sang:

Clifford, Clifford, Number Nine,
Your old dogwood doin' fine.

The producer-director made only a few small points. Jay Hebert's name was misspelled on the scoreboard in Middlecoff's basement—the scoreboard that would be superimposed on the live screen.

"Jay Hebert's name is always misspelled," said Dolph. "We've tried to get him to change it to Herbert."

There had been a little too much talking over the intercom, Frank said. "Let there be one leader." He asked around if Jack Schneider had enjoyed himself and did anyone know when the big boss was heading back to New York? Schneider had left, someone said.

"Kid never did have stamina," said Frank.

Chirkinian went on to say that he hoped there would not be too many green jackets—Masters committeemen—in the control truck tomorrow to tell him all about the mistakes he was making. And finally he announced that the show would begin thirty minutes before air time so they would all have a flying start and be warmed up.

"That's about all," he said. "Good luck tomorrow, and since I'm going back in the dry-cleaning business, let's win this one for me, okay?"

Frank Chirkinian looks almost like Hollywood's conception of a TV director. He is a natty little man, dark-complexioned, with black, wavy hair, horn-rimmed glasses, alligator loafers, jazzy clothes and a 10-handicap. This would be his eighth straight Masters production for CBS. His earlier training had not been in sports. A native of Philadelphia, he had been in the army, done a year at Penn and two years at Philadelphia's Columbia Institute. In Philadelphia he had directed just about everything possible—musicals, news, drama, public affairs, variety and circuses. Along the way to CBS in New York, he had become a golf nut, and this had certainly shown in his work at Augusta as well as on the *CBS Golf Classic,* the best of the canned golf shows.

Chirkinian's job at Augusta was far from enviable. Few creatures, electronic or otherwise, are more imposing than a TV control truck. The one at this Masters was a blinking monster of fourteen screens, large and small, color and not, of live pickup, videotape and stop-action. Frank's job was to watch them all simultaneously while keeping in constant touch with commentators, assistant directors and technicians on his headset, and select which of the different shots to put on the air.

Physically, the network's setup as air time approached for Saturday's one-hour show on the third round was this: Chirkinian was at his table in what television romantically calls the hot truck. He was seated between an assistant director, Roland Vance, and a technical director, Sandy Bell, whose job was to punch a button when Frank said "Take one" or "Take three" or whatever picture he wanted on the huge panel before him. Also in the truck was Lou Scanna, the engineer in charge of the whole rig-up, the man mainly responsible for all of the plugs being in their sockets, the strewn cable and so on, and one of the few men in the world who knew how a person got a picture on his screen at home. MacPhail and Dolph were present, of course, to worry.

Another big truck was situated down near the 16th green, and squeezed in there were Bob Dailey, a fine director in his own right who rates up there with Chirkinian, CBS's Tony Verna and ABC's Malcolm Hemion and Andy Sidaris, as the elite of sports directors. Dailey was acting as Frank's assistant. It was his job to punch up the action from the 15th, 16th and 17th holes as best he saw it, and ride shotgun on the commentators at those locations. The commentators—talent, they are called, perhaps because they earn eighty-four thou a year—were all on their towers in their blazers, and Middlecoff was in his basement, frequently saying to Frank, "I'm here if you need me, Doll."

As show time drew close Chirkinian sat calmly calling up test shots—the scoreboard, Jack Whitaker, various greens, competitors walking along fairways, the gallery.

"Fellows," said Chirkinian in his headset, "let's remember to keep sight reference at all times, and keep silent on the shots. We've got these tees and fairways miked for audio, so I want to hear it when they swing."

He glanced at one of the screens and noted that a cameraman

had playfully trained his lens on a shapely, bell-bottomed spectator.

Frank cupped his hands and called out, "Barr-a-cuda!"

Bill MacPhail got nervous and left the truck to step next door to a VIP trailer and get a Coke, and when he returned he asked Frank if he was happy with the opening that Whitaker had been rehearsing earlier in the day.

"The gray eagle will be fine," said Chirkinian. "I'll stick some spurs in him just before we go on, anyhow."

Dolph, trying to think of something useful to do, leaned forward and reminded Chirkinian that he should use as much stop-action stuff as possible because Paley liked it.

"Paley who?" said Frank, without turning around.

Just then Roland Vance, earphones on, stopwatch uplifted, papers spread out before him, announced that it was just seven minutes to go. At about the same time the truck door opened and several CBS friends invited themselves in to stand in the back. They were Dave Marr and his wife, Susan, and Charley Conerly, the ex-Giant quarterback, and his wife, Perian, a pretty plantation owner from Houston named Eloise Rowan, Jerry Danford, then a salesman for WCBS-TV, and Bill Brendle, the publicity man, who began taking drink orders.

"What's the story on the bigger truck we ordered?" Dolph cracked.

With everyone crammed in Chirkinian lit his ninety-seventh cigarette of the day, sat up a little straighter in his chair, adjusted his headset like a bomber pilot engaging some flak and said that great thing that TV people enjoy saying so much.

"One and a half 'til air," he said.

As Roland Vance started to wave his arms and shuffle his papers, Chirkinian began talking to his crew. "Whit, we've got a hell of a tournament. The scores are close. Everybody's in there with a shot at it—Palmer, Nicklaus, all the big guys ... Hey, you fellows downstairs! I want that scoreboard up to date *right now*. ... Get the stop-action ready. ... We'll get into that pretty quick, Cary. ... Bobby, your guys all set? ..."

Vance practically shouted, "Ten seconds! Stand by."

Chirkinian relaxed and spoke quietly. "Good luck everyone, and good show."

"Roll Augusta music," cried Vance.

Suddenly on the big color screen surrounded by all of the smaller screens in the truck, there was Jim Jensen and what might have been a wisteria behind him. It was the taped opening.

"Good afternoon," said he. "I'm CBS News correspondent Jim Jensen. Because of the importance of the program you are about to see, it is being brought to you with a reduced number of commercials, and . . ."

Jensen concluded the opening with the line that was a cue for Jack Whitaker to take it live. "May you enjoy the show you are about to see," he said.

"We're on!" shrieked Vance.

"Go, Jack," said Chirkinian. "Go, Babe."

Jack Whitaker took over, and in his distinctive, elegant style began bringing the tournament into focus. Nicklaus had led the first round. Paul Harney and Peter Butler had taken over the second day, and now, today, the big guns were making a move.

Just then, a knock came on the door of the control truck and Yvonne Connors, a CBS secretary from the VIP trailer, poked her head in. She said that Bill MacPhail was wanted on long distance. It was Jack Schneider back in New York.

"Oh, Christ," said MacPhail, getting up.

"Where do you want the body shipped?" said Dolph.

MacPhail, who is a member of the very famous baseball family, returned in a few minutes looking as if he had just heard a rumor that Mickey Mantle's hobby was needlepoint. He smiled weakly and sat down. "Guess what Schneider wanted?" he said.

"I'm sure he didn't want to know why Jensen called himself a correspondent," said Dolph.

MacPhail said, "I just told him it was a conspiracy involving some foreign powers and the CIA would furnish us all with a full report later."

Back on the panel of screens the tournament was beginning to tighten up. The leaders were creeping into view in this corner and that. This is when a director ages. He is likely to have two or three key dramas at hand, and, of course, he can only show one at a time. The trick is knowing the sport and the tendencies of the athletes—exactly how long Nicklaus will take on a putt, when Palmer will stop hitching his trousers and hit a drive, how much study Sanders will give to a chip shot.

Chirkinian seemed to be doing remarkably well in spite of the periodic irritant of Roland Vance shouting something like, "Two minutes past ideal commercial."

To Bob Dailey, the assistant director in the truck down at the 16th Chirkinian said, "Better whip your boys a little, Bobby. They're dragging along, and this is pretty exciting."

Frank went to Whitaker.

"A little more schmaltz, Jack, on the closeness of the race." Frank then dramatized his voice and slowly, mimickingly said, "You could cut the tension here with a hot butterknife."

Dolph and MacPhail let out a whoop.

"It's the wide world of Jim McKay," said Dolph.

Now a crucial moment approached. Jack Nicklaus had come to the 18th tee and Arnold Palmer was back on the 16th, both of them struggling to catch the current leader, Gay Brewer, Jr. The audio picked up a devastating whack as Nicklaus drove into the woods. The camera caught Palmer's shot biting into the 16th green and curling toward the flag.

Palmer striding onto the green made a spectacular image in color, and Bob Dailey had it. Somehow the lighting on Palmer, the emerald turf mingling with the shade of the pines and the pond and the flowers in the background combined to represent, in Chirkinian's mind, everything the Masters was.

"Look at that Picasso!" said Frank. "Good shot, Bobby."

The producer-director's ecstasy was interrupted by Yvonne Connors again rapping on the truck door and peeking in.

"I don't know what to do," she said. "Mr. Roberts just called and said the TV set in his cottage isn't working right and he wants somebody over there to fix it *immediately.*"

"Terrific," said Chirkinian, glued to his screens.

MacPhail looked at Dolph. Dolph looked at MacPhail. They both turned and looked at Lou Scanna, the chief engineer, as if to ask if he had a screwdriver. "Yeah, yeah," said Lou, getting up. He edged toward the door, poked his head out and called to a technician. "Hey, uh, somebody go over to Roberts's house and kick the set or something," he said.

Jack Nicklaus at the moment was having worse problems. He was virtually out of sight in the woods at the 18th fairway. Middlecoff's voice then came into the truck. "Frank," he said. "We're gonna *have* to get big Jack in those woods. This is a real important shot."

"Thanks a lot, Doc," said Frank. "I'll see if I can hit a couple of trees with Armenian lightning."

As Nicklaus thrashed around in the woods Palmer was preparing to putt for his birdie at the 16th and Chirkinian stood up.

"Need a little luck here, babies," he said.

Palmer stroked the putt. "Whit, throw it to sixteen," said Frank. The ball rolled toward the hole. "Ready two, and open the fairway on eighteen," he said. "Take two." Nicklaus slashed from the woods, and Palmer's ball neared the cup. "Take remote." Palmer's putt narrowly missed. "Take three." Nicklaus's ball bounded into a bunker. "Take remote." Palmer grimaced. "Gimme a closeup, Bobby." Nicklaus emerged from the woods. "Take one." And Chirkinian sat down.

It had been only thirty seconds of show-biz torture but an excellent moment in good production.

When CBS did its first Masters in 1956 it used only six cameras, all of them trained on the greens, and Bud Palmer

164 THE DOGGED VICTIMS OF INEXORABLE FATE

was the lone commentator sitting on the 18th and describing the other holes from a monitor. Chirkinian encouraged making it a more sophisticated production his first year, which was 1959.

At that Masters CBS increased the number of cameras to 12, and Frank deployed them so that fairways and tees could be shown, and he upped the number of commentators to three. A year later he began miking the tees and greens. Conduits were put underground to eliminate the cables stretched everywhere for Arnie's Army to trip over. Frank also devised the plus-minus cumulative scoring system that Clifford Roberts himself adopted for the big leader boards (red for under and green for over par). By 1965 Frank had fifteen cameras, helicopter footage, hole diagrams, videotape reruns, stop-action, the TNT Eidophor, more commentators and improved camera positions. And he now had a dedicated, experienced crew.

Everyone thought the Saturday show was beautiful, and with a certain amount of justification, the evening was once again devoted to tension-relieving. There was not so much moving around, however. A couple of downtown bars were visited, but the hard core of tension relievers flopped down in the MacPhail-Dolph-Brendle house, or P. J. Clarke's South as it came to be called, for a fine-old-fashioned dinner of fried chicken and Scotch. It was there that Jack Whitaker and a writer friend who had been loitering around all week completed a parody they had been working on as a tribute to Chirkinian. It would become the underground Masters theme song for the next few years.

To the tune of Steve Allen's *This Could Be the Start of Something Big*, it went:

> You're walking around the course,
> You're on the veran-da.
> You're looking for Chen Ching-po,
> Or Cobie LaGrange.
> You're looking for Downing Gray,

Terry Dill or Rod Funseth, say,
This could be the Masters in the spring.

You're standing on seven-teen,
You're up on a tower.
You're looking for Up-de-graff,
Tutwiler or Hunt.
When there in a fair-way dance,
You come upon Lion-el Platts,
This could be the Masters in the spring.

With Randy Glover,
You discover,
It's a thrilling day.
And Har-old Henning is the nicest guy.
And Peter Alliss, Michael Bon-al-lack and Dicky Sikes,
With Ramon Sota will be pass-ing by.

You're walking around the course,
You're on the veran-da.
You're looking for Chen Ching-po or Cobie LaGrange.
If you wander all eight-teen holes,
Maybe you will find Neil C. Coles,
This could be the Masters—oh, yes,
This could be dis-astrous—oh, yes,
This could be the Masters in the spring.

On Sunday CBS had the telecast scheduled for an hour and a half but, unlike the old days, it was geared to stay on, hang the expense, until the Masters had a champion. Not too many years ago TV had a habit of bidding farewell to the excitement when its allotted hour was up, and if Sam Snead happened to be bent over a putt for a possible win, that was tough luck.

"We're different now," MacPhail explained Sunday morning. "We're cleared to run over into prime time if we have to. And if there's a play-off on Monday, we'll be here. In fact if there's a sudden death after the playoff Frank thinks we could cover it remote." MacPhail wasn't sure how—perhaps with Whitaker snapping Polaroid shots from a golf cart and

Frank preempting Cronkite's news to show the stills. Talk of sudden death made MacPhail sick to his tum tum.

The program opened Sunday with the same dramatic count-down procedures of the day before. A couple of new spectators were in the hot truck, each of them wearing a green jacket. They were crouched down near Chirkinian, presumably to see to it that CBS didn't screw up anything.

"Do they know anything about television production?" someone discreetly asked Jack Dolph.

"Taught Chris Schenkel everything he knows," smiled Jack.

Things went along in an orderly fashion for a while, but then the Masters burst apart with the excitement that it always seems to provide on Sundays. Gay Brewer's lead was far from secure. Tommy Jacobs had moved up to contend. Nicklaus still had a chance. So did Palmer.

Feeling the drama, Chirkinian's voice began to pick up some emotion and strain that it had not previously shown. A delicate ear detected something of a bark. Buzzing Bob Dailey, he said, "Let's drive these commentators a little, Bobby. The players are nervous. There's tension out there. This is the big one."

There was frantic activity everywhere on the closing holes. Nicklaus birdied the 14th, Jacobs birdied the 15th, and when Brewer could only make a par at the 17th, there was the distinct possibility of a three-way tie. Chirkinian leaped up and clapped his hands during all this, and, coming back down, he remembered that he had alerted Whitaker to make a specific point about something or other. But he had now forgotten what.

"Just vamp, Jack," said Frank. "Go."

Whitaker vamped about tension, azaleas, Bobby Jones, Augusta, the veranda, and seemed about to launch into a soliloquy on the old open-cockpit days of aviation when Chirkinian rescued him.

Tighter grew the tournament. Palmer blew a short putt on the 17th, and fell out of it. But Gay Brewer now came up the 18th fairway to a seven-foot putt for a par that might lock up the championship.

"This is it, Doll," said Middlecoff over the intercom.

Chirkinian said to Whitaker, his anchor man, "This is it, Jack. This is the most important putt of Gay Brewer's life."

And Whitaker said to Videoland, "This is the most important putt of Gay Brewer's life."

If it was, that was too bad, for Brewer missed the putt. He was thus in a tie with Tommy Jacobs, and Nicklaus, too, could tie if he could manage pars on the last two holes. Jack played deliberately, just missing a short birdie at the 17th and driving safely off the 18th tee.

"I want to really hear that sound," said Frank, getting poised for his big finish. "When Jack comes up the fairway near the green, I want to hear the crowd. I want some emotion. This is a hell of a finish . . . This guy may birdie the hole, and I want a reaction . . . I may have a reaction . . . Who's got Nicklaus in the pool, anyhow? . . ."

Nicklaus had a tremendously long birdie putt on the 18th for a win, and it seemed that a pay-off was assured, but Chirkinian wanted a buildup.

"Jack," he said. "There's Brewer and Jacobs, watching from the edge of the green. They have no other recourse but to watch, right? . . . Wait! Don't repeat that crap."

Frank, giggling at himself, wheeled in his chair toward MacPhail and Dolph. "My resignation will be on your desk tomorrow morning," he said.

Nicklaus rapped a fine putt that came down from the back of the green and curled slowly toward the cup, dying away just at the lip, amid Chirkinian's chaotic shouts of, "Take one, take five, take three," and the agonizing groan of the gallery on the audio.

Whitaker rapidly did a résumé and a wrap-up and the show signed off, and Dolph spoke for everyone in the truck when he said, "I don't suppose we'd do anything like have about nine thousand cocktails?"

Compared to the roaring finish of the previous day, Monday's play-off was tame. The network managed to make the most of it though. Nicklaus was pretty much in command by the time they came on the air. Jacobs was hanging in with a chance, but Gay Brewer had played like Chirkinian. The show had some fill in it—a lot of taped replays of Sunday action, and some Middlecoff lectures on big Jack's swing. But it worked all right.

At one point, Chirkinian got annoyed at a couple of camera shots. One had been an intimate closeup of a spectator's hand. "What's *this?* Frank said in the headset. "I want Jacobs and you gimme a *hand?*" Another time, a green-jacketed official had marched out in the center of the 17th fairway, right in front of a camera, and obscured Nicklaus from view. "That's it, that's it," said Chirkinian. "You and me, Mr. Green Coat, we'll swing along down to Wall Street together."

There was only a dim chance that Jacobs could make up enough strokes on Nicklaus to force a sudden-death play-off, but Lou Scanna had put in motion the sudden-death preparations, just in case, when Nicklaus and Jacobs had been tied through nine holes. Now he had a question.

"Frank, is sudden-death canceled?" he asked.

Chirkinian roared with laughter, and the hot truck gently swayed.

"Lou, you're beautiful," he said.

"Well *is* it?" said Scanna. "My guy's on the headset and he says it's not only getting dark out there, they've taken out the pins everywhere and they're watering the greens."

The truck exploded with laughter again.

"That's the bottom line," said Dolph. "That's the merciful ending we've been waiting for."

Had Nicklaus not maintained his lead and won the 1966 Masters, it would surely have been the most fascinating sudden-death in golf history. It would have been played Tuesday morning, and CBS could have done it as a two-minute commercial on a *Leave It to Beaver* rerun.

Several weeks later, after all concerned had recovered from the battleground that was Augusta, Frank Chirkinian was in Toots Shor's one evening and happy as an Armenian dry cleaner who had discovered the white knight. He had accepted an Emmy award for CBS sports. It had not been won for the Masters—which was a shame—but for the *CBS Golf Classic*.

And the awards committee had also presented an Emmy to NBC and ABC sports. A three-way tie, like the Masters had been. Still it was an Emmy.

"Who'll ever know?" said Frank. "Anyhow it doesn't look bad on the hood of the car."

Wide Open

I'm gonna be a Spaniard instead of a Mexkin as soon as I get some more money.

—LEE TREVINO,
on the eve of winning the
U.S. Open championship

Super Mex is what he called himself. Super Mexkin. A laughing tub of enchiladas in bright red socks with a caddy-hustler's game from Dallas. That was Lee Trevino. Then came the cross-handed sergeant, Orville Moody, who had a name like a bowler or a dragstrip mechanic and who didn't even have a hometown to be poor from. Just Sergeant Moody from fourteen years of Fort Hoods and Koreas. And, suddenly, there they were, implausibly and inconceivably, out there among the striped ties and gold pins, the blue coats and armbands, enhancing the tradition of the Nobody in that incorrigible old shrub-judging and weed-stomping contest known as the United States Open Golf championship. Gentlemen, play away. Mexkin, play away. Sergeant, hit it.

Here was the Open, as it is so simply known, almost seventy years old as it neared the end of the 1960's, crammed with all the class and propriety, the crustiness and aplomb that men like Bob Jones and Ben Hogan, like Harry Vardon and Gene Sarazen, like Jack Nicklaus and Arnold Palmer, had given it. Here was the Open, exaggerated into the greatest tournament in the world, played from year to year on only the most aristocratic and brutal courses, offering a title which guaranteed a wealth and fame that no other golfing event could match. But there came these two Nobodies, this Mexkin at Oak Hill in Rochester in 1968 and then this sergeant at Champions in Houston in 1969, serving as a reminder that the Open is for *all* the people and that somebody must have been right a long time ago when he said that nobody wins the Open, it wins you.

Before the Mexkin and the sergeant most enthusiasts of the game thought they knew what the Open was supposed to be. Some club named Oak-something got doctored up to look like a Scottish moor, a group of men who looked like delegates to a world money conference moved onto the veranda, a flag went up and Ben Hogan won for the two dozenth time while Sam Snead lost again. Before Hogan it was always Jones. And after Hogan it was a blend of Boroses, Caspers, Middlecoffs, Nicklauses and Palmers. Somebodies.

Oh, of course, there would be these metaphysical years now and then when players with names like Lee Mackey, Bob Gajda, Bobby Brue, Rives McBee, Les Kennedy and Al Brosch would seize the first round lead or shoot a course record the second day. But they would follow up those rounds with characteristic 91's and return to their club jobs back in Willoughby, Ohio. A couple of them *had* won, as Sam Parks, Jr., did in 1935 at Oakmont and as Jack Fleet did in 1955 at Olympic, but those occasions were so rare that they were written off as the natural catastrophes that occur to any lasting institution. A catastrophe every twenty years is not so bad. Even a little quaint. ·

Thus, one got used to an Open and knew exactly what to expect of it. Every year in mid-June didn't we read stories something like the following:

OPEN FIELD MAY REVOLT

OYSTER BISQUE, N.Y.—A glittering field on the eve of the National Open golf championship agreed today that there is so much exotic plantlife bor-

dering the narrow fairways of historic old Baltus
Oak Country Club that only a malnourished hippie
could walk down the middle of them without snag-
ging his britches.

During today's final warm-up round two foursomes actually got lost in the foliage of the back
nine holes and wound up at a Southampton lawn
party.

Gardner Dickinson, chairman of the PGA tournament players committee, said he was withdraw-
ing from the championship because he had never
learned how to hit golf shots out of waist-high
asparagus.

The irate Dickinson said, "If this kind of thing
doesn't stop we might not have a spot on the tour
for the USGA next year. The sponsors may have
the tents, but the players have the dog acts."

UNKNOWN LEADS OPEN

OYSTER BISQUE, N.Y.—Jesse Ray Rives, an un-
heralded driving range pro from Hoot, Utah,
grabbed the opening round lead in the National
Open here today with a sizzling even-par 70 on
historic old Baltus Oak, the course where Bobby
Jones first wore knickers.

Rives, who wore coveralls and a straw hat with
a band on it which said "Root for Hoot," birdied
the first nine holes and blew out a full row of lights
on the IBM scoreboard, and although he bogeyed
the entire back side for a 44, his score held up
against an array of glamorous challengers.

Incredibly, Rives took only six putts for the
round, tying a record set by Bob Rosburg. He tied
another Open record held by Don January when he
holed out eight sand wedges.

Rives, 25, said he would feel better about his
chances if he weren't so lonely so far away from

home. "I wisht my uncle Clyde and my pet bobcat
was here," he said.

OPEN JOLTED BY SECOND
MYSTERY MAN

OYSTER BISQUE, N.Y.—R. J. (Bo) Mackey, an obscure pro at a putt-putt course in Clump, Calif.,
seized the halfway lead in the National Open here
tonight when he added a 65 to his first-round 81
for a 36-hole total of 146, only 6 over par on historic
old Baltus Oak, the course where Walter Hagen
had his first hangover.

Having teed off at 5:14 A.M., Mackey was one
of the day's early finishers at 4 o'clock in the afternoon as the field of 150 moved along briskly despite
the 101-degree heat. Sweating out his lead in Baltus Oak's non-air-conditioned clubhouse, Mackey
had some anxious moments until shortly before
midnight when defending champion Jack Nicklaus
came in.

Nicklaus had threatened to overtake Mackey until the 17th hole. Jack finished with a horrendous
13 and then a 15 on the last green when his children
persisted in clinging to his back when he swung
the club. He failed not only to catch Mackey but
to make the 36-hole cut.

"I'm tired of golf," Nicklaus said. "All I really
want to do anymore is go to family reunions and
take my kids to Astroworld."

First-round leader Jesse Ray Rives also failed to
make the cut, largely because a lurking animal—
believed by some to be a bobcat—swallowed his
ball on the 10th fairway.

Mackey, who wore khakis and a tool dresser's
helmet, confessed that he had received a lot of help
in molding his game. He said he owed a lot to the
crew on the B. W. Roberts No. 2 oil rig in Clump.

They had encouraged him to leave town, he said. He also specifically singled out two men who had pieced together his compact swing: Ralph Tibitt, his ex-warden, and Roy Sangry, his parole officer.

UNKNOWN LOG JAM IN OPEN

OYSTER BISQUE, N.Y.—Billy Tom Riddle, an assistant pro from Harper Valley, Tenn., playing in his first professional golf tournament, tied for the 54-hole lead in the National Open here today with four amateurs, all from the powerful University of Houston. Their score was 223, only 13 over par on historic old Baltus Oak, the course where Harry Vardon tripped on a dining room carpet.

Best known of the Houston collegians was Rex Zark, who has been the Western, Trans-Miss, Southern, North-South, Broadmoor, British and Idaho State amateur champion every year since the age of 9. The other talented members of the Texas team are Kermit Blank from Albany, N.Y., Babe Stimmett from Seattle, Wash., and Joel Wuthergrind from Worcester, Mass.

None of the leaders could rest easily, it appeared, for only 16 strokes off the pace, poised to make one of his patented stretch runs, was Arnold Palmer.

The championship was struck with an indelicate misfortune during Saturday's third round when R. J. (Bo) Mackey, the putt-putt pro, was disqualified on the first 9 holes of his round. A USGA spokesman said Mackey had been warned repeatedly since Thursday to refrain from making obscene gestures and comments to women in his gallery but that he had refused to heed the warning. "We had no other course of action to take," said T. Phillip Carter duPont Lawrence, a USGA vice-president.

"This, after all, is the Open championship. Not Orlando."

HOGAN WINS UNPRECEDENTED NINTH OPEN

OYSTER BISQUE, N.Y.—With the coveted National Open championship all but sewed up, Arnold Palmer caught his backswing in a flowering banyan today on historic old Baltus Oak, the course where Tommy Armour once bought lunch, and Ben Hogan, looking tanned and fit despite his 67 years, breezed past him to win an unprecedented ninth Open.

Palmer caught his swing in the tree at Baltus Oak's 17th hole and had to be rescued by a demolition team from the Corps of Engineers. Palmer was unable to complete the round and the tournament, and thus he will have to endure sectional qualifying again next year.

"It's pretty disheartening to know you can finish 10–10 and win, and then not even be able to play," said Palmer.

Hogan shot a flaming 67 in the final round for a 72-hole total of 301, only 21 over par. Hogan's round was the lowest since architect Robert Trent Jones had revamped Baltus Oak, placing a number of Bunkers in the center of some tees and forcing carries of 280 yards or more over water.

There was a moment of pure drama at the final green after Hogan finished, flashing his familiar outgoing, quick-smiling expression. Hogan went over to Jones and shook his hand until the architect knelt down, uttering a bit of a whimper.

"I brought the monster to its knees," said Hogan.

Sam Snead, who mailed in his scores, again finished second.

None of the third-round leaders managed to finish. Billy Tom Riddle, tormented by the sight of his first gallery, picked up at the 3rd hole after striking his ball 21 times in a bunker. The entire University of Houston team, including Rex Zark, quit after 9 and mysteriously departed for West Lafayette, Ind., the site of next week's NCAA championships.

Palmer was one of several blowups as the Open pressure mounted late in the day.

Billy Casper needed only to play even bogey over the last 9 holes to tie Hogan, but he suffered a sneezing fit because of pesticides which had been sprayed on the fairways and shot an incoming 46. A man of great inner peace, however, Casper smiled and said, "Boy, it looks like the Lord got up on the wrong side of the bed today."

Miller Barber, who kept swallowing diet pills throughout the round, could have parred the 72nd hole for victory, but he hit a 5-iron an amazing 240 yards over the clubhouse and the massive marble statue on the veranda of T. Phillip Carter-Hughes Bentley McCarver duPont Lawrence, Sr. "Well, you get pretty revved up out there," said Barber.

Finally, Julius Boros, chewing on a weed and sipping a can of beer, nonchalantly tried to backhand 3 successive putts on the final green, missed them all, and lost by the same margin as Casper, 2 strokes.

As Hogan accepted the unprecedented ninth Open trophy in a moving ceremony at the putting green and in turn presented the USGA with his full set of clubs and his wife Valerie for the Golf House museum, some 30 players were still out on the course, completing the last 9 holes in the dark. Word circulated momentarily that one of them,

Frank Clack, a driving range operator from Davenport, Iowa, could tie Hogan with 2 birdies over the last 4 holes. Officials, however, dismissed the news as wild, malicious rumor.

In its only other action of the day the USGA announced that next year's Open had been awarded to the Upper Course at historic old Baltus Oak, the club where Jug McSpaden first wore sunglasses.

As strange as this imaginary Open may seem, it is no more strange than many which had been played since a nineteen-year-old named Horace Rawlins won the first one in 1895 at Newport on October 4 with rounds of 91–82—173. Just about every established star has played as carelessly in the Open as he has played splendidly, and Open blowups have been more numerous in golf than doddering foursomes.

The statement may seem foolhardy, but both Bob Jones and Ben Hogan, the grandest players the Open ever produced, managed to lose as many Open championships as they won, and officially they captured four apiece. Hogan unofficially can count five, for in 1942 a Hale America National Open was played at the Ridgemoor Club in Chicago for the benefit of several service organizations, and Hogan won it. The championship is listed in the USGA record book, and Hogan received the same kind of gold medal for winning it that he was presented for winning in 1948 at Riviera, in 1950 at Merion, in 1951 at Oakland Hills and in 1953 at Oakmont, but no one credits Hogan for having taken a fifth Open.

Except Hogan.

A number of us journalists who loiter around the sport like to recall with relish an afternoon when Ben was sitting in a locker room at Cherry Hills in Denver, having failed in a bid for the 1960 Open championship, the tournament Arnold Palmer won with a crushing 65 over the last eighteen.

Someone said to Hogan, "Ben, do you think you'll *ever* get that fifth Open?"

"Sixth," said Hogan. And the conversation ended.

It does not appear likely that any golfer will ever post a better continuous record in the Open than Hogan. With his game styled to narrow, target-type courses—Open courses— he had a stretch of playing in sixteen straight Opens from 1940 through 1960, never finishing out of the first ten. The record reads: fifth at Canterbury in 1940, third at Colonial in 1941, first at Ridgemoor in 1942, fourth at Canterbury in 1946, sixth at St. Louis in 1947, first at Riviera in 1948, first at Merion in 1950, first at Oakland Hills in 1951, third at Northwood in 1952, first at Oakmont in 1953, sixth at Baltusrol in 1954, second at Olympic in 1955, second at Oak Hill in 1956, tenth at Southern Hills in 1958, eighth at Winged Foot in 1959 and ninth at Cherry Hill in 1960.

Hogan worshippers also like to point out that Ben missed five Opens during his prime—three because they were canceled during World War II, the 1949 Open because of his automobile accident, and the 1957 Open because of a shoulder injury.

Even in losing Hogan dominated the atmosphere of a U.S. Open. Always the big favorite, he tended to create as big a stir with his near-misses as with his victories, so much so that the winner, whoever he might be, was looked upon as a man "touched," or someone who had lapsed into what came to be known as an "Open coma."

Among Hogan's more famous losses were these: a three-putt on the 72nd at Canterbury in 1946 to miss tying with Byron Nelson, Vic Ghezzi and Lloyd Mangrum; a four-wood that crazily bounced out of bounds as he led the field in the third round at Northwood in 1952; the miracle of Jack Fleck's birdie-par-par-birdie finish to tie him at Olympic in 1955 and Fleck's subsequent 100-to-1 shot victory in the play-off; a thirty-inch par putt on the 71st at Oak Hill which curled out of the cup in 1956 and cinched the title for Cary Middlecoff; and a wedge shot that failed to clear a pond by an inch on the 71st at Cherry Hills in 1960 when he was tied with Palmer.

All of this made the Open Hogan's tournament, which in turn gave the championship a class and importance it might not otherwise have attained. Two decades earlier, Bob Jones had done the same thing.

Jones played in only eleven Opens, but his record was fantastic. He was eighth at Inverness in 1920, fifth at Columbia in 1921, second at Skokie in 1922, first at Inwood in 1923, second at Oakland Hills in 1924, second at Worcester in 1925 (losing a play-off to Willie MacFarlane), first at Scioto in 1926, eleventh at Oakmont in 1927, second at Olympia Fields in 1928 (losing a play-off to Johnny Farrell), first at Winged Foot in 1929, and of course first at Interlachen in 1930 when he scored the Grand Slam.

One of the least remembered things about Jones's Slam is how close he came to failing in the Open at Interlachen in Minneapolis while playing some of the best golf of his career. For one thing, he half-topped a spoon shot at the ninth hole of the second round and it went directly into the lake. But then it skipped across, rather miraculously, and got Jones a birdie instead of a six. For another, he had to birdie three of the last five holes on the final eighteen, including a forty-footer on the 72nd, to edge out Macdonald Smith by two golden strokes.

In the pre-Jones era of the Open, there are three years well worth mentioning, all because of the brilliant Englishman Harry Vardon and what he meant to the growth of the game.

There is first the year 1900, Vardon's first to tour the U.S. in a series of exhibitions. He concluded his trip by playing in our Open at the Chicago Golf Club, a chore he did not particularly warm to. Our Open at this time, of course, was of no more importance to Vardon than, say, the Singapore Open is to Jack Nicklaus today. But Vardon played and naturally Vardon won. The way he won, however, demonstrated the utter disdain that he held for the title. He casually whiffed a putt on the final green, shrugged, and still walked off with the championship. Vardon next returned in 1913 with his friend Ted Ray, a large man who was considered the world's second-greatest player. The U.S. Open had gained considerably in stature by then, but not so much that Vardon and Ray weren't supposed to smother the field at The Country Club in Brookline, Massachusetts. And smother it they did with the lone exception of a twenty-year-old, wide-eyed, home-grown amateur named Francis Ouimet.

To the astonishment of everyone, including himself, Ouimet finished the tournament birdie-par to tie Vardon and Ray. He then walked home, slept a comfortable thirteen hours, got up, walked back and shot 72 to Vardon's 77 and Ray's 78 in the play-off. The legend is that Ouimet's feat made golf front-page news in America, but the truth is that his conquest hardly got onto the sports pages of any newspapers outside of Boston and New York. It would be inaccurate to say, however, that the deed did not eventually help popularize the game along the Eastern seaboard.

Vardon's last appearance in our Open was in many ways one of the great accomplishments of his career, which included the taking of no fewer than six British Opens—the *real* Open of his day. This was in 1920 at Inverness in Toledo, Ohio. Vardon was fifty years old, but he thoroughly dominated the tournament. In fact he led by five strokes with only seven holes to go. Unfortunately a vicious gale came up, and Vardon played those holes in even fives, allowing the larger and stronger Ted Ray to overtake him and win by a stroke. It was a shame that Vardon could not have crowned his career with that victory in his fiftieth year, for he was, by all evidence, the best swinger until Jones. He was so perfect in the swing, in fact, that Walter Hagen once admitted, "In times when my own swing would leave me, I could bring it back by remembering Vardon and trying to imitate him."

The period between Bob Jones and Ben Hogan—the Thirties—can safely be regarded as the goofiest era of the Open, a decade into which champions like Lee Trevino and Orville Moody would fit perfectly.

No sooner had Jones retired than the Open responded to his absence in 1931 by producing the longest golf playoff in history. Billie Burke and George Von Elm had to play seventy-two grinding extra holes at Inverness before Burke won by a single stroke.

In 1932 Gene Sarazen found himself seven strokes behind with twenty-eight holes left to play at Fresh Meadow in Flushing, New York, so he promptly swept over those holes in 100 strokes, which included a final round of 66—nine under par in all—and which of course produced a victory.

A year later a lightly regarded professional named Olin Dutra, who also happened to be suffering a severe stomach ailment, put on an equally impressive stretch drive. He was eight behind with thirty-six to go, and all of the leading players of the time were ahead of him at Merion, including Sarazen.

One by one Dutra passed them all to defeat Sarazen by a stroke, thanks in large part to a triple bogey seven Sarazen made at Merion's 11th hole, which thereafter earned fame for its Baffling Brook.

If Sarazen could suffer a blowup, so could lesser men, the Open having by now become the one championship in golf that a winner could truly cash in on where endorsements were concerned. Perhaps Jimmy Thomson, first of the long hitters with the steel shaft, had dollar bills in his eye when he three-putted away his one and only chance at a major title in 1935 at Oakmont. Thomson even managed to four-putt one green in the last round to allow the absolute nobody Sam Parks, Jr., to win.

In 1938 at Cherry Hills a dashingly handsome and personable player Dick Metz, was gradually running off from the field through fifty-four holes. At this point he was told that an Open victory would get him a glamorous movie contract. Metz promptly shot 79, and the quiet, brooding Ralph Guldahl took his second Open in a row.

The Thirties concluded with Sam Snead's first and most often discussed Open tragedy. Snead came to the 72nd hole at Spring Mill in Philadelphia, with par five to win and a mere bogey six to tie. Nothing to it. Except Snead came apart in a fairway bunker, took a disastrous eight, and Byron Nelson went on to win. Snead never fully recovered from that experience in the Open, and thus he never won America's biggest championship, although he won nearly one hundred other titles.

"If I'd won that one I might have won ten others," Snead frequently said.

The post-Hogan phase of Open history belongs pretty much to Arnold Palmer—right up to the Mexkin and the sergeant.

Palmer won his only Open championship in 1960 at Cherry Hills in a typically Palmer way, with a rousing 65 in the last round.

Throughout the 1960's, however, the Open would never be his again, although it would several times *almost* be his. He had to three-putt twelve greens at Oakmont to fall into a tie with Jack Nicklaus and lose the play-off in 1962. He had to blow to a wild 77 in the third round at Brookline in 1963 to fall into a tie with Julius Boros and Jacky Cupit and lose the play-off to Boros. He had to blow a seven-stroke lead on the last six holes to drop into a tie with Billy Casper in 1966 at Olympic and lose that play-off.

The fact that it seems impossible for Arnold Palmer to win another Open somehow is partly the reason why the victories of Lee Trevino and Orville Moody seem all the more mysterious.

Golfing America had a legitimate question: how could a Mexkin and a sergeant win a tournament that the country's darling couldn't?

The answer of course is as elusive as the perfect round of eighteen birdies, and the thing that makes the game itself so irritatingly unfathomable at times.

There was Lee Trevino at Oak Hill, cracking jokes to his gallery and the press, acting as if just being *close* to the leader, Bert Yancey, was good enough for a Mexican from Dallas, an impoverished lad who had never won a tournament and who in fact had been on the professional tour only a little more than a year.

For three days it was Yancey's championship, clear and simple. He was golf's best putter, everyone agreed, and everyone knew how much Yancey *wanted* the Open, and his slow, smooth swing was considered to be among the more picturesque of the game's bright new stars. He would be a splendid Open champion. And he was beginning to ge used to the idea himself. After the third round interview with the press, he quietly asked a friend, "How did I sound?"

Meanwhile, Trevino against the backdrop of Oak Hill's yawning clubhouse and verandas—a place which seemed to combine all of the elements of Wuthering Heights and Jay Gatsby's mansion at West Egg—was an oddity, golf's credibility gap. Well, it had been fun to have him up there challenging, saying things like, "I'm gonna be a Spaniard instead of a Mexkin soon as I get some more money."

But he couldn't win.

Oh really? All the Mexkin did on Sunday was go out on Oak Hill paired head-to-head with Yancey the way a hustler likes it and turn that pretty swing into a wreckage of broken rhythm and disturbed concentration. Yancey began missing putts and Trevino began making them.

Lee would ask his followers, who already had assumed the name of Lee's Fleas, "What am I doin' out here? I don't know if I'm gonna hook it or slice it." The crowd would whoop and holler, "Whip the gringo."

Trevino buried Yancey over the first nine holes that day and he then stood up to a late rush by Jack Nicklaus, who was playing behind them. At his rear, the crowd would explode for a Nicklaus birdie, but Trevino would respond with a wisecrack and a slashing recovery shot out of Oak Hill's weeds.

"I was tryin' to get so far ahead I could choke and still win," he said later. "But I had to keep playin'."

And suddenly all Trevino had done was not only blast Bert

Yancey into a trauma and win the U.S. Open, he had shot a fourth consecutive subpar round, a 69—which had never been done before by Hogan or anybody, four subpar rounds in the Open—and his total of 275 merely tied the seventy-two-hole record set the previous year by Nicklaus.

Now here came all of that instant lore. Yeah, Trevino had come out of a hustler's game in Dallas, and sure he could play you with a Dr. Pepper bottle, using it fungo style and putting with it like a pool cue. Try him. For money, try him. He said his name was Super Mex and that some of the pros knew him before this, even if the public didn't. He sent a few of them home from El Paso in a Greyhound bus when they came out there to try him. What's that? Oh, the Band-Aid always on his forearm? Oh, that covered up the name of an ex-girlfriend that he once had tattoed on. "I get rid of 'em when they turn twenty-one," he said. The red socks and the red shirt he wore? "That's my payday outfit," he said. Finally, Trevino didn't know whether he had proved that Mexicans can play golf, but he thought he had proved that one of them can.

And that was Super Mex, the unlikeliest Open champion ever—until a year later.

Here now came Orville Moody to compound the felony at Champions in Houston. Like Trevino, the sergeant had never won a professional tournament, aside from a few Korean Opens, and also like Trevino he had only been on the PGA tour for slightly more than a year. Nor did his cross-handed putting method particularly recommend him since no man had ever putted cross-handed and won more than a kick in the ass with a cold boot, as the saying goes.

As Oak Hill had been Bert Yancey's tournament for three days, Champions had belonged almost exclusively to a tour veteran, Miller Barber. Barber was not an exciting player, with the loop in his backswing, the dark glasses he wore and his quiet, keep-to-himself nature. But he was solid, he had been a winner on the tour, and to see him up there in front at Champions was no real surprise.

Champions was playing long and tough and the humidity was at times unbearable, but Miller Barber had destroyed par for three days. He was four under, sitting on 276 in other words, and if he didn't come back to the field on Sunday, the championship was over.

Orville Moody, who was thirty-five and had spent fourteen years in the army, was the nearest man to Barber, and they were paired together on the final day, just as Trevino had been paired with Yancey.

"A guy like me can't think about going out and winning the National Open," Moody said that morning. "I'll just play along as best I can and see what happens."

He said he had liked the army, that the army had been good to him. He had made staff sergeant E6. He had gone in the first time for six years because of a girlfriend that done him wrong. "A kid don't know what he's doin' sometimes," he said. Then he reupped for three more years because he didn't know exactly what he would do if he got out.

By then, he said, he had become a pretty good golfer and he thought he'd like to try the tour. So in 1962 he got out of the army again, rounded up a likely by sponsor for a try at the tour, qualified for the National Open, went to the Open and missed the cut. "My sponsor came down a little on the money he promised when I blew the cut," Orville said. "So I went back in the army." Total time out: two weeks. Amount of time back in: five years.

Moody had played the tour most of 1968, but he had won only $13,000. He seemed to have a good, sound game, however. His swing was compact and smooth-looking. He had fair distance. He stood up to the ball well. But there was that business of the putting stroke.

"Anything over six inches long, my grip comes loose if I putt normal," he said. "I'm just a lousy putter, so I got to go cross-handed."

Moody arose on the morning of the last round and drove with his wife and his two children about an hour out to

Champions from a Holiday Inn across town. Obscure motels are where Nobodies stay. He reflected briefly in the locker room about the fact that he was playing pretty good. "I'm hittin' my irons exactly where I'm aimin' 'em," he said. "I guess I ought to start shootin' for the pins."

So he went out with Miller Barber and just played steady golf. He played 72 golf, two over. He played 281 golf, one over at Champions. But it was more than good enough. No one broke par on Sunday. The wind came up and the flags were tucked behind bunkers and ponds, and Moody's 72 was quite a score for a guy in contention. Miller Barber, meanwhile, got too conservative, too cautious. Bogey after bogey assaulted him, and after nine holes Moody had the lead.

"Miller kept tryin' to cozy it," said Orville. "He knew a seventy-three or four was all he needed, but he knew he was in the National Open too. It isn't easy out there."

It seemed easy enough for Moody. When he got to the last hole he needed a par four to beat two other contenders who had slipped up on Barber, Bob Rosburg and Al Geiberger.

All he said to his caddy was, "I got to get me a four here somehow." He nailed a driver down the middle, then he split the green with a five-iron, just twenty feet from the flag. Two more putts would do it, except that the first putt stopped about fourteen inches short. Moody looked at it and turned his cap sideways, the way a man does when he's made a dumb mistake and knows it. But he walked up to the short one, took no time, and dropped it.

Maybe the Open daze made that par for him and maybe not. Maybe the Open coma won it for Lee Trevino. Back-to-back Nobodies is asking a lot for us to believe. But perhaps there is something more to it. It is just possible that the right player can come up to the right course at the right time. The fairways bend to his shots and the greens suit his stroke. Somehow he also gets to thinking that he *can* win and, more important, that he *deserves* to win. In the case of Trevino and

Moody, it may also be that a little bit of disrespect for the institution and the establishment doesn't hurt anything. Trevino did it with an obvious brashness and defiance. Moody did it with a cold sort of you-can-bet-me-if-you-think-you-can-play attitude. They were both hustlers and a hustler likes a big game, and there is no game bigger than the Open. Looking back, they even made it look easy, and one had to be reminded of that old story about the Turnesa family. They had learned the game as caddies where their father was a greenskeeper, and when it once looked as if Joe Turnesa might win the 1926 National Open some members of the club, having heard the news on the radio, rushed out on the course where the father was clipping grass. "Mr. Turnesa," one of them cried. "Joe's winning the National Open."

"Why shouldn't he?" said the old man, without looking up. "All he's ever done is play golf."

Maybe it's as simple as that, after all, for a Jones or a Hogan, or a Mexkin or a sergeant.

Out There with Slow-Play Fay

Where I came from, a so-called lady golfer was always something to be hollered at, like an overheating '53 Buick blocking traffic, or a sullen waitress who couldn't remember to put cheese on the burger and leave off the onions, the dummy. Hey, you. You up there on the green with the legs like tree bark, and the schoolteacher skirt and the one-foot putt. It's *good*. I give you the putt, all right? So take your 135 shots back to the Mixed Grill and jump into your vodka martini with your nitwit husband who took your father's thieving money and built the country club and won't let you play here but once a week—in front of *me*. Go shell some peas or crochet an afghan or do whatever women ought to be doing instead of cluttering up a golf course. Fore! *Fore, Agnes Zilch!*

That's how it was growing up back in Texas. The most fun was to stand back there with your guys and then, after all the yelling and waiting, everybody would cut loose with a three-iron. And then when the shots would burn into the green and go between the putting stances of Slow-Play Fay and Play-Slow Flo, and when they would hop around like an assortment of Ruby Keelers, we'd sink to the knees of our khakis in aching laughter.

We had it all worked out in our minds that we belonged on the course and they didn't. We were there to sharpen up for the Goat Hills Invitation and they—the women—were there to keep us from becoming the future Hogans and Nelsons. "Women golfers are meece," we said, referring to our plural of moose.

We never asked to play through. We just did it, often while they were studying their chip shots. And there would always be one of them, a slightly rotund, menacing, scowling soul who would challenge us. "Don't you boys know anything about manners?" she would say.

We would all very wittily ask each other if we knew anything about manners and, while we putted out, we would discuss it. One of us would say he thought he used to know something about manners, back when manners lived over on Hemphill near Kenny Don Minter, who couldn't beat nobody. Manners was pretty good, we would say, but he had a tendency to snap-hook it when he got moved up in cash. We would be going on toward the next tee and the big lady would still be after us. "I know who you are, and I'm going to tell your parents," she would say.

One of us would say, "That's gonna be a lot of phone calls because we all come from broken homes."

The big lady would usually turn out to be somebody I'll call Mrs. R. F. Zinger, 14 times city champion and president of the women's district golf association. She would be the first lady ever to pass the local bar exam, the first lady pilot, a former Curtis Cup alternate, an ex-national spelling-bee champion, the daughter of the city's first four-term mayor, the author of a textbook on the history of the Colorado River and the architect of the town's new West Side freeway system.

With Mrs. R. F. Zinger lecturing after us, we would bound off down the fairway, having successfully played through, but of course a couple of us would insist on calling something back at her from out of slung-wedge distance. "Miz Zinger eats Maxflis," somebody would shout. And somebody else would holler, "In an unraked bunker."

Such was my fondness for women's golf in those days. Not to suggest, however, that my attitude would be changed by a certain maturity or my advancement into newspaper work.

Anyone who ever did time on a newspaper sports desk is familiar with the type of phone calls you get from lady golfers. Mine usually came when I was listening to the Kentucky Derby and the horses were at the post. I would get the call from Mrs. Simcox reporting the net 77 that Mrs. Slocum shot to win the local women's golf association's Tuesday Flag Tournament.

"I'm *sure* it was a net 77," Mrs. Simcox would say. "Let's see. She bogeyed 1, double-bogeyed 2. . . ."

Yeah, yeah, yeah.

I guess my most favorite phone call of all time—true story— went something like this:

Me: Hi, sports fans. Pegler here. Runyon's out to lunch.

"Sports department, please."

This here's it.

"Is this the sports department?"

Take it on one, Hildy.

"Hello? Sports department?"

Hi!

"This is Mrs. J. D. Stephens calling for Mrs. R. F. Zinger, the president of the women's district golf association. Mrs. Zinger asked me to call you because she said you always wanted the results of our weekly tournaments."

Oh, good.

"Mrs. Zinger said you liked to print the results."

Well, Mrs. Zinger looks out for us pretty good.

"Mrs. Zinger said to tell you that we played our weekly blind-flag bogey event today, and I have the results."

You played a what?

"Our weekly blind-flag bogey tournament is what Mrs. Zinger called it."

What exactly is that?

"Well, it was sort of complicated, but we all played and I have the winners here."

Fine. What was it again?

"It was our weekly blind-flag bogey tournament, a different type of event that Mrs. Zinger thought up."

O.K.

"I'm not sure I can explain it, but we all played 18 holes and then Mrs. Zinger figured out who won."

O.K. Just start with the winner.

"Well, first place in the championship flight was Mrs. R. F. Zinger. . . ."

It was inevitably my experience that women didn't actually play golf. They casseroled it. They all stood there in front of my gangsome, poking at two-inch putts. They all had woefully slow, four-piece backswings with curious hip moves. They took the clubs back so far that the shafts whipped them on the shoulder blades, and then they lunged forward and the club heads plundered into the earth and the balls went dribbling off into the weeds.

A lot of the time I figured it was the way they dressed that made them play so badly. And slowly. They all wore those goofy things on their feet that weren't socks and came up just above the shoe tops and reached down below the anklebones. Ugly. And they wore straight skirts that hit them below the knees, with white blouses that were too tight, and big-brimmed hats with red bows.

Then there was the cackling in the clubhouse. After their rounds, I noticed that most women golfers could get into the booze better than most men. Several times I thought I saw two women having a bitter fight across a table, but they were just chatting over their Manhattans—or whatever women drink—about curtains and drapes.

I understood, of course, that there were supposed to be a lot of women golfers in the world who weren't like the ones I had always been exposed to. I knew about the Babe and Jameson and Suggs and all that. The lady pros. I knew they had a tour of their own, but I also knew what most guys felt about it: you would've bet that every one of 'em out there on the women's pro tour could overhaul a diesel truck if she put her mind and energy to it.

In recent years I have been presented with a number of chances to visit a women's pro tournament instead of hanging around the men's tour all the time. Each time I gingerly managed to escape, and the assignment most often fell to an associate in the golf department, a child star who writes too well for any of us to loaf much.

"You ought to go see 'em," he would say. "They're great."

Wrong. Got to stay with the guys, I would insist. Tom Weiskopf is getting ready to issue his first quote of the year, and I don't want to miss it.

"It isn't like you remember it," my colleague would argue. "Most of them are cute and friendly, and they can play like hell."

Well, one of these days, I would say. Can't now, though. Got a biggie coming up in Pensacola. Eichelberger's moving up on the point list. McGee's ready to bust out. Crampton smiled the other day. All very exciting with the men.

To be candid about it, one of the things that kept me away from the LPGA tour was the knowledge that the girls don't exactly travel the caviar circuit in terms of towns. I mean, do you want to spend a week in Shreveport or Waco? Take your shot, Alamo, Calif. or Winchester, Va.? Horsham, Pa. or Prospect, Ky.?

Also, the names of their tournaments were troubling. They all sounded like stock-car races. For example, there were things like the Shreveport Kiwanis Invitational, the Johnny Londoff Chevrolet, the Len Immke Buick, the Springfield Jaycee, the Lincoln-Mercury and the Quality Chek'd Classic. How did they miss Darlington and Daytona? What was Sandra Haynie driving these days? A modified Spalding with dual grips?

Then it happened. My young associate said he thought there might be a women's event coming up that I'd like. The $50,000 Sealy-LPGA Classic. Sealy like in mattress.

That's *funny,* I said.

"No, seriously," he said. The men's tour was quiet, after all. Terry Dill wouldn't be changing his grip for another week or so. Dick Lotz still had the same putter. Bert Yancey had postponed his annual interview till July.

"And it's in Las Vegas," he said.

That was the magic word. Vegas. Now, I know that to some people Las Vegas is not all that fascinating. To some, it's Baghdad-by-the-Copperheads, the mob's idea of chic, a neon-lit asylum, the blonde-wig, no-bra, no-brain capital of the Western world. To others, such as me, however, Vegas comes up as the only civilized city in the U.S., because it's the only one where there aren't a lot of lightweight lawmakers, trying to tell you that you can't eat, drink, gamble or fall in love between two a.m. and noon. So I take Vegas whenever I can get it, even if I have to fool around with women's golf.

Judging from the number of blue Sealy blazers around The Desert Inn during this full week in May, there weren't many mattresses being sold anywhere. Sealy was venturing into golf for the first time, and the company had selected a women's tournament to sponsor for what it believed to be a tidy statistical reason. Women make or influence nine out of every 10 mattress purchases, said a Sealy press release. Furthermore, the release pointed out, "Research confirmed that the millions of people who enjoy golf conform to what Sealy believes is the predominant purchaser of its Posturepedic mattress."

There was an early moment at The Desert Inn, when I saw all of the lady pros attacking the slot machines, that this terrific headline came to me:

CAPONI POUNDS POSTUREPEDIC PAR.

It didn't take long, in Vegas, for me to realize that one of the major differences between lady pros and men pros is that lady pros scream a whole lot more at a dice table. On the first night in town I was trying to have a quiet drink in the lobby bar at The Desert Inn with my old friend Bud Erickson, a former employee of the Detroit Lions and Atlanta Falcons who had been cast into the unlikely role of executive director of the LPGA, when we heard these female noises ringing through the casino.

"I think those are my people," Bud said.

We looked and there they were, nine of them, jammed around a dice table as if it were a washrag sale. One of them—Gerda Boykin, her name was—was shooting, and she had just rolled a seven. Almost everything in The Desert Inn stopped for the next few moments as Gerda Boykin, an attractive brunette who was once the only lady pro in Germany, made three more passes with the dice amid a chorus of some of the best shrieks since Arnie first hitched up his trousers.

What had happened was, a bunch of the girls, including Judy Rankin and Pam Higgins and this Gerda, had formed a syndicate on the tour a few weeks before Vegas. Every time one of them three-putted in a tournament, she put $1 into a pool, and they had this pact they would take the money to Vegas for the Sealy. And on the first night there, one of them—it turned out to be Gerda Boykin—would shoot the bundle at craps for three, maybe four rolls. They went in with $60 total, and the nine of them came out with an average of $40 after Gerda got through.

Bud Erickson said, "Pretty good story, huh, right off the bat? Nothing like that on the men's tour, I guess."

Right, I said. You can't find nine guys who'll speak to each other.

"Lot of good stories out here," said Bud. "There's a girl named Diane Patterson who used to be a trapeze artist. She took up golf after she quit The Flying Viennas."

Really?

"Got a kid named Pam Barnett who throws her wig around when she gets mad, instead of breaking clubs."

Good.

"How about the Watusi Kid? Donna Caponi. She'll dance all night and play great golf."

Hmmmmm.

"Got a couple of Japanese girls on the tour now. Chako Higuchi and Marbo Sasaki."

Ah, so.

"Hey," said Bud. "How about Sharron Moran? She's really attractive and she does these hat tricks. She's always wearing a different hat on the course. She must have 20 or more different hats."

Z-z-z-z-z-z-z. Oh, excuse me, Bud. Almost dropped off there for a minute.

The Sealy-LPGA Classic had an odd format. It was a 72-hole tournament for the girls, of course, with a hefty $10,000 going to the winner. Well, that's big for the women. It's a shrug for the guys. Anyhow, John Montgomery, the tournament director, had it all worked out that to make it different—to give it something extra—it would be played sort of like the Crosby in reverse. The lady pros would have *men* partners every day in what constituted four separate Pro-Ams. In other words, each day the girls would play for some extra cash, and the amateur men would compete for what appeared to be just about all of the Steuben glass that had ever been steubed.

On Wednesday evening John Montgomery ran down the list of all the glittering male types from sports and show biz who had been invited to participate. There were Joe Namath, Glen Campbell, Mickey Mantle, Joey Bishop, Don Adams, Joe DiMaggio, George Blanda, Jerry Lucas, Fred Williamson, Joe Williams, Tige Andrews, Fred Biletnikoff, Peter Marshall, Jim Lange, Dale Robertson, Joe Louis, Vic Damone.

"And you," he said.

I said uh-duh-*who?*

"You play at 8:42 a.m. with Donna Caponi and Glen Campbell," John said.

Later that evening my lovely wife, whom I shall call June, and I were trying to decide where to go in Vegas—I was torn between "Vive Les Girls" at the Dunes and "Geisha'rella" at the Thunderbird—when she asked what I was going to wear tomorrow morning because they would be a gallery.

The usual, I said. My basic-blue button-down with the sleeves cut off and bush jeans. Maybe the gray sweater.

"You'll smother to death and look stupid," she said. "How's your game?"

Terrific, if I don't shank, I said.

"Then *don't* shank," she said. "What'll Glen and Donna think?"

Relax, I said. What do show-biz guys know about golf? And forget Donna. This is hardly the Masters, you know.

You could probably say that the crowd was fairly large around the 1st tee, most of them there to see Glay-yun. We stood around for a little bit, posed for pictures and waited for the P.A. to announce our pairing. Donna Caponi came over and said, "You and Glen both have eight strokes. We've got a chance to win this today. We'll just play loose and see what happens."

I told Donna that the tournament itself was the most important thing, where she was concerned. We'd try not to bother her, me and Glen, I said.

"Listen, we're going to have fun," she smiled.

Donna teed off first and whipped it about 240 down the middle with a pretty solid swing, and it suddenly dawned on me that she was, after all, the U.S. Women's Open champion of the past two years.

Glen Campbell stepped up next and flogged it about 260 down the middle with a very good swing, and I wondered where in the hell *that* came from.

I don't recall a great deal of applause when I was announced on the tee, but I do remember teeing up the ball, backing away for a practice swing and seeing my wife over behind the ropes. She was trying to tell me something in a whisper, hoping I could read her lips. Which I could. She was saying: "Take . . . off . . . the . . . dumb . . . sweater . . . Dummy."

That didn't bother me, however. I opened up with the tee
shot I always open up with—a howling slice which, when last
charted, was headed so far out of bounds that Glen Campbell
said, "Fore on The Strip."

The provisional drive I hit was the same old second effort,
a boring hook that hammered its way into the nearest fairway
bunker.

"That completes our clinic, folks," Campbell said. And we
were off.

It wasn't the most comfortable triple-bogey 8 I've ever made
because, by notable contrast, Campbell put a spoon up near
the green in two and had a couple of leisurely putts for a
birdie. Donna raced over and kissed him.

Look, I'm just one, I said. Can I play through?

"If you're not going to *try*," my lovely wife said, "then I'll
just go on back to the hotel and wait for you by the swimming
pool."

By the end of the 3rd hole I had cost our team a net birdie
by missing a two-foot putt—specifically, my wife said, because
I refused to take a cigarette out of my mouth before I stroked
the ball, and I had smashed another drive out of bounds and
made a double bogey.

"You have a good swing," Donna Caponi was kind enough
to say, "if you'll slow it down about four speeds."

Yeah, I know what to *do*, I said. It's just that sometimes,
if you drink a little. . . .

"You'll be O.K.," Donna said. "Just take it back low and
slow."

A little later my lovely wife came over and said, "Can I go
get anybody a Coke, or a *golf shirt*, perhaps?"

Billy Casper frequently plays in a sweater in warm weather,
I pointed out, rather testily.

"You're soaked under that thing," she said. "Yuk."

I'll tell you what else is making me hot, I said.

There were those in the gallery who, were they willing,
could testify that for the next several holes everybody in our

threesome, including the dummy, played pretty well. Donna
Caponi certainly wasn't any Slow-Play Fay or Play-Slow Flo.
She was hard at work on a 71. Glen Campbell, the celeb, was
in the process of carving out a surprising 72. When I finally
started helping, our team chewed its way down to serious
under-par figures. My moment of real glory came at the 13th
when I got into a good drive, and a decent eight-iron, and
then casually dropped a 15-footer for a birdie. Smoking. Donna
raced over and gave me a birdie kiss, the crowd clapped, Glen
patted me on the damp sweater and I looked around for the
wife. Wasn't there, naturally. Had gone to get another Coke.
Figured.

You blew my birdie back there, I told her.

"Well, thank goodness for *something* good," she said. "I just
wish you hadn't picked *today* to play so badly."

Hold it, I said. It's not all that bad. I'll be about an 82
with a triple bogey and a double bogey. Take away those two
holes and. . . .

"Glen's played just great all the way," she said.

. . . it's down to about a 77 or so, which isn't all that. . . .

"He's really hit some wonderful shots."

. . . bad, actually. And I've made a few pars. It isn't exactly
like I never hit a single. . . .

"I love his shirt and pants. Aren't they good-looking?"

. . . shot, all day long. I mean, it's not exactly my *profession*,
playing golf. Considering that I only play. . . .

"Did he say he'd get us a table for his opening tonight at
the International?"

. . . a few times a year, living in Fun City, whereas certain
show-biz guys don't have anything to do but play a guitar and
hang around Riviera and Lakeside. . . .

"Isn't he the cutest thing? And so nice and friendly."

. . . and, anyhow, you sure missed seeing a good birdie back
there.

Nobody I've ever known in my entire life has ever won a

Pro-Am. I have played in maybe 7,895 of them over the past 25 years, with any number of fine partners—guys who could really play and guys who had a bundle of strokes to use—and I have very often been "the leader in the clubhouse;" as the TV commentators say, but before nightfall every one of these Pro-Ams has been won by a bunch of guys from Sacramento or Tampa. The pro would be an unknown, and his amateur partners would consist of a real-estate developer, an electrical contractor and a priest. They would be 24 under par.

Obviously, then, it was quite silly for Donna Caponi, Glen Campbell or me to think that our measly little round of 14-under would win anything on that first day. And of course it didn't. Marilynn Smith had a team that featured Jerry Lucas, the basketball star who had just been traded to the Knicks. Jerry was so delighted with the trade that he went out with his 12 handicap and shot a two-under 70—gross—just like most of the 12-handicappers I ever knew back in Texas. They won laughing.

At the daily cocktail party and prizegiving, where all the Sealy folks got to work on their autograph collections and wondered where Joe Namath was, Jerry Lucas apologized and Donna Caponi confided that she was taking a party of 12 to both Glen Campbell shows that night.

For Friday's round the dummy got himself a golf shirt, his wife stayed at poolside, he drew for a pro a nice young married lady from Midland, Texas named Judy Rankin who had captured three LPGA tournaments of late, and, for his other partner, a guy from Tampa with a long drive and a lot of strokes. Guy named Bill. Land developer. I thought we were a lock.

For a long time we were. Bill from Tampa was a cheerleader who called our pro "Judy, baby," and liked to take out a nine-iron for a five-iron shot and announce, "If it's only 170 yards, a nine's plenty for me, baby."

We played the back nine first and didn't cause any particular commotion until the 18th (our ninth) when I did one of those things we all did every week when we were 15 years old. I holed out a chip shot for an eagle.

From up on the TV tower, where the Hughes Network people were rehearsing, Bob Toski was giggling. "Where'd you learn that?" he called down. "In a subway?"

Our gallery consisted primarily of one: Walter (Yippy) Rankin, Judy's husband, a golf widower, a big, good-natured guy who sells insurance when he's not applying body English for his wife's putts.

Somewhere on the incoming nine, Yippy Rankin made the mistake of telling us, "You know, you-all are 15-under and that's leading. I think you can win it today."

The ninth hole at The Desert Inn course (which would be our last) is an unprintable annoyance as far as I'm concerned. You have two choices off the tee on this par-4. You can drive it into a pond on the left or out of bounds into some homes on the right.

Knowing we had it all wrapped up, then, Judy Rankin promptly hit her drive into the pond, and I promptly hit mine out of bounds. None of this seemed to bother Bill from Tampa, however. He just stepped up and split the fairway with a boomer. Nine-iron to the green.

"I'll handle it, baby," he said.

When we reached Bill from Tampa's tee shot, we could see the scoreboard and absorb the fact that our team *was* leading. I reminded our partner that he had a stroke on the hole, on top of everything else, so there was no point in being brave. Just a little flip up there to the big, safe part of the green and two putts would give us 16-under, more than we needed. That'll be a sweet $500 for Judy Rankin and some Steuben for the good guys.

"Don't worry, I'll put her right up there, baby," said Bill from Tampa.

Who cold-bladed it out of bounds, and we finished tied for second.

• • •

Saturday's round was fairly uneventful, except for the fact that
I was paired with some of the best set decoration on the new
ladies' tour. She was Donna's sister, Janet Caponi, who wears
hot pants and helps make the LPGA look a lot different from
the way I remembered it. Donna had taken the lead in the
Sealy Classic itself, and we spent a lot of time asking for reports
on her round. It was hot and windy, and the round passed
as slowly as you might guess it would for somebody who
had now been in Las Vegas for five days, which is the equivalent of 17 years. I was sadly over-Don Rickles-d, over-Bill
Cosby-d, over-Juliet Prowse-d, over-dinner-and-late-show-d,
over-black jack-d and soundly asleep on each and every backswing.

John Montgomery and Bud Erickson decided that I created
something of a minor problem for Sunday's final round. They
had quite an athletic event on their hands, what with Donna
Caponi holding a one-stroke lead over Janie Blalock, who had
a sweet personality and a fine, fine game, and Sandra Palmer,
an old friend of mine, as it happened, from Texas, who had
yet to win her first tournament. And bunched together right
behind them were all of the other top lady pros: Sandra Haynie,
who had just won three in a row, Marlene Hagge, Jo Ann
Prentice, Kathy Whitworth, Peggy Wilson, Pam Barnett,
Margie Masters, Judy Rankin and Carol Mann.

Not only were the girls going out there on Sunday and
battling it out for what was a big payday for them, they were
going to have to play threesomes: two lady pros with one celeb
of sorts. For example, Montgomery and Erickson (and Sealy)
thought it would be nifty for national television if there was
a Glen Campbell or Joe Namath in every group of girls. And
no writers.

"Let's face it," Bud Erickson told me. "You're not much
of a TV attraction."

Just blurt it out, Bud, I said. No need to doll it up.

"How about 7:37 a.m. with Mary Lou Daniel and Jan Ferraris?"

I said I thought I'd be off the tables by then. Fine.

Part of the offering Sunday, to keep the men stimulated, was a competition for a huge chunk of Steuben shaped into the form of a trophy, The Heart of Variety Cup, they called it. A man took his handicap and used it, and took the best holes he could get from his two lady pros, and all of that counted as *his* score, best ball.

Inasmuch as I was a dew sweeper that Sunday, Mary Lou and Jan and I got around rather swiftly. In fact, we finished at 11 o'clock just as Donna Caponi, Janie Blalock and Glen Campbell were teeing off. Mary Lou and Jan had been excellent companions and pretty impressive shotmakers, I must admit.

Maybe I particularly liked the two of them because I beat them with a light-running 75. From memory. In any case, our combined scores gave me eight-under for the round, and I was the leader in the clubhouse.

"Hey," John Montgomery said. "You're the leader in the clubhouse."

That's right, Byron, I said. Now back to you, Chris.

When you finish early you get to be the leader in the clubhouse for quite a long time. At The Desert Inn, I suppose I was the leader in the clubhouse for, oh, three or four hours. As a matter of fact, I was the leader in the clubhouse for so long that I finally started worrying that I might win.

There is no rule, of course, which says the leader in the clubhouse can't leave the clubhouse. So I went out on the course to watch Donna, Janie and Sandra Palmer throw the lead in the Sealy back and forth in pure melodramatic fashion. Hell of a tournament. They were each making one immense pressure shot after another while the Namaths and Campbells tried to stay out of the way.

Presently, after glancing at a scoreboard, I realized that I was a *co*-leader in the clubhouse. Although I had finished ahead of a split end, some guy from *Petticoat Junction*, another guy from *Mod Squad,* a fellow from *Bracken's World, The Dating Game* man, a couple of pro quarterbacks and the guy from *The Hollywood Squares,* I had suddenly been tied by Mr. Dithers, or an actor named Charles Lane.

Then it all fell apart. Namath, Mantle and Campbell went by me, and then here came Don Adams with 18 strokes and a couple of pretty fair partners in Sandra Haynie and Marlene Hagge. He would win by a stroke.

"You're tied for fifth in the clubhouse," my wife said.

The Sealy-LPGA Classic came down to the very last hole where Sandra Palmer, who had never won a tournament, held a one-stroke lead over Donna Caponi, directly behind her. As Sandra hit her second shot into a front bunker by the 18th green, Donna smashed a big drive down the fairway. Everybody figured it would go into sudden death.

I curiously found myself standing out there halfway up the fairway watching both, pulling for both; for my old friend Sandra from the old home town, the ex-college cheerleader whom I had first seen play when she was 14; and for my new friend, Donna, the dancer, in many ways the solidest player of all the girls.

My wife said, "You've got to admit this is pretty exciting."

Big deal, I said. Ten thousand dollars. Nicklaus gets that much for marking his ball.

"You're phony," she said.

Yeah, I know, I said. But keep it in the family. It's an image deal.

About then, Sandra Palmer hit a slightly stupendous bunker shot that took two hops and rolled straight into the cup for an eagle 3; for all of the whoops, all of the glory and the biggest chunk of the cash. For victory.

I saw her later. She was still in semi-shock from her first win.

"Did you have fun?" Sandra asked. "I hope you got to see that we have lots and lots of really fine players out here and some awfully nice people."

That's true, I said.

"It's great you could be here. I hope a lot of the girls have told you that," Sandra said.

They had, and it was embarrassing.

"See you again somewhere?"

I grinned and said I'd have to check the towns first. See what the bus schedules were like. And the diners.

Sandra laughed.

"We'll see you again," she said.

Pro of 52nd Street

Claude Harmon not only taught me most of what I know about the golf swing, he took me out of Argyle socks.

—DAVE MARR,
holding court on 52nd Street

On one of those dazzling nights in Manhattan that a visitor from Minerva, Ohio, might classify as being heavy on the celebs, Dave Marr, a young man from the robot life of the professional golf tour, stepped into one of his favorite 52nd Street restaurants and began moving through the glitter like, let us say, Sandy Primetime.

It was a tired room, filled with those ever-present clusters of familiar midtown drinkers: Giant fans, Jet fans, Met fans, high handicappers from Winged Foot, broadcasting immortals, ex-athletes, magazine folk, network worriers, directors, producers, panelists—all sorts of people who sometimes pass for celebrities when there isn't a real heavyweight on the street. But suddenly the room seemed to be refreshed by Marr's arrival.

Tanned and beaming, resplendent in his double-breasted blue blazer, trim and handsome, all Guccied and Dunhilled, Marr shot his hand out in varying directions as he greeted individuals and groups at the bar up front, working casually toward a table in the rear. All around, there were happy blurps of worship: "Hi, Dave," "Hey, pro," "Put it in the vise, champ." And all around, there were friendly, happy needles:

"Missed the cut, right?" "Got arrested for impersonating a golfer, right?"

Marr grinned and pushed along, accepting a vodka and tonic from somebody, lighting a cigarette, shaking hands. Laughter trailed after him, for he, too, was dropping lines.

"Hey," he said to Mike Manuche, the proprietor. "Did you read where Arnold's been talking about the governorship of Pennsylvania? Man, I think that hip injury must be movin' up to his *head*."

By the time he reached his table, he had enough pals with him to play a good game of half-court, and the table quickly expanded like a bar at 5:42 P.M. All sorts of people had been in lately and asking about him, Marr was told. Alex Webster, the Giant coach. Frank Gifford, Bing Crosby. Bob Newhart. Tucker Frederickson. Don Meredith. Paul Hornung.

"A great thing about my line of work," Marr said to a friend. "I'm O-and-eighty but nobody's singing 'Good-bye, Davey.'"

And so Dave Marr was at home, doing his thing, holding another seance in sport, being his charming, likable, entertaining self, getting on the outside of his share of cocktails, being, for whatever it may be worth, the pro of 52nd Street. Later on, when he would move to other bistros in the big city, *his* city now—to Jimmy Weston's no doubt, perhaps to "21," Duncan's—a hearty band would follow and others would be collected. The end would finally come in the early morning. It would be signaled mercifully by the placing in front of him of that salvation of Western man: the bacon cheeseburger. Dinner at last. It would come in the back room at P. J. Clarke's after all of the golf tour's problems had been threshed out, after the future success of the New York Giants had been assured, after the city had been saved, the wars ended, the new books discussed, the world's oxygen preserved, the pollution problem solved. Surviving another evening on the town, the final triumph, would be shared with Marr by such stay-awakes as Danny Lavezzo, the owner of Clarke's, by maybe Jack Whitaker, the broadcaster, by an old ex-Giant or two, and surely Jimmy Martin, a stock broker and world philosopher, and perhaps myself.

The point is, Dave Marr would have done it again. His thing, whatever it is. This thing of just being alive and being around, laughing a lot, knowing everybody, being known, reveling in the fact that although he is just little Dave Marr out of Houston by way of Claude Harmon and golf shop flunky—just another of those steady, faceless guys on the PGA tour—he can move through the big town like the emcee of a talk show, like Arnold Palmer *should,* considering Arnold's fame.

And done what? On such nights as these, had Dave Marr only proved that he can drink and go back to the Hartford Open and hit five-irons? Proved he can stay up later than Joe Namath? Proved he knows more people than Paul Hornung? Proved he is the check-grabbing champion of the fashionable East Side? Well, let's see. Maybe part of this. Maybe all of it. But then again maybe none of it. Maybe David Francis Marr was only having a good time with friends, genuine friends, who constitute much of his real wealth. He is *not* just another pro exempt from qualifying, and he knows it, and an inner circle knows it and, after all, what other pro wears Guccis and always leaves you laughing?

Dave Marr would go back to the grind of the tour to finish twenty-third of course, to miss the cut perhaps, to *not* win another tournament, to become one of those hundred or so players out there who hit very good shots but who are not Arnold Palmer or Jack Nicklaus or Gary Player or Lee Trevino or Billy Casper, or even, in terms of crowd recognition, Tom Weiskopf or Johnny Miller. But he would go back and make the stylish living. He will play well enough to pay for first-class air travel, for the best hotel rooms in the best hotels, to be able to "whip out" for the restaurant checks, the theater, the nightclubs, the moving around town, the clothes, and all that. In this sense Dave Marr is a bigger winner than he ever thought he might be.

But he knows the way it is. Attention to oneself in pro golf is not easily gained except by winning—repetitious winning. And even then it can be difficult as evidenced by the public's slow warm-up to Jack Nicklaus. Nobody wins more than Nicklaus but the public for a long while said ho-hum, over-looking the fact that Jack is pleasant, at times witty and thoroughly likable. It has been said that Palmer did it not just by winning but by fighting a course in his furiously dramatic way. Tony Lema drank champagne and did it. Chi Chi Rodriquez danced on the greens and did it. Doug Sanders wore wild clothes and did it. Billy Casper ate buffalo meat and did it. But on the intolerant surface Dave Marr occupies the role of so many others. He hasn't done it outside of New York and Houston and when he comes down the fairway with Mason Rudolph or Frank Beard or Charley Coody, the crowd wonders who is who.

And so it goes for most of the so-called stars of the game. Aren't they robots in a curious way who plod along pondering their destinies as someday club pros? Their personalities tend to be the same: uncommunicative. Their look is the same: blue shirt, white cap, gray slacks. Their wives are the same: simple but nice, with outdated hairdos. Their politics are the same: unphilosophically conservative. Their food is the same: steak, baked potato, salad with Roquefort. And their com-plaints are the same: Palmer's gallery is a pain in the ass, Nicklaus plays too slow, Trevino talks too much, Sanders is dizzy, the pins are brutal, the travel is expensive, the caddies are lazy, and where the hell is the courtesy car the tournament chairman promised?

The weeks grind into months and the months grind into years. A major championship breaks up the routine with its abnormal excitement and pressure—"Boy, the press is really here"—but there are only four of those, the Masters, the

U.S. Open, the British Open and the PGA, and then it's
back to the real tour, back to the Buick Opens. It is back
to the blurry dreariness of Holiday Inns and Imperial South
Motels. Take the kids out by the pool. Give the wife some
money to go shopping. Is there anything good on television?
What was the name of that Polynesian restaurant? Frank
Beard wants to get up a bridge game. Ken Still wants to
go to a ball park. Man, did you see that chick following
Raymond Floyd today? Christ, it's hot in Chicago. The lady
scorer is a sun-scarred Wasp and the friendly, ingratiating
chairman made a million dollars selling hydraulic jacks so
how come his blazer doesn't fit? Why in the hell can't a
contestant get a table in the dining room? Who let all those
kids inside the ropes when we came off the 18th? Boy, Jack
Tuthill better get on the ball. The greens are grainy and
the rough is a zoo. The TV crew will cost you two shots
at least. How about getting paired two straight weeks with
Jerry Barber? The fairways are too high, the greens are too
damp, and Jesus, Dave Hill never shuts up. If Nicklaus is
anywhere near his game he'll win by six. If he isn't, then
it must be Casper's turn again. It isn't Dave Marr's. It
never is.

But it beats working, they say. It's the golden goose, they
say. Just make the cut every week and you'll break Byron
Nelson's money record of 1945. What does the touring pro
do that's hard? He plays golf six days a week and not exactly
on public courses with a pull-cart. He hangs around country
clubs with rich guys and takes down $40,000 if he can't play
at all. Where's the grief? California in the winter, Florida in
the spring, the big cities in the summer. Couple of trips to
Europe or the Far East. Some TV stuff. Some appearances and
exhibitions. Snappy clothes for cost or zip, a big bag, four
dozen pairs of shoes, three dozen new balls every week from
the companies, courtesy cars, limousines and drivers, air travel,
celebrities, room service, lolling around on verandas, parties,
outdoors, fresh air, vodka and blondes, playing a game, for

God's sake, and calling it work. Let the brooding dummies overhaul diesel trucks for a living and see how they like it.

One of the engaging things about Dave Marr is that he understands the paradox of the tour better than his contemporaries. It *is* good when you reach a certain plateau, he will say. Everybody likes attention, being made to feel important. The money is there. Status is there. But it is also a terrible grind, almost an addiction, that bleeds the brain, puts a strain on the family, and keeps the ego bouncing like a basketball.

"Your ego is everything," Marr has admitted. "And if you don't get that pumped up regularly, you can't last."

The pro is an athlete above all else, Marr explained, a special kind of athlete who has to control his emotions. Most of his strain is mental, but much is physical about his sport. Play six straight rounds of golf *walking* and you will see that the pro's legs have to be in decent shape. Stand close to a pro hitting an iron shot and look at the deep, slashing divot he takes and you will see that good golf requires some strength. Few things in sport move any faster than a clubhead going through a ball when a touring pro makes a pass at a shot. Whether the player has an easy swing, like Marr, or a gritty one, like Palmer, there is real speed involved at contact—one of the things which separates the pro from everybody else at the country club.

"There's no doubt that the mental part of the game is the toughest," Marr said. "Trying to keep the dog from comin' up in you when you're in shape to win. But when guys tell me there's nothing physical about playing the tour, well, man. I start thinking about all the travel, aside from the practice. Follow me around for two or three weeks and I'll guarantee you, you'll be a tired mother."

Restoring the ego is the constant concern, according to Marr. Small things can do it—a kind word from a respected player, a series of good rounds. The driver can come back from the dead, or the short irons. The putter can get hot. But the best source for the nonwinner is a new venue each week. You're starting all over with renewed faith. There is new hope, new anticipation. You have a whole new set of friends. Different admirers are fawning over you, oblivious to the fact that you missed the cut last week. There's Garner Dickinson, who wears a cap like Hogan. There's Gay Brewer, the guy with the pug nose. There's Art Wall; he makes holes in one. There's Bob Rosburg, who uses a baseball grip. And isn't that Dave Marr? Didn't he win something once? The PGA, or something?

"You can play real good in a tournament and even if you don't win it, it'll carry you a week or two," says Marr. "A win, of course, can carry you for weeks or months. And a major championship can carry you a whole year, or longer, depending on what you make out of it. There's a very depressing feeling when the year's over and you no longer hold the title. It's back to what have you done lately? But if you've put the title to work it'll stay with you for a long time."

Dave Marr is the perfect example of the young man who has, of necessity, put *everything* to work in order to carve out a nifty existence that he had no right ever to expect. He has nothing spectacular about his game other than a picturesque swing. He has no length, and his putting is absurdly bad. Inside the ropes he has no special charm. He is just another guy in a Jantzen shirt and Foot Joy shoes, slight of build, expressionless, blond, good-looking and usually one or two over on the scoreboard. Ronnie Runnerup, his good pal Frank Gifford calls him, to which Marr says, "who'll ever forget old number fifteen?"

How, then, could this man have become the tour's best-liked, most personable, articulate socializer—golf's major link with television, Hollywood, Broadway, the Palm Beach party and maître d's throughout the broad plain of America? Why is it always Dave Marr with Paul Hornung in the Palm Beach Club? At Tucker Frederickson's party after a Giant game? With Arnold Palmer and Don Meredith at John Murchison's cookout in Dallas? With Dick Shawn at the Pine Inn in Carmel? With the lead columnist or broadcaster in every town? With all of those vice-presidents at Ruby's Dunes in Palm Springs? With Bing Crosby at Manuche's in New York? With Bob Newhart at Shor's? With Alex Webster and Charley Conerly and Gifford at Clarke's? Why him?

"Because I lived in New York," smiles Marr.

That, of course, is part of it. Keep Marr back in Houston where he started and none of his accomplishments—the PGA championship in 1965, mainly—would have mattered nearly so much. He would not really still be "Claude's boy," meaning Claude Harmon, the man who gave Marr most of everything; his opportunity to work at Winged Foot and Seminole, to learn the game, his sophistication, his introductions to the big town and his friendships with real millionaires in Palm Beach, Palm Springs, Westchester County and Long Island, and not just the pretenders. He would never have known New York.

"Claude Harmon not only taught me most of what I know about the golf swing, he did something almost as important," says Marr. "Man, he took me out of Argyle socks."

Claude Harmon, noted for his teaching, has had a lot of protégés, as everyone knows, players who shuttled in and out of Winged Foot, leaving for the tour with infinitely more knowledge about the game, but Marr is surely Harmon's favorite for at least three reasons. First, Dave did more with less, and Claude watched him rise from sweeping out the shop to bon vivant along 52nd Street. Second, he was immensely popular, both around New York and Palm Beach (when Claude would transport his staff to Seminole in the winter). And third, Dave *stayed* in New York, even after making it on the tour. It was only later, much later, that he chose Houston again.

Marr could have lived anywhere, of course, after proving that he could survive on the tour with a victory now and then in Seattle or somewhere and steady checks. He could have gone to Florida as many did, or to California or to Dallas, a convenient place to "get out of" when you have to roam about the country, or he could have gone home to Houston where he had turned pro at nineteen, foregoing a college scholarship.

There were close ties in Houston, not just his mother, who had worked in a Howard Johnson's as a waitress after his father died, or two younger brothers and a sister, but several cousins named Burke who were involved in golf, Jackie Burke being one.

"That was hardly what I'd been working for, to get back to where I started," says Marr. "Houston is where I couldn't beat anybody even as an amateur and where the wolf was at the door. It's Jackie and Jimmy's town. Man, I had to go East and pick on those Italian assistants before I could find anybody I could beat."

New York is where he had to be. THEN he could go home. On his own terms.

"All of my old friends on the tour—Mason Rudolph and Johnny Pott and Tommy Jacobs, we came out together, sort of—thought I was crazy living in the East. They said, hey, man, where do you go fishin'? What do you do for black-eyed peas and ribs? I just told 'em, hell, if I live in Clarksville, Tennessee, how am I gonna see the Giants play on Sunday?"

Marr talks with a twinkle and a grin, explodes with boyish laughter at a funny line, his or someone else's, and sets himself apart from most of the pros by not taking his game too seriously in conversation. Football occupies much of his talk, and good food, good books, the theater, politics, current events. His golf talk is dotted with expressions that he either picked up from Burke or Demaret or spewed out himself.

"Always fade the ball. You can't talk to a hook," he says. To someone who strikes a low shot or tops one, "I didn't think you had enough runway for a minute." Or, "I'll take anything in the air that doesn't sting." To a spectator or a marshal or a scorer standing in his way: "Sir, would you mark yourself, please, while I try to get this one up?" After starting a round with a mini-hangover: "If I try to leave the hotel tonight, put out a contract on me." To Arnold Palmer about his wardrobe: "You think Latrobe Dry Goods would make up some of those slacks for me?" On Tommy Aaron blowing Roberto De Vicenzo's scorecard at the Masters: "What player on the tour would you *least* want to figure your income tax?" On Orville Moody winning the U.S. Open after Lee Trevino: "What does it matter who Orville is? At least he brought the title back to America."

Marr further authored two spontaneous comments in the course of tournament play that have practically become legend; at least they seem to get repeated endlessly in locker rooms and 19th holes and in New York saloons.

Once, it seems, Dave was paired with Jerry Barber in a tournament in Florida, and Barber is never an easy pairing. He can be very slow and meticulous as well as contrary. Marr, who manages to overcome his own temper tantrums rapidly because of his wit, nevertheless can get "hot," as he likes to put it, and lash back at anybody. So on a particular hole Barber, after hooking atrociously, quickly looked over at Marr and said, "Your foot moved."

And just as quickly and coldly Dave said, "When I *walk*. I put the first one here and then the next one there, and pretty soon, I'm moving."

And then there was the day in Augusta, during the last round of the 1964 Masters when Marr came to the final hole paired with Palmer, who was winning the championship by six strokes.

Marr himself was playing superbly and was, in fact, about to finish in a tie with Nicklaus for second, all of it on the glory of national television, a condition that Dave insists created more fame for him than all four of his tour victories spliced together.

At any rate, there stood Palmer and Marr on the last tee, chatting. They were waiting for the big crowd to clear so they could drive up toward the 18th green. Marr and Palmer were already good friends, and Arnold was delighted to see Dave doing so well.

Just before teeing up Arnold glanced over at Dave and said, "Anything I can do to help you here?"

"Yeah," grinned Marr. "Make a twelve."

A year later Marr helped himself to a small part of the glory that Palmer and a few others had been wallowing in by winning a major championship. With sheer tenacity overcoming his lack of distance, and while enjoying a week of unbridled confidence, Marr fought off Nicklaus and Casper and won the PGA on the big course at Laurel Valley in Pennsylvania. It was sort of the American Dream come true, and in his moment of triumph, for all of his cynical wit, Marr could not fight back a tear. All he could think of were the hours, days, weeks and years of sweeping out golf shops, selling cashmeres, giving lessons to the inept, slowing down his swing, struggling to get rid of the dog in him and rejoicing over $400 checks. Now here was a major championship, something few golfers achieve, and something *most* players on the tour will never achieve.

"All I could think of was that the title was for everybody who had helped me—Claude, Robie Williams, Jackie, all the men at Winged Foot who first put me on the tour," says Marr. "The $25,000 was for me, and the prestige was what I would spread around New York and see what it could bring."

It brought a good deal more than it would have anyplace else, to be sure. Dave Marr has been reaping rewards ever since, appearing on TV as one of ABC's commentators, in ads, playing exhibitions, being a "name" he had no right to be. One little thing he originated then is still paying off. In New York, he decided that a corporation or two would like to have twenty of its important clients enjoy a round of golf, a clinic and lunch with a top pro—him. Dave arranges the game and the club. He plays three holes with each group, thereby putting himself into the company of everyone in the course of a full round, and he tells his jokes, and drinks are enjoyed, and all of the friends of Union Carbide or Allied Chemical go home happy. He, of course, is paid a fee, and he plays as many of these in a year as he can promote.

In golf it is acceptable to put down the PGA championship as sort of the low rent member of the Big Four. The Masters and U.S. Open have more prestige and enjoy much broader coverage, and the British Open has the PGA up on the front tees where tradition is concerned. But there is hardly a better title to win for the journeyman pro, mainly because once you are a PGA champion you never have to qualify for another tour event.

The PGA is also, quite possibly, the hardest of the four to win because it annually has the toughest field. A great many good players don't get invited to the Masters, and a good many don't qualify for the Open, and an awful lot of Americans do not make the effort to play in the British Open. But *everybody* is in the PGA, and this, after all, is a championship glorified by such winners as Walter Hagen, Gene Sarazen, Ben Hogan, Byron Nelson, Sam Snead, Gary Player and Jack Nicklaus and made all the more intriguing by a list of some nonwinners. Arnold Palmer hasn't won it, nor has Billy Casper or Gene Littler, and Jimmy Demaret, Cary Middlecoff and Lloyd Mangrum never won it, for some instances.

"Say it again," grinned Marr. "This is my ego trip for the day."

Another thing the PGA championship did for Marr was put him on the Ryder Cup team, which is sort of the Oscar awards of pro golf every two years. He went to England and helped lead the Americans to another victory over the British at Birkdale, one of the toughest courses there is. On the wall of his den in Houston is a sketch made by a British artist showing every shot played by Marr and Palmer when they teamed up in one of the Scotch foursome matches, a round in which Dave and Arnold shot eight under fours.

"Anyone who says they don't think the Ryder Cup is thrilling can bust me," he said. "I didn't know how I'd feel until I got there on the first tee and listened to "The Star-Spangled Banner" and then "God Save the Queen." Man, I wanted to throw a block on one of those U.K.'s."

A man does not stay a major champion, of course, except perhaps in his own home, surrounded by his trophies, and

Dave Marr knows it. Since 1965, he has had to be content with such modest successes as teaming up with Tommy Jacobs to win the CBS Golf Classic, and tying with Frank Beard for the thirty-six-hole Music City Open in Nashville, a gigantic feat for which he received a five-hundred-dollar guitar.

But despite the fact that too many years have sped by since he last won a tournament he remains devoted to the tour. It is partly because the money is so good, partly because he believes he can still play championship golf, partly the fun, and partly his interest in the game.

David's wife Tallie, his second wife, would probably be happier if he quit the constant grind, if they could travel only to the places they liked, *when* they liked. Every wife of every pro would enjoy having it that way, once the initial glamor has worn off. But that is not the way it can ever be.

For a while, Marr suffered through a period of his career wondering if the tour had not cost him a wife and three children, wondering if his first wife, Susan, had not been right when she accused him of "choosing golf over life." He finally realized their marriage would have headed in the same direction, regardless. He was admittedly lost for a while, but suddenly there was Tallie—an attractive, sweet-natured and witty girl with the Southern attitudes and accents of himself.

Marr said, "We all have to face the problem of the future. How good are you? Can you stay out there with the big hitters? In my case, I can play my best but I might not win if I don't hole everything because Nicklaus can slop it around and out-birdie me. Do I take a club job? I'm still young. I think I can still play good enough to win. You come close a few times and you *know* it. You go through a tournament playing super, but you don't win. So you look back and see one missed putt of about three feet on each nine holes. That's eight strokes you lost by, but you played good."

Dave Marr suffers the dilemma of all of the nonimmortals. But he is mostly what the tour is made up of. A man with style, temperament, knowledge, and all the shots, but one who rarely wins. Still it is not so true that as Marr goes, so will go the rest. He has a more complete background than most, coming up as an assistant, coming out of a golf family, being exposed to Claude Harmon, Jack Burke, Jimmy Demaret, still taking a deep interest in the well-being of the game and worrying about its public relations. Somewhere, there is a special place for him, perhaps as another of the great, personable teachers that Claude Harmon is, backdropped by New York, thrust into all of the glamor he seems to find there.

And then again he might start to win. Wouldn't it be nice to play consistently, he thinks, the way he did in the 1969 Open at Champions in Houston? Shoot 286, close to the top, and pick up the good check every week. Be patient, playing fairways and greens, and let the putts fall where they will. Get your $70,000 a year in prize money and do another forty thousand on top of that in extras.

"That's fine," said Marr. "But as Claude has always said, you can't turn it on and off. Only Hogan could do that. You've got to be totally committed to the tour, out there working all the time."

What truly keeps someone like Marr out there, whether he knows it or not, can best be told by reciting an incident that happened in Houston in the summer of 1969. It happened during the U.S. Open, in which he played superbly, enjoying one of those pleasurable spurts of his, surrounded by all sorts of old friends and relatives.

Completing the first round, he came to the 18th hole needing to hit a four-wood to the green to get his par 4. Standing behind the green was a friend, chatting with a rather well-known spectator—Ben Hogan, wearing, as Dave later said, his Marty Fleckman cap.

Marr hit a tremendous shot, cutting a high four-wood out of the rough and onto the green, a shot which bounded up to within three feet of the flag for a birdie. The crowd had exploded appreciatively, and, afterwards, Marr asked the friend what Hogan had done.

"What'd the Hawk say when I cut one in there for three on eighteen?" Marr grinned.

"He said it was too much club."

Dave Marr, the pro of 52nd Street, broke up.

"I guess that's what it's all about," he said. "That's where it all is."

The King and Us

Golf Go Away.

—THE KING OF MOROCCO,
hitting a slice.

What could happen in the middle of this story is that the writer might decide to hurl Morocco to the ground and ravage it. Nothing obscene, mind you. Just a gentle, loving tussle in a platter of *couscous* while his heart thumps ecstatically and the neckcloth on his Foreign Legion cap billows in the soft Marrakesh breeze. The thing is, Morocco grabs you here, right here, like a haunting song. But even before I went there on a golf assignment—uh huh, golf among the Arabs—I had been carrying on a rather violent affair with the country. Casbahs and French Legionnaires had done it. And harem girls. And Humphrey Bogart running a bar in Casablanca. What chance did I have on a visit? None, of course, which explains why I shall soon be rejoining a group of contented Berbers in Tiznit, there to enjoy the quiet life of carving silver gunpowder horns and perhaps helping tend the greens of the Robert Trent Jones course that King Hassan II is certain to have constructed one day in the Atlas mountains.

I thought I knew what to expect in the way of golf in Morocco. I knew the king was building courses as if he had heard that Palm Springs was opening a racket club in Agadir. I was aware he had also been flying in Claude Harmon between nines to put some altitude on his low darters. But a golf course there, I felt, would have to combine all that was beautiful and serene about the St. Louis zoo and the battle of the Kasserine Pass.

For example, it was easy for me to envision this wondrous par-4 where one drove from a nest of cobras, aimed for a meandering camel on the right, drew it back between a couple of Sahara dunes and hoped to avoid being stymied by the only living palm in the country. The second shot would require a full carry over an old Nazi ammunition bunker, would have to bounce safely over a herd of sheep, glance off a mosque and come to rest on a putting surface occupied by acrobats, storytellers and clusters of veiled women.

In all of my stupidity, in fact, I have to confess that I didn't really know where Morocco was. I knew it was over there somewhere in Africa or Arabia, somewhere in the land of Yvonne de Carlo and Peter Lorre, in the land of dark, narrow streets, magic rugs, tribesmen and a lot of guys wearing tarbooshes and trying to buy a visa.

I had inquired of Claude Harmon, "What do you do over there besides get your jewels stolen and watch Sydney Greenstreet auction off your wife?"

Like myself, Claude tends to exaggerate, but he has an excuse, having devoted his career to curing the slices of millionaires, presidents and kings. In any case, his reply was encouraging.

"It's the most beautiful country in the world," he said, "next to the good old U.S.A. And it's just as friendly as can be. You're gonna eat it up like a drive and a wedge. And, hey. The king is my man."

Claude Harmon was the king's man, actually. For a couple of years Claude had been going over to Morocco to bring Hassan II's game down from 110 to 85. Claude had been getting permission from his two clubs—Winged Foot in the summer and Thunderbird in the winter—to go over and watch the king take divots in Rabat, Marrakesh, Casablanca, Fez, Tangier, anywhere there happened to be nine holes hidden inside the palace walls or tucked away on a hillside or creeping

through a palm grove or seared by the Atlantic or Mediterranean sun. This led some of Claude's friends to invent a slogan
for him: have overlapping grip, will travel.

Originally, according to Claude, the king wanted Tommy
Armour because he had come into possession of an instruction
book by Armour and decided to invite him over. Tommy
thought about it but eventually declined, his friends joked,
because he discovered that Morocco wasn't in Westchester
County.

Claude, the king was told, had a reputation as the most
accomplished teaching pro in the U.S., a man who had once
captured the Masters (1948) even though he hadn't played in
a single tournament all that winter, who could go around
Seminole in something like even 3s and in his later years had
taught such power brokers, statusmakers, Bob Hopes and pa-
triotic Americans as Dwight Eisenhower, John F. Kennedy
and Richard Nixon.

Anyhow, that is the rough background on how this all got
started. Claude and the king are mostly what this story is all
about, but there will be something of Morocco in it too. I
hope, and, of course, in the minor role of casual typist and
thorough-going tourist there is, clearing the throat, me.

I find it fascinating that of the few monarchs left today—
24 by my last count—one is not only captivated by golf but
has sort of bent himself toward making his country one long
par-5—to promote tourism—and has, at the same time, developed a very special relationship with an American pro.
Claude Harmon had made four trips to Morocco before I joined
him there for his fifth. During this period of almost three
years Claude and the king had exchanged more gifts than
words. Claude had not known exactly what to expect in the
way of reward until after his first visit. "I went out of goodwill," he said. Goodwill became a thousand a day plus expenses. Plus as many swords, daggers, plates, trays, leather
goods and small jewelry as Claude could admire during his
freetime shopping tours. Claude would pause to glance at

something, a guide would notice it, he'd tell the king, and it would later arrive at Winged Foot.

A Mark III Continental arrived at Claude's home one day, and so did a cigar box full of cash—in case Claude wanted some undeclared income. "I declared it all," said Claude.

Things also turned up for Claude's wife, Alice, and for the country clubs he represented. For straightening out a duck hook, one might presume: some antique jewelry and a Moroccan belt for Alice. And then for ironing the curl out of a slice, one might also presume: a $25,000 silver tea service for Thunderbird and one on its way for Winged Foot.

But what could one give a generous monarch, Claude often wondered.

"I don't know," I told him once. "His very own junta?"

On each trip Claude would take along dozens of golf clubs and bags and shoes to pass around among the king's friends and aides. He would take the king a wedge or putter or odd club he might not have seen or heard about. He once had Ben Hogan make up a few dozen balls with "King Hassan II" engraved on them. He also had Hogan make an engraved set of clubs. Claude carried over balls, clubs, head covers, gloves, wedges, sand irons, weird putters, even a set of gold Winged Foot cuff links.

Morocco's oldest course is in Marrakesh and it consists of 18 holes woven through lovely woods, with occasional glimpses of the snow-peaked Atlas mountains. One doesn't find a swimming pool or tennis courts at Royal Golf de Marrakesh. In fact, one seldom finds any people there at all, much less caddies. You lug your own clubs and hope to find an Arab mowing greens along the way to tell you where the next tee is. He might say something in Arabic, like, "Carrock, a-loc, a-loc," which I took to mean, "Tees are where you find them."

But it was handsome, quiet and pleasant, and always there were the mountains rising above the palms and poplars. The holes, as on all of the courses, aren't tremendously long, which does much for the golfer's ego. But I gather that no one spends much time looking for a stray shot in the uncultured rough, unless, of course, one has a fetish for disturbing cobras.

As one of the world's leading cobra haters, I had two experiences in Marrakesh that scarred the soul. First, entering the orange-walled city by car, having driven three hours from Casablanca through some amazing scenery changes—from dunes to brilliant green hills and over streams the color of café au lait—I came upon two grinning Arabs under a tree, waving at me. I stopped. They stood up. I smiled back. They pointed at two buckets they were holding. And smiled again. I smiled again. So they reached into the buckets and lifted out two wriggling, unhappy cobras.

"A-mock, car-rock, a-loc," one of them said, still smiling.

"Car-rock you," I said, and sped away.

Later on, in a square named the Djemaa-el-Fna, I found their mates.

Like 50,000 other people, I had been milling around the Djemaa-el-Fna, looking for the missing letters in the name and observing fortune-tellers, magicians, medicine men, gamblers, acrobats, Saharan dancers, donkeys, camels, children sitting and listening to story tellers and vendors cooking snails and sausages, when an Arab tapped me on the shoulder. He pointed to a carpet spread out on the dirt and to a basket turned upside down.

"Hmmm," I said. "Beeg black cobra? One dollar American?"

The Arab grinned delightedly, lifted up the basket and out he came, King S, to rear up, swell up and do his thing. And then out from under the carpet came another. Terrific.

"That's great," I said, putting a dollar in his hand. "Now do you happen to have a magic carpet to get me back to America?"

Like every other place on the globe, Marrakesh is finding itself being modernized. Only two blocks away from the Mamounia Hotel, a mammoth place of elegance and gardens said to have been Winston Churchill's favorite, is a Holiday Inn and a friendly neighborhood Avis office where a cute Arab attendant wore a miniskirt as short as any on a cocktail waitress along the Sunset Strip. Sadly, one thing is unavoidable in Marrakesh. You can't sit in a hotel lobby having your mint tea without overhearing an American in a summer sport shirt reaching to his navel, crepe-soled shoes and a Midwestern accent telling a Frenchman about his funfilled days at the University of Ohio and what a damn hard time he was going to have trying to fit three sons-in-law into his roofing company back home.

The best golf course in Morocco for anyone, king or peasant, lies about 40 minutes north of Casablanca, on the Atlantic. Royal Golf de Mohammedia, it is called. The resort town is Mohammedia, naturally. A couple of large luxury hotels sprawl on the beach, and there is a yacht basin, but the main attraction appears to be the golf club. The course is flat but heavily wooded and quite scenic along the bay, where the 9th and 18th fairways lie adjacent to the water. (In Casablanca proper there is another course to which the tourist has entree, but the serious golfer would be just as well off hitting a few chip shots in a public park. This is the Royal Golf d'Anfa, a nine-hole layout inside a small racetrack.)

But Casablanca had far more mystery when it was situated on Warner's back lot than it seems to have today. I couldn't find Rick's Café American or Ingrid Bergman or anybody.

There are only four other golf courses that any Moroccan knows about in his country. One is a nine-hole course in Tangier that is notable for only one thing. Playing it with Claude on an occasion a year ago, the king warmed up by hitting a few pitch shots onto a tennis court and then by driving a dozen or so balls off a cliff toward the Rock of Gibraltar. Another course is in the Tyrolean-type village of Ifrane, an hour or so by car from Fez. It isn't much—"A hotel par-3 that hasn't been mowed in a week" pretty well describes it—and the king plays it only rarely. Then there's the Royal Guard in Rabat and Inezgane in Agadir, both nine-hole layouts.

So much for the courses that the public sees. There are others that only His Majesty and those who loiter with royalty can see and play. These are courses Hassan has had built inside the walls of his various palaces. There are nine holes, fully lighted, within the main palace in Rabat. There are 18 holes behind the walls of the summer palace on the Atlantic in Skhirat. There are nine holes inside the palace grounds in the ancient town of Meknès. And nine more inside the palace at Fez. All of which add up to 45 more than most of us have for working out our duck hooks in private.

As the guidebooks say, Fez is the "heart of Morocco," the onetime capital, the spiritual and intellectual center of the country. Thus, it was more than appropriate that in Fez, which is about as ancient as a place can get and not be in China, I finally caught up with Claude and his pupil.

One of the king's cars, bearing a driver who believed himself to be the Arab equivalent of Cale Yarborough, had transported me the 125 miles from Rabat to Fez in, like, zap. There a two-engine plane was landing at a deserted airport. Out of the plane stepped Claude and his personal guide-friend-envoy for this particular trip, the Moroccan Consul General in New York, Abdesslam Jaidi.

Jaidi spoke good English and good everything else, so the heat was off. Jaidi's job was largely that of entertaining Claude and seeing that he got where the king wanted him to be each day. His job was also to bargain for Claude in the Casbahs and try to prevent him from buying every brass tray and Moroccan carpet in existence.

"Claude, you can't cure the economic ills of our country singlehanded," Jaidi would say.

"Don't you understand?" Claude would reply. "I *love* your country, Monsieur Jaidi."

Fez is cradled by hills, but it crawls up the sides of some
of them, its old fading cream structures and brown ruins ringed
by rich green beauty. For all of its age, you can do things in
Fez you wouldn't dare do or try to do in, let us say, Mexico
or Spain—like eat anything, drink the tap water and get one-
day dry cleaning. It is simply a remarkably pretty, enchanting
and friendly city with all different kinds of lofty balconies and
dark dungeons to dine and drink in and gardens to stroll in.

The Casbah or medina—or old city, as they call it—is twice
the size of any other in Morocco and twice blessed with atmosphere. Deep in the Casbah of Fez one can wander into a
doorway, be led through damp corridors of carpet and leather
to the antique jewelry room, there to be offered a chair, a glass
of hot mint tea, a plate of cakes—and a pipe. Two puffs and
you buy the whole store.

Frankly, despite all of Claude's stories, I didn't really know
what to expect from His Majesty. And when the day came
that I would be invited to accompany Claude inside the palace
walls at Fez and there to stroll the nine holes with him—as
Trent Jones had done six times—I was a little nervous.

"I hope there's some atmosphere around," I said to Claude.
"I mean, it would be kind of nifty to see a king play golf
around some ruins or something."

Claude said, "How does twelve hundred years old grab you?"

Inside the burnt-orange walls of the palace at Fez there was,
sure enough, a nine-hole golf course. It had grass that was
green. It had smooth putting surfaces with pins. Rough. Water
hazards. A couple of par-5s. And all around it were these 20-
to 50-foot walls, looking as though they had always been there,
as if Idriss II, or somebody, had known a long time before the
Scots about the rut iron.

On days when Hassan plays golf, a lot of people turn up.
Mostly, they are aides and servants and simply close friends.
Claude, Jaidi and I got there a few minutes ahead of His
Majesty, and I got to notice a great deal of hustling about by

everyone. A couple of Harley-Davidson carts were driven out, one carrying three sets of clubs, all belonging to King Hassan, the other carrying refreshments.

Several Arabs wearing fezes and djellabas neatly spread out a dozen pairs of golf shoes from which His Majesty would make a selection. They also spread out half a dozen sweaters in cellophane wrappers for the same purpose.

A number of men with briefcases stood by, obviously hoping to conduct some business between swings. Some diplomats, the Moroccan chief of world affairs and an official of the police were there, as were the head of the paratroopers and a very good Moroccan amateur. These last three would play with Hassan. Claude would walk around and give a tip now and then.

Suddenly something dawned on me.

"Listen, uh, Claude," I said. "How do we greet his Majesty? I mean, I know I don't say, 'Hi, King! How's your mom and them?' Do I kneel or what?"

Claude said, "He's quite a fellow. A young man. Tough. Well educated. Speaks a lot of languages."

"So what do I do?"

Claude said, "He's a king, you know. No mistake about who the *king* is."

"Yeh, I know," I said. "So?"

"You're an American," Claude said.

"Yeah, right."

"Well, you just walk up to him and stick out your hand and say, 'How do you do,' and look him right in the eye."

"Oh, good," I said. "Then I don't have to bow and kiss his hand like I would Hogan."

I don't know whether I expected the palace gates to open so King Hassan could gallop in on an Arabian stallion with a hundred Bedouin warriors, or what. But I do know that I didn't expect him to arrive driving the lead car in a motorcade himself, and for that car to be a Chevrolet station wagon.

"He loves cars," Claude whispered. "He'll turn up in a

Maserati tomorrow and a Volkswagen the next day. He's probably trying this one out. Probably thinking about buying a fleet of them."

Everybody lined up to greet the king, including all of the people in all of the limousines behind him. The custom is that the king sticks out his right hand and a Moroccan gets to kiss the back of it. If the king holds him in favor, he also gets to kiss the palm. Very close friends and family get a back, a palm and a cheek. This went on for a while and then Claude shook hands and forthwith presented his writer pal.

Following Claude's advice, I self-assuredly stepped forward, took King Hassan's hand, looked him straight in the forehead and said, "Good Majes, your morningsty. Real pleasure. Fine. Sure is."

He was a bit tiny for a king, I thought. About five-six. He was swarthy and had black sideburns stealing down in mod fashion from thinning hair on top that he combed straight across. He was pretty mod, all around, in fact. He wore a pair of tight, pocketless flairs and buckled loafers, and he had gotten out of the car in dark granny glasses. I decided that he could pass easily in Beverly Hills for the script supervisor on a hit TV series.

He moved around briskly, choosing his shoes and sweater. But he didn't put them on. Somebody else did that for him. And the singular job of one valet was to hold an odd-looking instrument that resembled a large pair of tweezers. It was a cigarette holder. The king smoked a lot and rather than drop his cigarette on the ground between golf shots, he just held it out and the tweezers grabbed it.

Now he had a three-wood and went to the practice area to take several vigorous swings before the game. Claude trailed quietly after him with his hands folded behind his back. Two of Morocco's best pros, who have played in several World Cups, were present, and their jobs were equally divided. One selected each club for His Majesty, and the other saw that he never got a bad lie, even in the rough.

What most of this added up to, I realized, was that when kings play golf they never have to bend over.

The king's swing would not send Bert Yancey scurrying to the practice tee. He took a wide stance with both toes pointed outward. Wearing gloves on both hands and with his shoulder hunched up, he swung aggressively with a long, flapping backswing and a leaning-forward follow-through. Still, he hit some good ones, favoring a medium to low hook.

"Too fast," he cried of his swing a few times.

"Hmmm," Claude said, agreeing.

Turning to me, Claude said, "You can never let a pupil think you're disappointed in him. You can never let him think he isn't improving. The secret to teaching golf to someone is to show a deep interest in his game, no matter how bad it might be, and continually offer encouragement. If I just tell him one or two little things today, he'll be happy. I'll pick my spots."

The king, now ready, had a small surprise for us. He led us all, maybe 20 people, toward a corner of the palace wall, through an entranceway, up a long, high rock stairwell to the very top of the corner wall. Perched up there, overlooking all of Fez and all of the palace grounds, was a little grassy knoll— alas, the first tee.

"We tee off," said His Majesty, "from many centuries ago." And he smiled.

The first hole was considered a par-4, a straightaway drive, mindful of the wall running down the left side of the fairway with a small pond in front of the green. Although the king played it in four with a driver and a wedge, an American touring pro would use about a three-iron. It would be a par-3.

As we walked along on the first few holes, Claude explained that His Majesty likes a joke or two. Indeed, I noticed in one of his golf bags there was a pop gun.

"He'll sometimes sneak up behind somebody who's getting ready to tee off and shoot the gun between his legs, blowing the ball off the tee just as the fellow swings," said Claude.

"Hey, that's really funny," I said.

There had also been a day when one of His Majesty's golfing companions from the court showed up in wild, multicolored slacks. So the king ordered a pair of scissors, which were promptly produced, and went about cutting off the man's trousers above the knees.

Just before I got there, Hassan had played in Rabat with the Apollo 12 crew—Conrad, Bean and Gordon—Claude told me. "They didn't play too good. I told him, 'Your Majesty, they can play the big ball in the sky but they can't play the little ball on the ground.' He liked that."

Claude had said that although the king was never with you in the evening, he arranged, personally, most of your entertainment. And he always knew where you had been and with whom. Armed with this knowledge, I was not surprised when he asked, "How was dinner last night?"

We had gone to the home of a wealthy businessman of Fez named Mernissi. Whiskey and ice were displayed on a center table in the living room, a help-yourself favor to the thirsty Americans. Few Moroccans drink. Scads of servants moved about, passing snacks and placing incense burners on the floor. A Berber orchestra showed up and there was occasional dancing and singing. Scotch, incense and music do not necessarily make an American hungry, but Claude had warned the feast would be spectacular.

And here it came.

A tureen of soup first, with lamb and lentils and lemon. Then shish kebab. Then a smoking platter of lamb knuckles with artichoke stalks and lemon. Then a huge bowl of meatballs with lightly fried eggs on top, floating on a mixture of paprika or chili pepper. Tex-Mex-Moroc, I thought. Next came an equally large serving of whole chickens highly seasoned and swimming in juices. This was followed by an entire barbecued lamb. Then came the *couscous*, served on this occasion as a dessert with powdered sugar. Finally, there was fruit and hot mint tea.

We dined Moroccan style, which means that one eats only with the thumb and first two fingers of the right hand. Just reach in and rip it out.

For a napkin there is only your very own huge loaf of crusty bread. You wipe your hand on it, or tear off chunks and dip it in the bowls and platters. Moroccans know where the best pieces of barbecued lamb and seasoned chicken are. My hand followed theirs, to the point, in fact, that one or two of them began to pull off delicate, lean slivers of meat and offer them to me. "Fine. Sure is," I said.

To say the least, it was the best meal I've ever had.

And so when Hassan asked how our dinner was last night, I couldn't resist preempting Claude.

"It was marvelous," I said. "And what I think I'll do is cut off my right hand and open a restaurant in New York."

His Majesty laughed and repeated the remark to some aides.

"He likes a joke," I told Claude.

Along about here, the king's golf suffered a bit. From the 5th or 6th tee he hooked a high one over the palace wall and onto the Boulevard des Saadiens.

"Golf go away, Monsieur Har-moan," he said to Claude.

"Golf will come back," Harmon smiled.

Whereupon the king hooked another high one over the wall.

"Very bad," he said.

"Golf comes and goes," said Claude.

Whereupon the king hooked still a third drive over the wall.

"Golf is gone," he said, shaking his head.

"Golf will come back," said Claude.

"When?" I said to Claude.

King Hassan finished out the nine holes in something like 43. He hit a few more bad shots, but he also hit some good ones, including a fine three-wood to the last green, where he picked up his fifth par of the round.

He went then to the practice tee, chatted with his friends for a moment, signed a few documents, read through some papers an aide handed him and then began soaring several practice shots off into the distance.

They were remarkably straight.

The king looked up and smiled.

"Golf come back," he said.

As we were driven back to our hotel in Fez, we passed along the Boulevard des Saadiens. Through the car window I saw an Arab in a djellaba sitting crosslegged on the grass looking at an object in his hand.

It was most likely a golf ball that had "King Hassan II" engraved on it. But the Arab would not know what it was, I figured. And he would never understand what it might mean to his country.

Three Coins in the Ball-Washer

Hi there all you guys on the PGA tour in America with a putter in one hand, the keys to a courtesy car in the other, a practice bag between your knees, and a Big Mac in your mouth—which leaves nothing free for the sand wedge, the laundry, the two dozen Jantzen pullovers, and the wife. How's the dry cleaning service over by the bowling alley in the shopping center next to the high-rise apartments around the ice rink? The one across from the supermarket near the used car lot by the drive-in pharmacy on the way to the discount department store. Right there where you turn left on Route 542 at the pancake house on your way to the second round of the $200,000 Equity Funding Classic at Preston Heaven Golf, Tennis, Dancing & Condominium Sales Country Club where Bob Barbarossa clings to a one-stroke lead over Forest Fezler and Artie McNickle? How's it going? I was just sitting here reflecting back on things like the *Campeonato Internacional Abierto de Golf de Espana*—that translates into the Spanish Open, Arnold—and dwelling on the wine and the sidewalk cafes and the Mediterranean, and the whole European golf circuit itself, and, listen, I was wondering if any of your double-knits had come unravelled?

Excuse me a minute. Yes, Anselmo. More wine. It goes well with the jagged coast and the old lighthouse and the hills around Cabo de Palos. The golf is beyond the hills, no? Today they play the golf and tonight they eat the lamb. Is it not true, Anselmo? An Englishman says we must have "sips and dins with the Elegantini." Quite fun, he says. What of the Elegantini, Anselmo? Is Piero really a count? Was Valentin really a matador? Is Constantine still a king? Who is Coco? Go well, my friend. Go fast and true while I look out at the sea. And don't forget the wine.

This story could be a problem, seeing as how I tend to daydream. If you get lost now and then, write me in care of Fred Corcoran, American Express Pro-Ams, somewhere in a TWA holding pattern over Rome or Madrid, and footnotes will be forwarded. It is primarily his fault that I have kept turning up in all these funny places, and why I shall probably be returning, having been hooked.

"There's no golf in Europe," I told Corcoran at first. "Europe is for wars, novelists and perfume. What do you do? Throw three coins in the ball-washer?"

I reminded him that golf is played in Akron, Pensacola, Laurel Valley and Tallahassee by people like Bert Yancey, Hubert Green, Homero Blancas and Babe Hiskey. Biarritz was for Napoleon, and Crans-sur-Sierre was for skiers. La Manga was a thing on a tree or a vine, largely eaten by the natives, and Rome was a lot of ruins with pasta machines in the basement.

"Don't give me any of this French Open, Swiss Open, Spanish Open, or *Campionato Internazionale Open D'Italia* stuff," I said. "Which I think is the Italian Open in Berlitz."

He only smiled and gave me preferential starting times in the Pro-Ams.

At first it was work. Do you think for a moment that it is easy to tell a Gallardo and a Garrido of Spain from a Garrialde of France? A Barrios of Spain from a Barras of Switzerland? A Bernadini from a Grappasonni in Italy? A Dorrestain of Holland from a Kugelmuller of Germany? Do you think it is easy to talk to a European golf federation president?

A European golf federation president wears a dark suit and tie. Usually, his family manufactures something that everybody in the country needs. In the glass and concrete opulence of the La Manga clubhouse, he came up from my blind side.

"Allow me to say that I am Juan Antonio Andreu," he said.

"How do you do?"

"I am the president of the Spanish golf federation," he said.

"How do you do?"

"You have come a very long distance for the golf."

"Yes."

"You have come before to Spain?"

"Yes, but not for the golf."

"You have not come for the golf?"

"Yes. Definitely for the golf. But also to look around."

"We are happy everybody has come to Spain for the golf."

"Thank you."

"We are having a good tournament for you, do you think?"

"It seems funny to be in Spain for golf."

"Golf in Spain is funny?"

"I meant that it is very different for me. Different. Not funny—as in funny like my swing. Ha, ha funny."

Most golf conversations make me thirsty. I looked around the room for Ward Wallace, the publicity director of La Manga. He knew how to say J&B and water in Spanish.

We continued.

"You make the golf joke, no?" asked the man in the suit.

"Not really."

"And so. How do you find our wonderful course here?"

"I asked somebody. They said it was outdoors. Heh, heh."

"The course is very green."

"Yes. La Manga seems to have much water. Water, incidentally, is good for me to have in a drink with Scotch."

"You are here from Scotland?"

"No, no. I'm from New York City."

"I have been to New York."

"Good."

"Now you have been to Spain."

"Yes."

"And so. How did you watch the golf today?"

"I went out to see Antonio Garrido, the defending champion."

"Garrido does not go well this week."

"It was O.K. The man I saw turned out to be Angel Gallardo."

"Ah yes."

"On the other hand, it might have been Jean Garialde. Heh, heh."

"There are many fine golfers in Europe although some of them do not go well this week."

"Yes."

"Many in Spain now."

"I'm just getting to know them."

"You would like to know them?"

"First, I would like to know how you say J&B in Spanish."

"Jaime? Ah, yes. Jaime is Angel Gallardo's brother. Jaime is the plump one."

"That's very helpful."

"And so. How many people do you say watched the golf today?"

"Counting you and me?"

"I would say perhaps a thousand."

"Not quite so many, to be honest."

"Five hundred perhaps."

"Actually less, I would say."

"It was my thought that there were two hundred at least following Neil Coles."

"Possibly, if you included those having lunch in the clubhouse."

"Two hundred is very good for the first Spanish Open at La Manga."

"That's interesting."

"Here, we are somewhat remote and La Manga is new. But we will have the people one day because we are presenting much money."

"If you presented the money to the people, you would have many people, I think. Heh, heh."

"The champion must receive eight thousand dollars I believe."

"That's very good."

"Do you personally know Jack Nicklaus and Arnold Palmer?"

"Yes."

"And do you personally know Lee Trevino and Tom Weiskopf?"

"Yes."

"You must tell them about Spain."

"I'll tell them about the eight thousand dollars and the two hundred people."

The man in the suit said, "All golfers must like La Manga."

"Yes. La Manga and Cabo de Palos."

"You know Cabo de Palos?"

"After the golf, I go there to sit in the sun and daydream. Also have a drink."

"What do you prefer to drink?"

"Now that you mention it, if I knew how to say J&B with water and ice, I would drink that."

The president snapped his fingers.

"Senor, por favor! Uno ohta bay con agua sen gas con yelo, por favor."

It sounded like.

"Hold it," I said. "That's oh ta bay . . . con agua . . . seen gas . . . con. . . ."

"It has been my pleasure for us to have this talk about the golf. You must come many times to Spain for the golf and bring Jack Nicklaus and Arnold Palmer."

"Oh ta bay, was it? Oh ta bay, con gas . . . seen agua. . . ."

"I am Juan Antonio Andreu, the president of the Spanish golf federation. When you come to Spain, you must inquire of my presence."

"I think this could be the beginning of a beautiful friendship. Let's see. That was oh ta bay, con yelo, con gas. . . ."

As anyone might guess, golf on the continent of Europe has hardly ever been as popular as building castles or sitting around. Professional tournament golf dates back only to the first French Opener, *L'Open de France* of 1906.

Until the 1970's there had never been any sort of organized European tour. What there had been was a ragged, conflicting, confused, aristocratic, almost secretive schedule which only a few Garridos and Grappasonnis and British journalists knew about. Or, in the past, an occasional Walter Hagen and Henry Cotton.

To be honest, of course, the European tour for quite a while will have several mashies to hit before it can catch up with the Australian tour or the Asian tour or the South African tour or the British tour, much less the American tour, in terms of style, prize money, organization and competitive quality. But all of a sudden things have happened.

The evidence:

A regular continental tour has been scheduled in two parts, before and after the British Open, none of the events conflicting, and all of them compatible with the British PGA.

Six tournaments, the opens of France, Italy, Spain, Switzerland, Holland and Germany, have become part of the British Order of Merit—part of the British tour, in other words, helping decide Ryder Cup points, Vardon Trophy winner, and entrants to various invitationals.

Six tournaments (some of them the same) now constitute something called the American Express European Order of Merit. These tournaments offer special inducements to the professionals, such as a big pro-am, sponsored by American Express—and run by Ferd Corcoran of World Cup repute—and offering a season's prize to the most consistent player.

Prize money is increasing, led by the Italian Open and the

Spanish Open. Others have vowed to follow. With various corporations getting into the act, a race is underway among several federations to become the richest event on the continent. Big money—like America used to have.

Tony Jacklin, one of the world's five best players currently, has quit the American tour and joined the British and European exclusively, giving it glamor. A star.

The European tour has found a real friend and draw in Tony Jacklin. As a former U.S. and British Open champion the rules permit him to demand (and usually receive) $2,500 in appearance money, plus expenses, from most of the sponsors. He is ahead from the start, as opposed to his plight in America. And with the tournaments being closer to him, and travel cheaper, not to forget the purses increasing, his future is even more enhanced.

"I have to play bloody well for months in the U.S. to earn $100,000," said Jacklin. "And then half of that goes to taxes and expenses. I can make more in Europe and go to more exciting places. In the U.S., every tournament seems like the same place. In Europe everything changes. The scenery, the food, the people, the language, and the atmosphere. When the prize money gets even bigger, I think some American pros are even going to discover what I've already discovered. We're definitely moving toward a world tour."

France:

It is the summer of '72, which is not a film title. The Basque Coast. Bay of Biscay. Biarritz. As a thoroughgoing hedonist I am wishing they played L'Open de France right here in my suite at the Hotel du Palais. It is a castle on a cliff above the Atlantic. From the pool I can see the town and the beaches below, and French ladies in brushed jeans which sell for $100. From my balcony I can see Albert's, a loud, open-air restaurant where it seems like waiters walk on your table, believing it to be humorous, and where everybody sings, and where, finally, at the end of an evening, furniture or something is thrown onto the sand and sometimes set fire to.

At the Hotel du Palais one hurried through dinner nightly in order to have a cognac on the terrace and watch Albert's burn again.

Ben Wright of the *Financial Times* in London had dined at Albert's and smoldered while a waiter kept time to the music by beating on his table with a stick. He stared off at the fire and said to no one:

"If there was only the remotest chance that the odd French waiter could be pitched atop the flame. . . ."

Characters are emerging.

Arthur Crawley-Boevey is everywhere. In his blazer and scarf and cigarette holder and British accent, he seems like the best reason for planting tea in India. The British pros call him "Groovy Baby" and "Crawley Boozy." He is their field director on the European tour, and they say he has a liking for pink gin. They also say he has a habit of standing up to speak at dinners and thanking the Spanish Federation for all of its courtesies in Italy.

"Good show, the Continent," says Arthur. "Do a bit of walking about myself. Bit of history around, mind you."

Jean (Coco) Dupont is a road company Alain Delon. A Parisian bachelor, Coco has the time and energy to be secretary of the European Golf Federation and the French Golf Federation as well. Coco has probably done a lot to get the European tour organized. When you say his name swiftly it comes out "Go Go Doo Paw," and sounds like you know French.

I asked Fred Corcoran if Go Go Doo Paw was Mr. Big in European golf.

"He wears a 5F shoe," said Fred.

I asked Coco the same question.

Coco said, "I must make this worry, you see, about the

petty jealousies of our federations. It is not so easy. It is sometimes impossible. But not always. It is something we must do."

Dick Severino is more places at once than Arthur Crawley-Boevey or Coco Dupont. I say Dick Severino is a spy who uses his notepad, his camera and *Golf World* as cover. Besides, he lives in Beirut.

Dick Severino is a busy man in the golf cap of the tournament he is covering. He has an armband and a personal card which says "Golf Correspondent." He has a camera around his neck and a clipboard. He is athletic-looking and fast-talking.

"Great city, Beirut," he says. "I can go either way there. I can whip down to Inzai or over to New Delhi. The Seven Day War? I played golf every day."

Dick Severino knows everybody on the European tour, or any other tour. He knows Hugh Baicchi of South Africa and Baldovino Dassau of Italy. He knows Phillippe Toussaint of Belgium and Manuel Ballesteros of Spain. He knows Simon Hobday of Rhodesia and Mohammed Said Moussa of Egypt. He knows Vincent Fernandez of Argentina and Guy Wolstenholme of Australia. He not only knows them, he can *talk* to them.

"Watch this kid Dassau," says Dick Severino.

I have finally found *L'Open de France*. It is at a club called La Nivelle, and it is not a golf tournament. It's a garden party.

La Nivelle is a miniature golf club of 5,758 yards, par 69. It is surrounded by miniature white-washed villas with red-tile roofs. A street borders the course named Massy. It is named after Arnaud Massy, who came from Biarritz and won the first French Open, and who, in fact, remains the only continental ever to win the British Open. A few people are standing around eating sandwiches. Golfers are trudging up the 18th fairway pulling carts. Two elderly ladies are sitting on a bench. A soldier is asleep under a tree. Fred Corcoran is looking for a photographer.

"The prime minister is here," says Fred.

"Good," I answer. "Maybe he can tell us where the French Open is."

Wait a minute. Here comes an American off the 18th. It has to be an American because his sweater is new. It looks like Barry Jaeckel, out of LA. Not a bad young player. What the hell's he doing here? If this kid weren't pulling his own cart and drinking a Pepsi, I'd swear it was Barry Jaeckel.

"What are *you* doing here?" he asks.

"I was going to ask you that," I said.

"I don't know, man. I just paid my $15 and teed off," says Barry.

"How do you stand?"

"O.K., I guess. I just shot 63. Where's a good place to eat?"

In several different languages, the Press wants to know who Barry Jaeckel is, and he has left in a taxi. I am interviewed. I know the only player in the tournament Dick Severino doesn't know and he's leading.

Barry Jaeckel, 23. Son of the actor, Richard Jaeckel, who gets killed a lot in John Wayne's Marine squad. Caddied for Dean Martin, drove his golf cart. Martin sponsors him. Hasn't made the PGA school yet. Over here getting practice. Doesn't know that Walter Hagen and Byron Nelson are the only Americans who ever won the French Open.

It's Sunday, the last round. It must be because there's a cocktail party under some trees. Barry Jaeckel has a caddy, seeing as how he is in contention with some known quantities: Peter Oosterhuis, Brian Barnes, Clive Clark, and Roberto Bernardini. Pretty French girls are passing out free cigarettes. They wear brush jeans which cost eight million dollars in a local boutique. Fred Corcoran and Dick Severino are looking for each other.

Barry Jaeckel finishes birdie-par to tie Clive Clark for the French Open. They go to No. 1 for sudden death and Barry Jaeckel hits an iron six feet from the cup, sinks it for a birdie, and wins. Walter Hagen, Byron Nelson and Barry Jaeckel.

"Dean Martin will love that," smiles Barry.
Is he going to the Swiss Open?
"Do they *have* one?"

Switzerland:

Crans-sur-Sierre. High in the Alps overlooking the Rhone Valley. Postcard Land. A good course, leaping from Alp to Alp. Almost 7,000 yards, good condition, par 71. I don't really want to play in the American Express Pro-Am because I'm afraid I'll fall off.

Fred Corcoran, however, just happens to have a set of clubs, a preferential starting time, and a pairing with Barry Jaeckel and Jean-Claude Killy. I can play in my loafers. On the tee. The French Open champion, the ski racer and the idiot. Fred is looking for a photographer.

"It's at least 10,000 feet from here down to Geneva, Fred. I'm not swinging hard at any sidehill lies," I say.

Jackel laughs a lot. I smoke a lot and glance occasionally over the edges of the tees. Killy tries hard and worries.

"I golf like you ski," says Jean-Claude.

We don't win.

The Swiss Open is guarded jealously by Crans-sur-Sierre, which has always held it. A couple of families named Barras and Bonvin, who seem to own all the hotels and raclette and fondue in the village, see that it runs perfectly.

A band is marching through town wearing leather skirts, another cocktail party has started, seven watchmakers in black suits are making speeches, everybody is getting a trophy for simply showing up—and the tournament hasn't begun yet.

In case the press doesn't know where the Matterhorn is, or where to find the best raclette, somebody named John Allatini is around to help. He is an expatriate Yorkshireman of private means who says he greatly enjoys "having sips and dins with the Elegantini."

Ben Wright of the *Financial Times* says he quite agrees. "I try never to miss high season in Sardinia," Ben says.

The tournament begins and compared to France the galleries are enormous. Everybody follows Tony Jacklin for four rounds while Graham Marsh, an Australian, wins.

"Watch this kid Marsh," says Dick Severino.

Spain:

Spring of '73. La Manga Campo de Golf. Costa Blanca. An hour's flight and another hour's drive from Madrid. The Spanish coast is exploding with Fort Lauderdale condominiums and California developers. One day, from Valencia to Gibraltar, it will be air conditioned.

La Manga Camp de Golf is startling. In the midst of nowhere, tucked against some parched brown hills, looking out at the blue sea, a fortress looms. Inside: multi levels of glass, carpet and porches. La Manga sticks out like gun placements above elegant apartments hidden below like ammunition bunkers. Bars, cafes, sundecks, verandas, shops and fireplaces are here, over there, down this way, up there, around the corner. And always a view of the Mediterranean gleaming beyond the golf course stretching out in the valley below.

La Manga's American owner, Greg Peters, has flown in his props, like a movie studio. Five thousand California palms line the fairways of La Manga's 36 holes, standing guard over 14 artificial lakes, five-inch rough, and fairways only 30 yards wide. Is the big barranca cutting across the middle of it all a natural wonder or was it flown in as well?

Greg Peters has built a wonderland out of nothing, hired Gary Player, signed up the Spanish Open for the next five years, and bombed an ancient Spanish fishing village with Rancho La Costa instead of Hemingway.

The rise of the Spanish professional is well timed with the bursting forth of golf interest and golf architecture in his country. Robert Trent Jones got there first with Soto Grande and then Andalucia la Nueva at Marbella, but now there's La Manga, and even Jack Nicklaus has designed a course outside of Madrid. Meanwhile on the European circuit, only the British play consistently better as a group than the Spanish. And the Spanish are coming in swarms.

They are still led by Ramon Sota, the hunchback, slow-playing "bull of Santander," who once finished sixth in the Masters. But he has a lot of company now in the form of Gallardos, Garridos and Benitos, along with a stray Canizares, Ballestreros, Contreres and Valentin Barrios, who looks like a youthful Fernando Lamas and, having once been a film actor as well as a matador, is the only Spaniard who did not come up through the caddy pens.

There are at least three Gallardos, Augustin, Angel and Jaime, and two Garridos, Antonio and German, and four or five Benitos, led by Jaime. It is difficult for anyone, including Dick Serverino, to tell all of them apart, except for Angel Gallardo, a tiny, good-looking fellow with charm who beat Billy Maxwell and Lee Trevino in the Mexican Open a time back and says every shot and every course is "inbelievable."

There are those, mainly the British, who say they know how to explain the success of the Spanish players. They have cousins for forecaddies whose trouser legs are stocked with Dunlop 65's in case somebody gets lost in the rough. And they have Portugese caddies who can improve a lie with their feet.

Tony Jacklin remembers a Portugese caddy who could lift a ball instantly—first try—with his big toe and the one next to it. Tony kept finding these fantastic lies one day during a Pro-Am in Estoril. He asked a Portugese official about it. Yes, all of the caddies can do that, the man told Jacklin, so it evens out for everybody.

Uno birdie con foot con toe, por favor.

La Manga is set up for the British. The wind is making the course player longer, to its full par of 72. The rough is too deep for a Spaniard's flat swing, or a Portugese foot. Besides, the British know where to eat. Over in Cabo de Palos in an old house, El Cortejo. Exquisite lamb, roasted before your very eyes. And they know where to drink. In another old house down a dirt road in the middle of an open field. Open till dawn. No name.

Neil Coles, who drives to tournaments on the continent, who has a clerical exterior and Charles Dickens hair, is well in control. Other British follow: Jacklin, Craig Defoy, Peter Butler, Brian Barnes, Maurice Bembridge.

Coles wins handily at 282. A fine, underrated player, and a gentleman. Only one Spaniard, some kind of Benito, manages to break 290.

"We've crushed the Armada," says Arthur Crawley-Boevey.

Italy:

The Rome Golf Club at Acquasanta. Along the Appian Way. A horizon punctuated by ruins. Hilly terrain amid the old aqueduct. Smothered in charm, class, scenery, cuisine, and assorted Elegantini. And one hell of a *Campionato Internazionale Open D'Italia.*

Big money is up. There's $17,250 for the winner, the highest ever offered on the continent. A man named S. M. Constantino is entered in the American Express Pro-Am. So is a lady addressed as Marchesa Avril Rangoni-Machiavelli. They are paired with Jacklin, Queen Anne-Marie in the gallery, and if Fred Corcoran can't find a photographer soon, he may kill somebody.

Italian Golf Federation officials wear gray suits, dark glasses, and suede shoes. They whisper a lot with Count Piero Mancinelli, a golf course engineer, until recently the manager of Italy's future hope, Baldovino Dassau, and the publisher of a magazine called *Golf Selectzione.*

Piero looks sinister enough to be a real count, but he is a kind man and my friend. He steals his way around softly, and holds his cigarette like a double agent, but he drinks like an American. And he has cared about golf in Italy, almost singlehandedly, through the years.

Piero says, "We are in a position to make the Italian Open the biggest and best on the continent. How do we get more Americans?"

"Tell their wives about the Via Condotti, and tell them about the food at Sabbatini."

"This week we are up against the Tournament of Champions," Piero says. "These are bad dates. But there are no good ones. Next week we would be up against Pensacola."

"That's bad?"

Acquasanta is a tremendous golf course. Only 6,515 yards, par 70, dating back to 1903, but it is tricky as can be, sloping away here and there, narrow, demanding, optional—a Roman Merion.

"Nobody is going to break 280," says Jacklin, "and I've got the King on my side."

Constantine is following Jacklin's every shot, dashing to scoreboards for information on the leaders, telling him jokes and stuffing him with caviar nightly. All of the names are up front, and the crowds are large and excited. The weather is gorgeous and the course, surrounded by those ruins, is haunting.

It's Sunday and Jacklin is battling Peter Oosterhuis, the glamorous Valentin Barrios, and France's Jean Garaialde. The King is sweating.

He delivers the news. Oosterhuis has faded. Barrios has bogied the last two holes. Garaialde has bogied the last two holes. Tony needs a closing par four for 284 and victory. The 18th is a long hole, uphill, 473 yards. Jacklin drives nicely but his second misses the green. Great chip, four feet.

"If the little beggar misses this, I'm going deeper into exile than the King," says Ben Wright of the *Financial Times*. "My story's already written."

The putt drops.

Everybody is at the bar. Jacklin is buying drinks for whoever stops by. I think Piero and I are buying drinks for a King— and perhaps a marchesa or two. Arthur Crawley-Boevey wants to walk to the Coliseum. Dick Severino needs a ride to the airport. He suspects a war.

"And so, my friend," says Piero. "You have been to Biarritz and to Crans. Also to La Manga and Rome. And Portugal, too?"

"I haven't seen a Portugese Open, if that's what you mean."

Piero throws up his hands.

"My dear chap," he says. "You haven't seen anything yet. They have these caddies there who. . . ."

The Golden Bear

For several years I have slowly been watching Jack Nicklaus become the greatest golfer who ever lived or died. As a writer, it is something I shall treasure as I think back on all of the verandas I stood on at places like Pebble Beach, St. Andrews, Augusta and Merion, but there has been this very peculiar thing about it all. Now that Nicklaus has done it—statistically at least—there are a lot of people out there who don't want to give it to him.

The arguments go like this:

Bobby Jones won more big ones in a shorter length of time, and besides that, Jones quit early.

Ben Hogan was even a better competitor than Nicklaus, under heat, and Hogan certainly had a greater variety of shots in the bag. Hell, Nicklaus still can't hit a pitching wedge.

Walter Hagen was a better showman.

Arnold Palmer did more for golf and carried a heavier burden, being a "super celebrity" and everybody's favorite.

Harry Vardon invented the grip and had to swing with tree limbs.

Sam Snead has the best swing of anybody, even today, and Sam can still shoot low scores even though he's 108 years old.

When Jack plays good for 50 years, like Gene Sarazen, *then* we'll consider him.

He hasn't really toured the world like Gary Player, proving he can play off of grass, dirt, gravel and Arabs.

Nobody can match what Byron Nelson did over a certain period of time.

If they bet their *own* money, Jack probably can't outhustle Lee Trevino.

And on and on.

Well, there is some truth in all of these statements, of course. But it is history which decides who the immortals are, and as of this moment in the 1970's, Jack Nicklaus is the greatest golfer who ever lived or died.

The major championships tell us so.

Major championships are the tournaments which separate the greats from the near-greats. The tournaments which offer the most fame and fortune; which attract the most attention; which create the most pressure.

In Vardon's day, a major championship was the British Open, and then the U.S. Open.

In the era of Jones, Hagen and Sarazen, the majors were (for Jones) the Opens and Amateurs of Britain and America, and for Hagen and Sarazen, who were professionals, the same Opens, plus the National PGA.

Today there are four, known as the Big Four—the U.S. and British Opens, the Masters, and the National PGA. Everything else is a Tucson Open or a Dunlop Invitational, with no bearing on history.

Nicklaus began his career *wanting* to become the greatest golfer who took a divot. "I had the raw ability," he says. "I had the obligation to try."

This was proved when he twice won the U.S. Amateur and finished second in the U.S. Open although he was still in college at Ohio State. Already, he had two majors.

In the next 11 years as a professional, then, Jack had these goals to shoot at: Jones' 13 major titles, Hagen's 11, Hogan's 10, Palmer's 8, Sarazen's 7, Vardon's 7, Snead's 7, Nelson's 5. And one by one, they've fallen.

One of the troubles with writing about Nicklaus all the time, I have discovered, is that you're always confronted with statistics.

In story after story for Sports Illustrated, I would continually find myself recounting his major titles as Jack moved up on the record.

And now that he has it, I must belabor the reader once more with a table of facts and figures.

In what follows, you will find golf's all-time 10 major championship winners, along with their close calls, the times they finished second in major events.

The chart tells you where they won, and where and to whom they lost when they came close.

To me, the remarkable thing about these records is not that Jack has captured 14 major titles—one more than Jones, finally—but the number of times he has been second. Nicklaus has also been second more times than anybody else, including Jones.

This single statistic appalls me. Nicklaus has been first or second 25 times in major championships!

Small wonder I have typed his name so often, since I covered all but about three of those championships.

Dwell on the chart on the following pages and we shall come back and chat some more.

WHO'S WHO IN MAJOR CHAMPIONSHIPS

JACK NICKLAUS (14)

U.S. OPEN

Winner

1962—OAKMONT, Pittsburgh
1967—BALTUSROL, Springfield, N.J.
1972—PEBBLE BEACH, Del Monte, Calif.

Runnerup

1960—Cherry Hills, Denver
    (Won by Arnold Palmer)

1968—Oak Hill, Rochester
    (Won by Lee Trevino)
1971—Merion, Philadelphia
    (Won by Lee Trevino)

MASTERS

Winner

1963—AUGUSTA NATIONAL
1965—Same
1966—Same
1972—Same

Runnerup

1964—(Won by Arnold Palmer)
1971—(Won by Charles Coody)

BRITISH OPEN

Winner

1966—MUIRFIELD, Scotland
1970—ST. ANDREWS, Scotland

Runnerup

1964—St. Andrews
    (Won by Tony Lema)
1967—Hoylake, England
    (Won by Roberto De
    Vicenzo)
1968—Carnoustie, Scotland
    (Won by Gary Player)
1972—Muirfield, Scotland
    (Won by Lee Trevino)

NATIONAL PGA

Winner

1963—DALLAS ATHLETIC CLUB
1971—PALM BEACH GARDENS, Fla.
1973—CANTERBURY, Cleveland

Runnerup

1964—Columbus CC, Ohio
    (Won by Bobby Nichols)
1965—Laurel Valley, Latrobe, Pa.
    (Won by Dave Marr)

U.S. AMATEUR

Winner

1959—BROADMOOR, Colorado
    Springs
1961—PEBBLE BEACH, Del Monte,
    Calif.

BOBBY JONES (13)

U.S. OPEN

Winner

1923—INWOOD, N.Y.
1926—SCIOTO, Columbus, O.
1929—WINGED FOOT, Mamaro-
    neck, N.Y.
1930—INTERLACHEN, Minneapolis

Runnerup

1922—Skokie, Chicago
    (Won by Gene Sarazen)
1924—Oakland Hills, Detroit
    (Won by Cyril Walker)
1925—Worcester, Mass.
    (Won by Willie Macfarlane)
1928—Olympia Fields, Chicago
    (Won by Johnny Farrell)

BRITISH OPEN

Winner

1926—ROYAL LYTHAM, England
1927—ST. ANDREWS, Scotland
1930—HOYLAKE, England

U.S. AMATEUR

Winner

1924—MERION, Philadelphia
1925—OAKMONT, Pittsburgh
1927—MINIKAHDA, Minneapolis
1928—BRAE BURN, Newton, Mass.
1930—MERION, Philadelphia

Runnerup

1919—Oakmont, Pittsburgh
(Won by Davidson Herron)
1926—Baltusrol, Springfield, N.J.
(Won by George Von Elm)

BRITISH AMATEUR

Winner

1930—ST. ANDREWS, Scotland

WALTER HAGEN (11)

U.S. OPEN

Winner

1914—MIDLOTHIAN, Chicago
1919—BRAE BURN, Newton, Mass.

Runnerup

1921—Columbia CC, Chevy Chase,
Md.
(Won by James Barnes)

BRITISH OPEN

Winner

1922—SANDWICH, England
1924—HOYLAKE, England
1928—SANDWICH, England
1929—MUIRFIELD, Scotland

Runnerup

1923—Troon, Scotland
(Won by Arthur Havers)

NATIONAL PGA

Winner

1921—INWOOD, N.Y.
1924—FRENCH LICK, Ind.
1925—OLYMPIA FIELDS, Chicago
1926—SALISBURY CC, N.Y.
1927—CEDAR CREST, Dallas

Runnerup

1923—Pelham CC, N.Y.
(Won by Gene Sarazen)

BEN HOGAN (10)

U.S. OPEN

Winner

1942—RIDGEMOOR, Chicago*
1948—RIVIERA, Los Angeles
1950—MERION, Philadelphia
1951—OAKLAND HILLS, Detroit
1953—OAKMONT, Pittsburgh

(*Wartime Open but included in
record book)

Runnerup

1955—Olympic, San Francisco
(Won by Jack Fleck)
1956—Oak Hill, Rochester
(Won by Cary Middlecoff)

MASTERS

Winner

1951—AUGUSTA NATIONAL
1953—Same

Runnerup

NATIONAL PGA

1942—(Won by Byron Nelson)
1946—(Won by Herman Keiser)
1954—(Won by Sam Snead)
1955—(Won by Cary Middlecoff)

Winner

1946—PORTLAND, Ore.
1948—NORWOOD HILLS, St. Louis

BRITISH OPEN

Winner

1953—CARNOUSTIE, Scotland

ARNOLD PALMER (8)

U.S. OPEN

Winner

1960—CHERRY HILLS, Denver

Runnerup

1962—Oakmont, Pittsburgh
(Won by Jack Nicklaus)
1963—Brookline, Boston
(Won by Julius Boros)
1966—Olympic, San Francisco
(Won by Billy Casper)

MASTERS

Winner

1958—AUGUSTA NATIONAL
1960—Same
1962—Same
1964—Same

Runnerup

1961—(Won by Gary Player)
1965—(Won by Jack Nicklaus)

BRITISH OPEN

Winner

1961—ROYAL BIRKDALE, England
1962—TROON, Scotland

Runnerup

1960—St. Andrews, Scotland
(Won by Kel Nagle)

NATIONAL PGA

Winner

(None)

Runnerup

1964—Columbus CC, Ohio
(Won by Bobby Nichols)
1968—Pecan Valley, San Antonio
(Won by Julius Boros)
1970—Southern Hills, Tulsa
(Won by Dave Stockton)

U.S. AMATEUR

Winner

1954—DETROIT CC, Grosse Pointe,
Mich.

GENE SARAZEN (7)

U.S. OPEN

Winner

1922—GLENCOE, Ill.
1932—FRESH MEADOW, N.Y.

Runnerup

1934—Merion, Philadelpha
(Won by Olin Dutra)
1940—Canterbury, Cleveland
(Won by Lawson Little)

MASTERS

Winner

1935—AUGUSTA NATIONAL

BRITISH OPEN

Winner

1932—SANDWICH, England

Runnerup

1928—SANDWICH
(Won by Walter Hagen)

NATIONAL PGA

Winner

1922—OAKMONT, Pittsburgh
1923—PELHAM, N.Y.
1933—MILWAUKEE, Wis.

Runnerup

1930—Fresh Meadow, N.Y.
(Won by Tommy Armour)

SAM SNEAD (7)

U.S. OPEN

Winner

(None)

Runnerup

1937—Oakland Hills, Detroit
(Won by Ralph Guldahl)

1947—St. Louis CC
(Won by Lew Worsham)
1949—Medinah, Chicago
(Won by Cary Middlecoff)
1953—Oakmont, Pittsburgh
(Won by Ben Hogan)

MASTERS

Winner

1949—AUGUSTA NATIONAL
1952—Same
1954—Same

Runnerup

1939—(Won by Ralph Guldahl)
1957—(Won by Doug Ford)

BRITISH OPEN

Winner

1946—ST. ANDREWS, Scotland

NATIONAL PGA

Winner

1942—ATLANTIC CITY CC, N.J.
1949—RICHMOND, Va.
1951—OAKMONT, Pittsburgh

Runnerup

1938—Shawnee-on-Delaware, Pa.
(Won by Paul Runyon)
1940—Hershey, Pa.
(Won by Byron Nelson)

HARRY VARDON (7)

U.S. OPEN

Winner

1900—CHICAGO GOLF CLUB

Runnerup
1913—Brookline, Boston
(Won by Francis Ouimet)
1920—Inverness, Toledo
(Won by Ted Ray)

BRITISH OPEN

Winner

1896—MUIRFIELD, Scotland
1898—PRESTWICK, Scotland

1899—SANDWICH, England
1903—PRESTWICK, Scotland
1911—SANDWICH, England
1914—PRESTWICK, Scotland

Runnerup

1900—St. Andrews
(Won by J.H. Taylor)
1901—Muirfield
(Won by James Braid)
1902—Hoylake
(Won by Alex Herd)
1912—Muirfeld
(Won by Ted Ray)

GARY PLAYER (6)

U.S. OPEN

Winner

1965—BELLRIVE, St. Louis

Runnerup

1958—Southern Hills, Tulsa
(Won by Tommy Bolt)

MASTERS

Winner

1961—AUGUSTA NATIONAL

Runnerup

1962—(Won by Arnold Palmer)
1965—(Won by Jack Nicklaus)

BRITISH OPEN

Winner

1959—MUIRFIELD, Scotland
1968—CARNOUSTIE, Scotland

NATIONAL PGA

Winner

1962—ARONOMINK, Philadelphia
1972—OAKLAND HILLS, Detroit

Runnerup

1969—NCR CC, Dayton
(Won by Ray Floyd)

BYRON NELSON (5)

U.S. OPEN

Winner

1939—SPRING MILL, Philadelphia

Runnerup

1946—Canterbury, Cleveland
(Won by Lloyd Mangrum)

MASTERS

Winner

1937—AUGUSTA NATIONAL
1942—Same

Runnerup

1941—(Won by Craig Wood)
1947—(Won by Jimmy Demaret)

NATIONAL PGA

Winner

1940—HERSHEY, Pa.
1945—MORAINE CC, Dayton

Runnerup

1939—Ponomok, N.Y.
(Won by Henry Picard)
1941—Cherry Hills, Denver
(Won by Vic Ghezzi)
1944—Manito, Spokane, Wash.
(Won by Bob Hamilton)

What I can best say of Nicklaus now, I have already said in Sports Illustrated. The crucial year for him was 1972, when he was trying, and talking about, and nearly winning a modern Grand Slam.

It began at the Masters where I told the story of the tournament like this:

AUGUSTA, GA.: Poa annua and poa Jack. It was that kind of a week down in Augusta. Poa annua, honey, you been gone for so long, galavantin' around the countryside. Get in that kitchen and fix up those biscuits. Get off those greens you done made slicker 'n Sam Snead's head, and you stop botherin' Jack Nicklaus. And Jack, you come in this house. Land sakes if you're not out there acting like you never been here before. Out there playin' against yourself and the record book and Bobby Jones and all that nonsense instead of just settlin' down and winnin' this old Masters Tournament by 25 or 30 strokes like you supposed to do. You ought to be ashamed of yourself, Jack Nicklaus. And Poa annua, you just shut up and get in there with the pots and pans.

That's how it was. Poa annua and Jack Nicklaus in the Masters all week long. *Poa annua* is that weed grass that comes around every four or five years to infest Augusta and turn the Masters greens blotchy. It makes the greens uneven, bumpy, fast, unpredictable, unreadable and it sends the scores soaring higher than Nicklaus' career. And who is Jack Nicklaus? Well, he's more than ever the greatest golfer of our time; for after beating everybody else, last week he proved that he can even beat himself. He must be the toughest opponent he's ever faced.

Think of it this way. Jack Nicklaus won the Masters this time by three strokes in a manner that would do honor to all the crippled and wounded of highway intersections everywhere. But the thing is, Jack was supposed to win the Masters more than he was ever supposed to win it before. And, believe it or not, that makes it harder. Everybody sits around and talks about how the pros really get uptight over all the money they play for, but that is a myth that can be filed away with people who claim they see a goal scored in ice hockey.

A golfer playing against the record book, his aspirations, immortality, eternity, the Grand Slam, his own private ambitions, and even his own embarrassment is a man who has chosen a pretty strong lineup of opponents. Jack Nicklaus was such a person last week, and that is the only thing that made the Masters as close as it was.

That's what made Nicklaus come limping down the stretch over those last few holes, trying to play it cozy, trying not to let the Masters slip away to some guy who didn't want it in the first place. He went to the 11th hole of the last round with a five-stroke lead on the pack, which included somebody named Jim Jamieson, and *he* was supposed to get you excited? You've got to be drunker than most everybody under the umbrellas on the veranda.

Nicklaus was only worried about fate, a weird fate that would keep him from winning his fourth Masters, the 12th major championship of his life, moving him up ahead of Walter Hagen and now only one back of Bobby Jones. It would also put him another step closer to being, beyond any logical argument, the greatest golfer who ever lived, overlapped, interlocked or putting on *Poa annua*.

Fate tried hard, of course. It grabbed hold of Jack and made him three-putt the 11th hole for a bogey, three-putt the 13th for a par, three-putt the 14th for another bogey and, the third day in a row, play the 15th hole like a guy trying to move the hot dog to the hand with the binoculars in it. The 15th is a par-5 hole that Nicklaus could go back out to right now and with nothing but a driver and four-iron—forget the putter, he'll kick the ball—play four balls and make three fours and a three.

Put him in the Masters, though, and throw all that immortality up against him, plus the fact that he's going to be so humiliated if he doesn't win, and he'll go out there and make a seven on Friday, a five on Saturday, and on Sunday he'll make a six, always hitting some kind of second shot that threatens to bounce clear to the parking lot.

The fact is that the Augusta National course with its ruined greens played so difficult last week—the most difficult since 1966, when Nicklaus last won—that Jack could lead the field all the way after an opening 68 and afford the luxury of going 36 holes on Saturday and Sunday in three over par.

If Nicklaus' winning total of 286—only two under par—was not proof enough of the sad greens, how about the fact that only three other players broke 290, and one of them was Jamieson? His main claims to fame are that he comes from Illinois, across the river from Jack Fleck, and that he works with a set of clubs that includes a couple of Pings, three Spaldings, three Power-Bilts, a Hagen, a Hogan, three Golf-crafts and a putter he bought in a department store in Orlando.

It was an old-fashioned Masters, actually, including as it did the *Poa annua*, some wind, some chilly weather, a low round by Sam Snead, a hole in one by Charles Coody on Billy Joe Patton's 6th hole, the high scores, a variety of double bogeys and a few triple bogeys.

Constantly the big leader boards argued with one's intellect, especially on the first day, the most exciting of all: Snead, a 59-year-old man with a putting style that looks as if he's bending over to tie his shoe, had a 69. Then Coody with his hole in one at the 6th to put him four under par. So on the next hole he takes four shots—in the same bunker. Finally, Nicklaus, looking like the player he is. His eagle 3 at the 15th took command.

From this point on the only question that remained was whether Nicklaus would whip himself. Slowly, the *Poa annua* would take everybody out of it, forcing three-putt greens, making recovery chips and pitches next to impossible. Nicklaus succeeded because just enough of his game held together to conquer his mind.

His driving was good, but his irons were unsettling, and his recovery shots were pretty awful. What kept him on top was his attitude, his ability to smile at his own mistakes, his refusal to become demoralized by the *Poa annua* and the short putts he missed.

"Trying to play safe is the worst thing in the world," Nicklaus said. "I don't think I would have looked so bad there at the last if I'd been forced to throw the ball at the hole. When you start playing safe. . . ."

Jack admitted he had become a bit testy over the constant badgering he got about the Grand Slam, and the fact that his legs were never working right on his iron shots.

"You come here to savor the Masters," he said. "It stands alone. I don't think about winning the Masters as part of the Slam. You want to win the Masters because of what it means to the game; what Bob Jones meant."

He never truthfully worked out the problem with the legs. There was wind and when there's wind you don't use the legs as much; you swing more stiffly, occasionally eliminating the full follow-through. Each night Jack practiced until almost dark, testing.

"I've played better here and didn't win, but the course changes and the field changes," he said.

One change in this year's field was that it included Lee Trevino, who became a part of the proceedings even though he played golf like one of the aging members on the tour. He had not been to Augusta in two years and he had said a lot of things about the place. Clifford Roberts, chairman of the Augusta National Golf Club, cooled him, delightfully. After his third round, Trevino went to the press building and did his usual comic routine, but as he was leaving Roberts approached. Trevino stopped for a radio interview. Roberts stood by. It seemed obvious that he was waiting for Lee, and it seemed obvious that Lee was taking his own sweet time.

Roberts finally left, wandering up the hill to the clubhouse.

Lee started up the same hill and as he passed Roberts' office, Cliff stepped outside. Whether he noticed Roberts or not, Trevino kept walking. But a club member on Trevino's left hollered to him, pointing at Roberts. The two shook hands and Cliff said, "Have you got a half minute?"

"I got to do a TV thing," said Trevino.

There was an awkward pause and eventually the TV man said, "I'll wait."

Whereupon Roberts put his arm around Trevino and they walked into Roberts' office. They stayed there about 25 minutes and came out together. They walked up the driveway and into the main entrance to the clubhouse and into the Trophy Room where they stood and chatted about Bobby Jones' old clubs in the glassed-in case.

"He only hit two shots with the sand wedge," said Cliff, talking about Jones.

"I guess he played in a lot of rocks," said Trevino.

They chatted on and on, amid laughter and in a perfectly friendly atmosphere. And Trevino said he would definitely return to the Masters.

Roberts said, "I was decidedly charmed by that fellow. One of the nicest things about this week is that we've got our relationship straightened out."

And Trevino said, "I really enjoyed that. He's a nice man."

The attention paid to Trevino just went to prove how times have changed. Somehow it seemed that Augusta's alltime favorite, Arnold Palmer, was not fawned over as in the past. The crowds were his, of course, but Palmer had a ruling go against him, something that might not have happened for a long time. It occurred on the second day and it not only cost him a stroke but catapulted him into such a bad frame of mind it probably cost him the triple bogey that took him out of contention.

At the 9th hole on Friday Palmer had his second shot come to rest in a depression caused by a chair seat by the green. He thought he deserved a free lift. He played his ball and made a bogey 5. He next played a provisional ball and made a par. He then went to the back nine, the incident under review.

What angered him was that he knew, or believed he knew, that the chair had been occupied by a tournament official. If so, he reasoned, it was no different from a TV tower or something you can freely drop away from. The full rules committee said no, and this news was delivered on the 12th tee, before Palmer was about to play the most dangerous hole on the course, that marvelous par-3 over Rae's Creek. Palmer promptly hit an eight-iron into the front bunker, hit the bunker shot over the green, slashed back across the green into the front bunker again, blasted out and missed a three-foot putt for a triple-bogey 6. He snarled all the way—about the ruling, the bunker, the greens, all the ships at sea and the eight years since he last won a Masters.

Meanwhile, Nicklaus was left to join Palmer as the only other four-time Masters winner. And in so doing Jack established himself as a man who has now taken the tournament in just about every conceivable way. He took it coming down the stretch by a stroke. That was when he first won it, nine years ago, over Tony Lema. He won it by shooting records, a 64 and a 271 and by nine strokes. That was in 1965. He won in a playoff, and back to back, in 1966. And now he has won it clumsily, with a 68-71-73-74, frightened only of destiny and that old honey child, *Poa annua.*

And, of course, frightened by himself. The toughest opponent he has ever had to face.

Next came the U.S. Open where I sat down and wrote:

PEBBLE BEACH, CALIF.: The Grand Slam almost went slumbering with the abalone in Carmel Bay, or soaring with the winds above it, or hiding with the wildlife in the forests beside it. But the right man was on call all along and Jack Nicklaus kept a personal rendezvous by winning the prettiest—and in some ways the most important—U.S. Open Championship ever played. On the toughest course there ever was, he beat the best there are, Arnold Palmer and Lee Trevino, plus a few of the usual lurkers who would have had to wire their sixth-grade English teachers for a suitable quote had they finished first. He won when he simply had to win, he won spectacularly and he won at Pebble Beach, a golf course which on this particular week was as mind swerving as the serpentine 17-Mile Drive that leads to it.

Pebble Beach, in fact, almost played too great a role. For a while it appeared that the winner wasn't going to be a man, but the course. Pebble—good old monstrous Pebble, Double-Bogey-by-the-Sea—won every battle, one-on-one, even with Nicklaus. It was absolutely the ruggedest course of recent years for all four rounds, and the scores that it wrought in the 72nd Open from the very best players in the world more closely resembled those out of the early 1900s, when men used hickory shafts and swung in tweed coats, than anything in this broad-belt era.

Was that George Archer shooting 87 or Horace Rawlins? Was that Frank Beard shooting 85 or Old Tom Morris? Who *are* those guys? Where are we?

On the last day, Sunday, when a ripping wind produced the ultimate horrors, only Nicklaus could summon the patience and the game to cope with the place. It seemed he had saved his best golf for the final round, when the course and the elements almost eliminated golfing skills in more normal men. And while that closing 74 of his for the funny old total of 290 will not look so dazzling in the record books one day, it should be stated here and now that under the circumstances it was as brilliant as any man ever shot.

Par is what the course and the weather dictate, to borrow from our Scottish ancestors, and the truth of the matter is that par at Pebble Beach on Open Sunday was 76.6. That was the average score of the 20 low finishers in the championship, of the men who were even remotely in contention. And of the actual nine men Nicklaus had to beat, or all of those within five strokes of him after three days, his 74 was the best.

All this came from the player who had already won the Masters and was supposed to win the Open in his quest for a modern Slam, taking the Big Four all in one year. This was step two in what his old Columbus, Ohio pals, who follow him around as faithfully as other Columbus citizens dog the OSU football team, have begun calling the Fan Slam, meaning they get to go to all these places like Augusta, Pebble Beach and now Muirfield in Scotland for the British Open and Detroit for the PGA, and rent all these hotel rooms and houses and buy up all the good beef in town.

Jack, as is his habit these days, got a lot of history on the record at Pebble. It was his third Open title, but more important it was his 13th major championship, tying him with Bobby Jones. Here we go counting them one more time: three U.S. Opens, four Masters, two British Opens, two PGAs and two U.S. Amateurs. In his two championships this year, the Masters and Open, he has led or shared the lead in every round. Nobody ever did that.

Does this then mean that Jack Nicklaus not only is going to accomplish the Slam but do so by leading every single round of all four championships? Well, no achievement seems beyond his grasp. He was immensely ready for Pebble Beach, and even though golf is such a delicate game and the odds of winning are so overpowering against one human being out there, Jack accomplished exactly what he set out to do.

Before Sunday, however, some wondered whether he had not been propped up by fate for a dismal disappointment. He had shared the lead on Thursday with five other players who no longer mattered. He had shared the halfway lead with Kermit Zarley (one of the five) and four new guys. He had emerged with a tiny lead of one stroke by Saturday night but there were a lot of people near him. For glamour, there were

Trevino and Palmer, and for nuisance value there were Bruce Crampton and Zarley.

No one actually expected Zarley to win; he never has won much. And pitifully few hoped Crampton would win, for he carries, rightly or wrongly, the reputation of a grump despite his fine style and the money he has won. As one competitor joked about poor Bruce, "He's only done three things wrong in his life. Get born, come to America—and stay."

Obviously, the press and most of the fans were rooting for either Nicklaus, Trevino or Palmer, so everyone could call this the greatest Open ever played, which it was close to being. Sunday's pairings, strictly luck, put Lee in with Jack, which meant that Nicklaus was in a spot to be voodooed again by Trevino, who had whipped him at Merion last year in a classic head-to-head playoff. That was the day Trevino pulled out the toy snake and practically talked Jack out of the title, or so it seemed. And Lee was joking again at Pebble all week, even though he was in ill health for real, recovering from near pneumonia.

"The Bear thinks my pneumonia is a trick," Trevino laughed. Did Jack? Somebody asked him Sunday morning, "You think Trevino might throw a rubber bronchitis at you today?"

Nicklaus smiled. And with the confidence that only he has, he said quietly, "The only thing I'm going to throw at these guys today is my golf game."

No tricks worked for Trevino, although on the practice tee he tried, nevertheless. He kept hollering at Palmer, "Is your airline on strike? Your pilot told me he was tired of being hijacked to Tijuana."

And when Nicklaus came out to hit a few balls before the final round right next to Lee, the defending champion immediately started intentionally topping three-woods, trick shot style.

"Look at that," Trevino chirped. "I can't get 'em up, Jack."

Nicklaus did giggle appreciatively, but he was not to be too distracted from the thing he had come to the Monterey Peninsula a week early to do. Like win.

For a while on Sunday, it looked as if it might be laughingly easy. Very quickly, everybody started making bogeys and double bogeys. And when Nicklaus made his only really long putt of the week at the 7th green on Sunday, a 25-footer for a birdie, he was even par and two strokes ahead of the field.

One of the reasons Nicklaus was up there at that point was that he had managed to avoid the quick catastrophe, the double bogey, even the triple bogey, or albatross, throughout. A man like Homero Blancas, for example, would have been up there, too, if it hadn't been for such things. Blancas made more birdies than anybody, even Nicklaus, but for the 72 holes of the championship Homero could look back on just four holes and see nine whopping strokes lost to par. He made three double bogeys and one triple, and wound up only five shots back of Nicklaus.

But now it was Jack's turn. Suddenly, midway in the last round, Pebble Beach finally and brutally got to him. A gust of wind lashed at him as he drove from the 10th tee, now with a four-stroke lead, and there went the ball, the Open, the Grand Slam, all the preparation soaring out to sea—or so it seemed. There Jack stood in wind-whipped splendor, exposed as mortal. He dropped another ball, mortal fashion, and fired his next shot. It was gale-tossed and oceanward again, ending up on the edge of a cliff, but playable. He went to fetch it, and at this point Pebble Beach had backed him to the sea. It added up to a double bogey. Palmer had a chance if a putt would drop. And Crampton was hanging in there. Even Trevino could rally.

It was then at the 12th hole, a par-3, that Nicklaus demonstrated his relentless courage. He hit what he thought was a perfect three-iron right at the flag. It struck the green 10 feet in front of the hole but simply zoomed past it, and then bore relentlessly down a steep slope and out of sight in thick ground cover.

As Jack walked onto the 12th green, he scowled at P. J. Boatwright Jr., the USGA's executive director who was refereeing, and said, "What'd you do with all the grass?"

Nicklaus was referring to the fact that on top of everything else that makes Pebble Beach so dangerous, the USGA, for the final round, had seen fit to roll and triple-cut the small, wind-dried greens, making them next-to-impossible to hold or putt.

Later Jack would say, "I went to bed Saturday night thinking I had to shoot at least 70 to win. But this morning when I saw the first green and the wind, I knew it would be a tough son of a gun and I'd have to have patience."

Nicklaus found his ball in a dreadful lie on the 12th. He gouged at it, moving it slightly up the hill. He gouged again and sent it eight feet past the cup. That left him with a super character-builder, as they call it, to avoid another double bogey that might destroy his confidence totally. And although he could not know it, he was in danger of losing his lead altogether. At this moment two holes ahead, Palmer was lining up a makeable birdie putt which, combined with a Nicklaus miss on 12, would put Arnold a stroke ahead. As Palmer said later: "It certainly would have given me a more personal interest in the Open."

Indeed, this had been an extraordinary Open for Palmer. He began it with three straight bogeys and a 77, but exploded back into contention on Friday with a magnificent 68, a score nobody bettered in the tournament. A 73 on Saturday kept him two strokes behind Nicklaus.

For a while on Sunday it seemed possible that Palmer might catch his old rival. On the 1st hole, to shouts of "Go Arnie," he hit his approach seven feet from the flag. Thunderous cheers. Then he left the putt short. *Short.* Thunderous groan. He missed another birdie putt on two, but rolled in a 40-footer on the third, which put him just one stroke back. After that it was a struggle—he made no more birdies and finished with a 76—but then everyone was struggling out there, Nicklaus included, so that if Palmer could just sink his birdie putt on the 14th. . . . It didn't happen. Palmer missed. And Nicklaus did not miss.

If this single pressure stroke did not wrap up the championship for Nicklaus, then his classic one-iron to the 17th green most certainly did. Here is one of the killer par-3s in the whole world, and here was Nicklaus needing a safe par. Nothing more. Just a par.

He stood there for a moment, trying to stare down the wind. Bobby Jones, the Open, the Slam and none other than Bruce Crampton, who was still lurking. And then he hit a shot that made him look like a fighter who didn't want to win on points; he wanted a knockout. He hit the damnedest one-iron in history and nearly made a hole in one as the ball screamed into the gale, cleared the ghastly bunker fronting the green, crashed down right at the flagstick and simply sat there, two inches from the cup—and two championships away from what could be one of the most astounding accomplishments in the annals of game playing. So ended Jack Nicklaus vs. Pebble Beach. Crampton finished second at 293, Palmer third at 294. Trevino and Blancas had 295s.

In addition to the course, there were other hazards at Pebble during Open week. One was a thing called the 17-Mile Drive cocktail party. At various points along the Drive, there were affairs going on in private homes bordering the course. Some of them began at midmorning and when contestants stood over putts that demanded a certain concentration here would come—out of the woods—the cackling, clinking sounds of Bloody Marys being poured into the minds of the peninsula's mindless. One could only assume the parties were being given by tennis or horseback riding fans. They were no fans of golf.

Then there was the wildlife. On the very first day a spectator got trampled by a frightened deer at the 2nd hole. The graceful animal leaped out of the woods, took fright at the sight of people, if not the USGA rough, whirled and pranced right over a poor man. It is said the deer in his confusion did a little dance step on the man's head and then found his way back into the trees. The man was not seriously hurt.

Overall, Pebble Beach as an Open venue combined two atmospheres. There on the sea with the wind and changing weather and the high rough, it had much the character of the British Open. But at the same time, being so close to Carmel's Dutch doors and overquaint restaurants and bars and galleries, there was a sense of a championship being staged at a rich man's Disney World.

At the course itself, the Del Monte Lodge had a stately look, one that it never has during the Crosby. There were candy-striped tents and little white picket fences sealing off the insiders—the committeemen, contestants, press and sponsors—from the hordes. The USGA must have loved Pebble for a number of reasons. Not many Opens have been held where the committee people could stroll out their front doors and see the 18th fairway by an ocean; and where, also, they could take a short drive and play golf themselves at Cypress Point or Spyglass Hill.

For all of the setting's advantages, though, Pebble Beach turned out to be a not-so-wonderful place at which to watch a championship. By the very nature of its design, Pebble Beach is fine for TV—two dozen well-placed cameras can cover virtually the whole course—but a pretty awful spot for spectators. No fewer than 12 holes could be galleried only on one side of the fairway because of oceans and private homes and such things. Also, because Pebble's greens for the most part are slightly elevated, only the first arrivals behind the ropes could see the roll of a putt. Next time—and there will certainly be more Opens at Pebble Beach—the USGA will probably relent and erect bleachers around the course so that everyone can better view all of those double bogeys and albatrosses.

There were specific reasons for some of the funniest scores

ever posted in a major championship. The four basic ones were water, sand, grass and wind. Water, or rather the Pacific Ocean, was a factor on seven holes—the 6th through the 10th and then the 17th and 18th. Sand and the rough and the wind were factors on all 18.

The reason sand was such a problem is that the USGA filled the bunkers with loads of the stuff from Monterey beaches and then fluffed it all up. Shots dropping down into the bunkers plugged in. It was a miracle when anybody was able to get down from a trap in two.

The rough was not the most brutal the pros have ever encountered in an Open, but it might have been the toughest since Olympic back in 1955, again in northern California, where the grass in the rough is thick and tends to "cover" the ball. What the USGA did for—or against—Pebble Beach was take away a lot of driving areas the pros had been used to in the Crosby, forcing them to be more accurate.

Then there was the wind. It never blew wildly, as it sometimes does on, say, one day of the Crosby each year, but it swirled consistently throughout the four days—and from a totally different direction than in January. What this did was make Pebble a new course to the pros. For example, the Open wind helped on the rugged water holes, Pebble's own Amen Corner of the 8th, 9th and 10th, except for that odd moment Nicklaus suffered through on Sunday, but it hurt on the inland "coming home" holes of the 13th through the 16th.

The primary example was the 555-yard par-5 14th, normally a birdie hole during the Crosby. It was a monster at the Open. A double dogleg to the right with a roguishly bunkered green and a tee shot into the wind, it became not only a nonbirdie hole but practically a nonpar hole. Any pro who hit a Crosby-type tee shot would have needed two slashing sand wedges just to get back to the fairway.

All of these things turned Pebble Beach's back nine into the orneriest challenge most of the pros had ever seen. Their scoring reflected the fact. Players of high reputation were absolutely embarrassed. There were more nines in the 40s than there were in the 30s.

A book of case histories could be written about Pebble's atrocities that would make Edgar Allan Poe read like Nancy Drew. There were men who made birdies on Thursday around the early holes and got on the leader board and even held the lead who didn't make the 36-hole cut—because of the back side.

In the first round, Bunky Henry was one under par through four holes but finished the day 16 over with an 88. Frank Beard—a steady, tested player, right?—cooled Pebble in a swift 85–80. Archer's 87 was mind-boggling. And on and on it went, reducing touring pros to weekend hackers.

If all of this is a way of saying Pebble Beach was the real star of the Open, that's true. After all, only 10 men broke 300. Considering that Merion is maybe too short and Pine Valley is too tormentingly special, Pebble Beach might have proved that when it is in good condition, as it was for the Open, it is America's greatest championship test.

And it no doubt is a bit arrogant to say so, but Pebble did separate the ordinaries from the absolute best players there are today in both name and pocketbook. Isn't that what a superb course and a big championship are supposed to do?

Now the burden grows for Jack Nicklaus. He goes next to Scotland, amid more pressure, more talk of the Slam, more intense preparation. Another rendezvous with who knows what. When it was all over at Pebble Beach Sunday night, it was left to that noble ex-king, Arnold Palmer, to say best what lies ahead for Nicklaus. "From now on," said Arnold, "he's going to have trouble even going to the john."

Perhaps Jack did. In any case, history deserted him in Scotland. Where I stood up and wrote:

MUIRFIELD, SCOTLAND: He stood against one of those sand hills, one foot halfway up the rise, a gloved hand braced on his knee and his head hung downward in monumental despair. He lingered in this pose, with what seemed like all of Scotland surrounding him, with the North Sea gleaming in the background and with the quiet broken only by the awkward, silly, faraway sound of bagpipes rehearsing for the victory ceremony. This was Jack Nicklaus on the next to last hole of the British Open after another putt had refused to fall. It was Nicklaus in the moment he knew, after a furious comeback, that he had finally lost the championship and what might have been the grandest slam in golf. One more putt of any size on any of these last seven holes and Nicklaus would have completed what could seriously have been termed the most brilliant rally the game had ever known.

But one more putt did not drop for Nicklaus, and on the same hole minutes later one more chip shot *did* curl implausibly into the cup for implausible Lee Trevino. Finally, after all the shattering heroics last week at Muirfield, the whole world had a right to feel overgolfed and oversuspensed.

The honest fact is, there are two fairly incredible golfers today, Nicklaus and Trevino, and the two of them have been producing so many memorable major championships lately that it is getting hard to keep them straight. The last two U.S. Opens pretty much have been a Nicklaus-Trevino saga, and so have the last three British Opens. It may be well and good to keep talking about Nicklaus' 13 major titles, but think about this: since the 1968 U.S. Open, when he first became a winner, Super Mex has won as many big ones (four) as Nicklaus has over the same period. And, for all of that drama and suspense last week, it was still the happy Mexican who never stopped providing the comedy that the stifling pressure at Muirfield needed.

Trevino tossed out all the usual lines about God being Mexican or else Nicklaus would still be alive for the Grand Slam; about switching back and forth from the small British ball to the larger American ball and how the American ball always looked like a melon; about the castle he had rented for the week ("They got to have some kind of princess locked up in there someplace"); and about the lukewarm drinks the Scots are accustomed to ("No wonder everybody over here's so wrinkled up"). That was Trevino all week.

It probably can be said that Nicklaus waited too long to attack Muirfield, that he perished with his own conservative game plan on a course that played easier than he expected because of some unanticipated glory-be weather. When Jack finally turned aggressive for Saturday's closing 18, when he was six shots down and the lids came off his driver and three wood, he shot a 66 to tie the course record and, at one point, miraculously lead the tournament by one stroke. Jack will think long about the holes he let get away during the earlier rounds and he will dwell, too, on the six late putts that refused to disappear into the cups—a 12-footer for a birdie at the 12th, a 15-footer for a birdie at the 13th, an 18-footer for another birdie at the 14th, a four-footer for yet another birdie at the 15th, a three-footer for a saving par at the 16th and, the last gasp, the 20-foot birdie putt at the 17th.

Saturday, the oh-so-memorable Saturday, began with only four potential winners of this Open. Trevino held a one-stroke lead by virtue of a flood of Friday birdies. They came five in a row from the 14th through the 18th, including an astonishing hole-out of a sand shot at 16—which even Lee admitted should have been a double bogey—and the sinking of a 30-foot chip on the last green. Next was Tony Jacklin, who was up there despite a triple bogey during the second round; and then Doug Sanders, who was only four back despite a triple bogey of his own along the way. And finally Jack Nicklaus—if he could muster an old-fashioned Arnold Palmer type of thing.

Jack did exactly that. Through 11 holes, as he was being cheered madly by a rousing British crowd of 20,000, he seemed to be playing, at last, the definitive round of golf. He was perfect with every club, and he had pushed to six under par.

"Look at this," Trevino said to Jacklin as they went to the 9th tee. "Nicklaus has gone crazy. We're out here beating each other to death, and that son of a gun's done caught us and passed us."

Two little dramas of high order were going on at this point. Up ahead, the crowds were yelling for the Nicklaus Slam as he strode the length of the 11th fairway toward another short birdie putt. Back at the 9th, Trevino had told his caddie, "We're behind, son. Gimme that driver, we got to make something happen." Trevino absolutely killed his drive at the skinny 9th fairway. He then put a five-iron within 18 feet of the hole and made the putt for an eagle. Suddenly he was back to even par for the day, and back to six under for the tournament. And Jacklin, too, eagled the 9th, to stay within one shot of Trevino.

Nicklaus, meanwhile, tried to address the birdie putt on the 11th green that would put him in a tie with Trevino at six under. He heard the two roars for the eagles, backed away from his putt and smiled. Then he coldly made the birdie, and once more came an explosion of sound, this time from his own gallery. It was an eerie moment hearing those roars back to back to back. Trevino remembered later, "After our eagles at 9, I told Tony, 'That'll give Jack something to think about.' Then we heard his birdie roar and I said, 'I think the man just gave us something else to think about.'"

What can be said of Trevino and how he actually won? How can it be accounted for? Nicklaus worked for more than a week at Muirfield, while Trevino arrived late. Wearing a planter's hat and cracking jokes, he practiced only two days. "I brought this trophy back," he said upon arrival, "but I shouldn't have. It's just going back to El Paso."

The case certainly can be made that this was a lucky win for Trevino, unlike last year at Royal Birkdale when he destroyed the course with brilliant shotmaking. After all, he holed out four times—four—from off the greens during the course of 72 holes for his 278. And that is simply indecent.

On the second day he chipped in for a birdie 3 at the 2nd hole from 40 feet with an eight-iron. Then he holed his two ridiculous shots in the third round when he ran off from everyone but Jacklin. The first was from a terrible lie up against a bank in a bunker at the 16th. He had just dropped consecutive birdie putts of more than 20 feet at the 14th and 15th. Now he slammed his wedge into the sand. Out spurted the ball in a semi-line drive to take one harsh bounce and drive into the cup for a birdie 2. At the 18th, after two-putting for a normal birdie on the 17th, he chipped out of the weeds for a fifth straight birdie and a 66. "I think things like that happen to a man sometimes when he's trying," Lee said. "I was trying. I was aiming at the cup. I didn't come to Scotland to help Nicklaus win any Grand Slam. If I played golf with my wife, I'd try to beat the daylights out of her."

For all of this, it was one last chip shot that found its way into the hole that rescued Trevino from what looked, at the very end, like a certain victory for Tony Jacklin. Tony had won in 1969, and Tony could win again. Princess Margaret was there; wasn't this an omen?

Trevino had played the par-5 17th like a man choking on the trophy or a sausage roll or perhaps royalty. He drove into a bunker, poked it out, poked it again and then ran a short pitch over the green. Jacklin, meanwhile, was just off the green in two. He chipped on, leaving himself a good birdie chance. He was about to go to 18 with a certain one-stroke lead. Perhaps two. Possibly three.

"I think I might have given up. I felt like I had," Trevino said. "My heart wasn't really in my chip shot." Something was. It went in for a saving five. Jacklin, having watched all these crazy shots of Lee's go in for two rounds, now did what was human. He three-putted from 15 feet. And that was that. Trevino got a routine par on 18 for his second British Open to go along with the two U.S. Opens he has won in his five years as a touring pro.

"I feel sorry for Tony, who played really well. And I feel

sorry for Jack. But Jack shouldn't have treated me like a butler when I had dinner with him the other night," said Trevino, still joking, still refreshingly Trevino.

In retrospect, one really has to wonder about Nicklaus' strategy, and Jack himself might well look back and question it. Maybe not, however. He is pretty stubborn about such things. He had a game plan for Muirfield and he stuck to it—at least until Saturday.

He arrived early to begin preparations for both the course and the smaller ball. There was nothing wrong with this—or else it could be said that he should not have arrived a week early at Pebble Beach for the U.S. Open. The argument that Jack was overprepared can be discarded. The final round proved as much.

There was tremendous pressure on him. The betting odds were an outlandish 2 to 1 before the championship even got under way and all of the Scottish newspapers were advertising the event as some sort of Nicklaus Extravaganza. *The Scotsman* (Edinburgh), for example, labeled its daily coverage, "The Grand Slam Open," with a portrait of Jack.

Muirfield has been called Scotland's best golf course by many authorities. This does not mean it is the toughest; that is probably Carnoustie in the wind. It means that Muirfield is the most elegant, the classiest, the most subtle, the best conditioned. It is not a long course; it has often been compared to our own Merion, given the right winds. There were one or two par 4s that Nicklaus could reach with a driver if he chose to try—and if he succeeded in hitting it straight enough. There were several others where he could reduce his second shot to a wedge if he hit with a big club off the tee. And there were par 5s he could surely reach in two blows.

Jack, having won at Muirfield in 1966 and sternly aware of the narrow fairways and numerous well-deep bunkers, had decided the only way to play the course was defensively, with caution and patience. He would one-iron it and three-iron it from the tees. On only five holes, depending on the wind, would his woods come out of the bag. "What happened, basically," he said afterward, "is that I didn't hit the other clubs straight."

It was only during Wednesday's first round that Muirfield played like a British Open course should—long, windy and rainy. Nicklaus' 70 that day was a mad scramble as he missed seven fairways on the only day his game plan made sense. When the unusually glorious weather set in on Thursday, Jack woke up and said, "Ye gods, I'll have to shoot 65 just to stay in it. The course will be a piece of cake." Muirfield was bright with sun, windless—and short. But all Jack did was go on missing fairways. Still, the field did not run away from him. And he was due a good round, wasn't he? "I haven't wasted any of my good golf yet," Nicklaus said Thursday night.

He didn't waste any on Friday either. The weather was even more wonderful, and there really weren't that many contenders for him to worry about. The first-day leader, Peter Tupling— was a Tupling worth more than a shilling?—had slipped back the way Tuplings should. A few other British surprises were still around but they wouldn't last. It was only Nicklaus against Trevino, Jacklin, Sanders and Johnny Miller, who had holed a three-wood for a double eagle, and perhaps astonishing Dave Marr, back from nowhere.

Everyone felt that Friday would be the day Nicklaus would explode. Not so. Jack was still missing fairways and was well out of it, two over par going to the 16th hole at the very time Trevino and Jacklin were at their hottest. It was only through a miracle of his very own, a chip in at the 16th, another birdie at the 17th and a struggling par at the 18th, that Nicklaus got home with a 71 and even par through 54 holes. Granted, in any other British Open that might have been fine. But Super Mex and Super Limey and the weather were seeing to it that this was no ordinary championship.

By attacking Muirfield, Tony Jacklin had met some tragedies, among them his triple bogey on the 13th hole the second day, but he had also stored up some birdies and eagles. Trevino had bounced between birdies and bogeys all along until nothing but birdies turned up late Friday in that mind-bending finish of his. And it seemed clear that Nicklaus had waited too long to change his strategy. But even after he had lost, Jack disagreed, contending, "I'll always believe I played the course the right way and just didn't play well. What can I do about a guy who holes it out of bunkers and across greens?"

He can keep trying for the Grand Slam, which might only exist in a dream, after all. At least as long as Super Mex keeps popping up to interfere with history.

Well, the Slam is still out there somewhere—giving Nicklaus something else to aim at. But at least he finally got old No. 14 a year later when he won the National PGA at Canterbury near Cleveland.

The night before he won, he was sitting around with some friends and business associates. They were worried that once again he wouldn't win; that he wouldn't get the 14th behind, and the ghost of Bobby Jones out of his mind and career.

They were all talking about going on an elk hunt in November, if Jack won. But somebody said, "Maybe we don't want to set it up yet. If you lose tomorrow, you may want to play some more golf during the rest of '73."

Jack thought about that. Maybe so, he reasoned. He paused and thought about it some more. He thought about how well he was playing. He thought about Canterbury.

"Book the hunt," he said.

"You'll Not Do That Here, Laddie"

It is statute an ordinit that in na place of the realme be there usit . . . Golfe or uther sik unprofitabill sportis.

—JAMES IV,
—to Parliament in Edinburgh, May 16, 1491

It was a gray, drizzly day like most others in Scotland and there was I, a lonely shepherd, strolling along a swollen dune by the North Sea looking for a wee stane to hit wi' a bit crook. Clumps of heather were up to my knees and the yellow-tipped whin was up to my chest, and I was up to here with my sheep because the little dumplings had wandered away. I had this crooked stick in my hand which I normally used to keep the dumplings in line. You know. Firm left side, eye on the tailbone, slow backswing—and whap. But they were gone and I was just ambling along when I saw this chuckie stane, as it was called, this round pebble. I also saw this rabbit scrape, as it was called, through an opening in the heather and whin. So I said to myself, "Self, why don't you take your bit crook and try to knock this here stane into that there scrape? And stay out of the heather because, boy, it'll make your hand

281

ring." Well, I guess I took it back a little outside because I cut a low one right into the garbage and almost never did find it, but anyhow, this is how I came to invent the game of golf a few hundred years ago.

There are those, of course, who claim that I did not invent golf in another life, nor did any other Scot. Some say the Romans did it long before me and called it *Paganica*, which I think, between you and me, sounds like a joint over on East 56th with a big tab. Some say the Dutch invented golf, or a game called *kolven*, which was similar. But no way. *Kolven* has to be a roll of veal stuffed with cheese and chives. Some say that even the French originated golf under the name of *jeu de mail*, but as any European traveler knows, this is a card game for the big players in Monaco. Actually, if the historians want to be picky, you could say that the Chinese a thousand years ago probably played a form of golf by batting a few snow peas around with chopsticks.

The fact of the matter is, golf is a Scottish game. It is naturally Scottish, as natural to our instincts as the seaside links land is natural to the setting. It was the Scots, after all, who took the game and did something with it when everybody else was busy making crossbows. We made the courses and the clubs, the balls and the rules, the trophies and the tournaments. We invented wind and rough, hooks and slices, bunkers and doglegs, and we were just getting ready to invent the overlapping grip when Harry Vardon, an Englishman, beat us to it.

We looked at the seashores, our links land, and said this is where the glory's at. Let the wet wind blow in from Denmark, or wherever it comes from. Let the incursions of the sea make the giant dunes and the tumbling valleys. Let the birds bring in the mixture of seeds that will grow our curious rough— the wiry, purple heather, the bulging whin, the dead fern we'll call bracken, and the green broom that does not have thorns to distinguish itself from the whin, or gorse. Let the rabbits and the foxes chew out the first fairways and dig the first cups, perhaps at St. Andrews where The Old Course lies today.

I don't know what the Romans, the Dutch and the French were doing around the 1450's—aside from waiting for the Bible to get printed—but us Scots were playing golfe then, and had been. At least we were when the kings would permit it, there being, from time to time, this nagging problem of national service. Had to go fight the English. Cancel my starting time.

There was this afternoon, I recall, when the game came close to being banished forever. As it happened, I was out on this moor at St. Andrews trying out a new Auchterlonie driving spoon at the 11th—the short hole, of course—when a King's guard raised up out of the whin and handed me a scroll signed by our monarch.

The scroll said, "It is decreetid and ordained that the Futeball and the Golfe be utterly cryit doune, and nocht to be usit."

"Guy never could spell," I said.

The guard pointed his crossbow at me and said that the King, Jimmy the Roman Numeral, meant business.

"The golfe is sik unprofitabill sportis," he said.

"Pal, you got that right," I said. "See that shepherd over there with the cross-handed grip on his bit crook? Well, he's got me out, out, out and one down."

"Don't be abusit," the guard said. "It is statute and ordinit that in na place of the realme be there Golfe in tyme cuming."

"Look," I said. "Smell that air. Gaze over this land. Great, huh? Who would want a guy to be hanging around a drafty castle waiting for an Englishman to scale the wall?"

"Aye," he said. "The aire is guid and the field reasonable feir. But can ya na handle the bow for archerie? Can ya na run or swoom or warstle instead?"

"I don't know, man," I said. "Let me put it your way. Here's the deal. I was drivin' the chuckie stanes wi' a bit stick as sune's I could walk."

He nodded his head as if he was beginning to understand. "Here's something else," I said. "I happen to know that a bow-maker in Perth is fixing up a set of clubs for the King right now. Why? Because the King sneaked out the other day to see what this game was all about and the Earl of Bothwell, who plays to a cool 23, brought him to his knees on the back three at Leith. The King's getting a pretty good price, too. Like only 14 s's for the set, whatever an s is."

The guard put down his crossbow and said, well go ahead and play if that was the case. And by the way, he added, did I want to buy "a dussen guid golfe ballis?"

"Hold it," I said. "You got featheries?"

"Aye," he said. "Guid featheries that cum from the Laird of Rosyth. Guid featheries stuffed with flock and wuid shavings."

"Four s's," I said. "And not an s more."

"Eight s's," he said.

"They're hot, man. Six s's and we both get out clean," I said.

He went for the six—you can always strike a bargain in Europe—and disappeared into the whin. And now that I had saved golf, I couldn't wait to try out one of the new high-compression featheries. I heeled up a good lie, and gave the shot a full body turn. Wow. Up, up, it soared—five yards, ten yards, twenty yards, and back to Earth, whatever that was, only a short rake-in from the 11th scrape, a par twelve. There is still a hole in the wind where I hit that shot, and I thought to myself, what a happy and golden time, indeed.

In a few more years, all of royalty would be playing golfe. There were rumors of Mary Queen of Scots shankering all around the fields of Seton when some said she should have been mourning the demise of Lord Darnley. Charles the First got a very bad press for being in a match at Leith when the Irish Rebellion broke out. A lot of Jameses and Dukes of York were seen swinging at Musselburgh, which still claims to be the oldest layout in the world and now sits inside a race course near Edinburgh. There was a Stuart or two spotted in a putting game at Leith, which is where The Honourable Company of Edinburgh Golfers got started before they built Muirfield.

All golfers, I think, should be indebted to a small group of us that got together in 1744—The Honourable Company. Looking back, I don't know how we managed it without George Plimpton, but what we did was form the first country club. Not only that, we sat down and wrote the first rules of the game, which we called the Articles & Laws in Playing Golf. At the time, some felt our days might better have been spent defending Culloden against the English, but it just goes to show how important we thought golf was.

Those first rules have been well preserved along with some terribly clever comments I made at the meetings as I spoke keenly above the roar of our first president, Duncan Forbes. The thirteen rules of our first code are as follows:

1. You Must Tee your Ball within a Club length of the Hole.
   (It's going to be uproarious fun, guys, waiting for somebody to drive before you can putt.)
2. Your Tee must be upon the Ground.
   (Nothing like teeing up the ball in the air for greater distance.)
3. You are not to Change the Ball which you Strike off the Tee.
   (The caddies will take care of this. When I tried to put down a clean one to putt the other day at St. Andrews, my man, Ginger Johnson, tugged at the sleeve of my cashmere and said, "You'll not do that here, laddie.")
4. You are not to Remove Stones, Bones or any Break Club for the Sake of playing your Ball Except upon the fair Green and that only within a Club length of your Ball.
   (Well, we'll get some pretty tricky breaks over the stones and bones.)
5. If your Ball come among Water, or any Watery filth, You are at Liberty to take out Your Ball, and throwing it behind the hazard 6 yards at least, You may play it with any Club,

and allow your Adversary a Stroke, for so getting out your Ball.

(Unless your Adversary doesn't see you do it.)

6. If your Balls be found any where touching one another. You are to lift the first Ball, till You play the last.

(I estimate the odds on this happening at, roughly, 9,768 to 1.)

7. At holeing, You are to play your Ball honestly for the Hole, and not to play upon your Adversary's Ball, not lying in your way to the Hole.

(I heard about this across the ocean in a place called East Hampton. They call it croquet.)

8. If you should lose your Ball, by its being taken up, or any other way You are to go back to the Spot where you Struck last, and drop another Ball, and Allow your Adversary a Stroke for the Misfortune.

(And if your Adversary has been seen taking up your Ball, you may strike your Adversary wi' a bit crook, teeing him upon the Ground.)

9. No Man at Holeing his Ball, is to be Allowed to Mark his way to the Hole with his Club or anything else.

(And if you do, man, the greens committee will wear your ass out.)

10. If a Ball be Stop'd by any person, Horse, Dog or any thing else, the Ball so Stop'd Must be Played where it lyes.

(Yeah, but the money up, how do you know if it's a real dog?)

11. If you draw your Club, in Order to Strike, and proceed so far in the Stroke as to be bringing down your Club; if then your Club shall break, in any way, it is to be accounted a Stroke.

(And your forearms will hum a merry tune as well.)

12. He, whose Ball lyes furthest from the Hole is Obliged to play first.

(This is a good rule, but I'll tell you, the public course players are going to relax it a little.)

13. Neither Trench, Ditch, or Dyke, made for the preservation of the Links, Nor the Scholars Holes or the Soldiers Lines, shall be Accounted a Hazard, But the Ball is to be taken out, Teed and played with any Iron Club.

(Oh, swell, Duncan. So how come you let me make eight passes at it yesterday in the Soldiers Lines with no relief?)

Well, you know what happens. You let one private club get started and down the road another pops up. The noblemen and lairds of Fifeshire couldn't stand it that we had The Honourable Company and some rules, especially, they said, when *everybody* knew St. Andrews was the cradle of golfe. So in hardly any time at all, they formed a group called The Society of St. Andrews Golfers, which later became known as the Royal & Ancient Golf Club. And you know what happened after that. They had the sport by the old gutta percha and never would turn loose of it.

A lot of arguments have gone on through the years about the history of the game, where it began, who molded the first cleek, and so forth. Over at Muirfield where The Honourable Company still hangs out—merely the world's oldest club—they say that the R&A would still be the Greensboro Jaycees if the Edinburgh code of golf hadn't been written. And at the same time, over at Prestwick on the West Coast, they like to say that the R&A wouldn't have anything to do but run the St. Andrews city championship if Prestwick's members hadn't decided to invent the Open championship and stage it the first twelve years of its existence. The Open championship, of course, is what we call the British Open today.

All I know is, every time somebody at Muirfield or Prestwick or Troon or Carnoustie goes out and finds an old track iron which had to have been made over two hundred years ago, somebody from the R&A will reach down into Hell Bunker or the Swilken Burn and find a club that is older. One envisions genial Laurie Auchterlonie, the honorary professional of St. Andrews, carving and hammering away these days, making an antique putter dated 1742.

What truly matters, of course, is that the whole scene is old—the gray clubhouses and the rolling land, the Minute Books and the scrolls, the wind, and rain, and heather, the dunes and swales, everything that makes Scottish golf what it is. It has been said by many that a golfer hasn't played the game until he has gone back where it all was, and where it all is.

It is a special feeling, I think, that calls the golfer back to Scotland as the sailor is called by the sea. Take me to the grave of Old Tom Morris, a voice says. Drive me around the Road Hole. Show me where the Wee Icemon chipped it in at Carnoustie. Lead me down the long, narrow 11th at Troon where Arnie made the threes. Let me hear the groan of the Spitfire ghosts at Turnberry. Carry me over the Sleepers at Prestwick. Bend me around the archery field at Muirfield. Drown me in all of these treasures of time once more in this, still another life.

The Scots themselves relish all of this more than anyone. It is in their faces as deeply as it is in their poems. They are constantly writing poems about their bunkers, and burns and braes. "The swallows are high in an empty sky, so let's to the tee once more." That kind of thing. Or, "There's none—I'll back the assertion with a wager—can play the heavy iron like the Major!" It has been estimated that more golf poetry exists in Scotland than heather. One particular effort keeps haunting me, maybe because I wrote it under the name of Sir Guy Campbell. It is titled "The Old Course Speaks," and I am grateful that J. B. Salmond preserved it in his book *The Story of the R&A.* It is written about St. Andrews, but it could be any links in the old country—guaranteed to hoist the enthusiastic golfer from any land out of his electric cart comfort and set him down on the creeping fescue of a Scottish links. Men have been known to pack as they read it:

> *I have heard the North Sea*
> *Ceaselessly withdrawing,*
> *Foot by foot receding,*
> *Through the Ages as they spent;*
> *Adding to my Loanings,*

My salt and misty loanings,
Gracious ground for Golfers,
Spread far for their content.

Gulls and Terns and Curlews
Left me rich guano;
Sand and silt and sea-wrack—
The Tilth that made my sward.
Cunningies then cropped it,
And foxes followed after,
Fashioning my fairways
And Greens for Golf's reward.

Winter, Spring and Summer,
Autumn, in their seasons;
Snow and haar and sunshine
With wind, and wave, and rain,
Tempered my whole being,
Brought me growth and vigour,
Bent, and, whin, and heather
To pattern my campaign.

Countless feet have worn me—
Children, men and women;
Multitudes have scarred me;
Come frost, come wet, come shine.
Service without measure,
Healing for my treasure,—
I renew at leisure.
The secret is mine.

Through long generations
I have watched Golf's pageant;
I have known its Powers,
And Princes in their prime,
Vying with each other
One year to another,
Yet for many changes
The Art is one with Time.

So it was and has been;
So it is and will be.

> *I abide unchallenged,*
> *And peerless is my Name.*
> *History behind me,*
> *I give all who find me*
> *Welcome and a Blessing,*
> *To the Glory of the Game.*

"So let's to the tee once more," I said to the customs official at Prestwick, having de-boarded my Pan Am flight from JFK. "The nature of my visit? Well, to receive a welcome and a blessing from the game. Actually, I have a meeting scheduled with Heather, Whin, Bracken & Broom, Incorporated, one of your very successful brokerage firms."

There was this tour that Keith Mackenzie, the secretary of the R&A, had worked out. Fly to Prestwick, the old World War II air base where everybody played 12 O'clock High, and motor from there down the West Coast to Turnberry, the Pebble Beach of Scotland. Stay at the Turnberry Hotel, which is the only thing there, and covers a whole hillside, overlooking the Turnberry course and the old Spitfire runways. From Turnberry, he said, one could reach two other very famous Scottish links—Troon and Prestwick—simply by driving once a day over the Electric Brae, a road which goes up when it appears to be going down. Cover the West Coast first, said Mackenzie, then move to The Old Course Hotel at St. Andrews where you can play The Old Course, right outside your window, and journey north toward Dundee and Carnoustie, or south toward Edinburgh and Muirfield.

"This is the best possible route for an American," said Mackenzie.

"But I'm Scottish," I said. "I'm just retracing my steps from a few hundred years before."

"Of course, dear chap," Keith said. "We're all Scottish when it comes to golf."

"Aye," I said.

"Simply marvelous tour," he said. "You'll see a bit of all.

Turnberry, for example, pitched right there on the Firth of
Clyde. Tees practically hanging on the water like Pebble. And
Prestwick with those slender fairways and blind shots, and
seven bloody five pars. Too outdated for the Open championship, of course, but, mind you, the Pine Valley of Scotland
in a way. And wonderful Old Troon. The 'postage stamp'
green. The very first sharp-angled dogleg. I say, Arnie argued
a good case there, didn't he?"

"Aye," I said.

"Then to the East Coast. That's your story," Keith said.
"You'll quarter in the Old Course Hotel, naturally, right where
the railway sheds were on the Road Hole. Walk out on your
terrace and spit in the Principal's Nose, by jove. With the
new bridge, you can reach Carnoustie in an hour now. Good
old somber Carnoustie, the Barry Burn and all that. And then,
of course, there's Muirfield. Marvelous place, Muirfield. Not
a burn on it, you see. Just one hundred sixty-five bunkers.
You'll see a bit of sand there, I'd guess."

"Aye, aye," I said.

"Best of luck," he said. "See you at St. Andrews when you
arrive. We'll have a bit of port. It goes well in the Big Room."

For some evil reason, some death wish that perhaps is concealed
within us all, the first thing a touring golfer is captivated by
in Scotland is the plantlife adjacent to all fairways. The heather,
whin, bracken and broom. Turnberry, my first stop, had all
of these other landmarks to dwell upon—holes hanging on
the Firth of Clyde, as Mackenzie said, the Spitfire runways
now bordered by wild flowers, a bird sanctuary on an island off
in the distance, the huge hotel on the hill where "God Save
the Queen" reverberated from the orchestra pit in the ballroom
at night through all of the tea rooms, and an RAF monument
at the 12th green commemorating those men from Turnberry's
aerial fighting and gunnery school who perished, their name
liveth forever with the group captain in the sky. But I was
preoccupied with the rough.

You find yourself having this running commentary with your caddy, as if he's a botanist in his checkered James Cagney cap, his coat and tie, and a scruffy face which hasn't been shaved since the last air raid. His name is Jimmy or Peter or Ginger or Tip or Cecil, and chances are he caddied for Hagen at Hoylake in 1924.

"What am I in here?" I asked the one at Turnberry on the very first hole. "Is this gorse?"

"Not likely," he said. "I think that's a bush."

Your caddy is a warm, friendly man who knows his golf. You swing once and he knows your distances. If he says the shot is "a wee seven," you'd better hit it wee-ly, or a dozen of you with machetes won't be able to find the ball behind the green.

Such a hole was the 4th at Turnberry, which bears the name Woe-be-Tide. It is a 170-yard one-shotter. You practically stand on the Firth and hit into a crosswind to a green about as big as your golf bag with more water on the left and hounds of the Baskervilles on your right.

"What am I in now?" I asked, having hit a Firthlock safely to the right. "Is this heather?"

"That," he said, "is gorse. You ca'na swing softly, sir and be way o' the gorse."

"Gorse is whin, right?"

He said, "Aye, the whins we call it. You can'na plant the whin and neither will the whin die. The whin is just here where it always was."

I took a forceful swing with a sand iron, moving the ball about one foot, and said, "Don't forget to show me the heather when we find some."

"Aye," he said. "That's heather you're in now."

You can't often find the ball in heather. It is a stubby dwarf plant, all matted and wiry, brown at times, purple at others. You can top a shot with a driver and, whereas in America the ball is likely to run for a hundred or so yards, if in Scotland it finds a cluster of heather only a few yards away, it will go flimp—and either disappear forever, or bound straight back at you.

I could see at least half of the ball there in the heather, and I took a full swipe at it with the wedge, so hard that the caddy counted all of the cleats in my shoes and the veins in my legs, and the noise I made sounded like the Stukas had returned to drop another load on the docks at Glasgow.

And the ball didn't move at all.

"When does my hand stop tingling?" I said.

Turnberry has one hole that is more magnificent than all of the others. It is the 9th, a 425-yard hole with a tee sitting back on an island of jagged rock, with rocks and water bordering it on the left where a lighthouse marks the farthest point of the course from the hotel. Off to the right, beyond the plantlife, is part of the old asphalt Spitfire runway. Behind the green is broom—whin without thorns—and little dabs of bracken, which the cows won't eat.

One finds in Scotland, however, that if the botany doesn't confuse you, the scorekeeping will. I drove well at the 9th, which means safely onto the close-cropped fescue grass which comprises all Scottish fairways. I reached the small green with one of my rare un-shanked four-irons, and I stole a putt of about twenty feet for a three. Then the trouble began.

"Is this a par-four hole?" I asked the caddy.

"No, sir," he said. "It plays to a bogey five."

"Then I made an eagle," I said.

"It can'na be an eagle, sir," he said.

"Well, what's par for the course?"

He said, "Bogey today is about seventy-six."

"But level fours is seventy-two," I said. "Shouldn't that be what I would call par?"

He thought a minute and said, "I reckon par to be about seventy-four today."

"What was it yesterday, for instance?" I asked.

"Oh, in that wind yesterday, par must have been seventy-seven or so."

I said, "Well, I think I just made an eagle."

"You did'na make an eagle, sir," he said.

"A birdie?"

"Not exactly a birdie with the helpin' wind, sir."

"A par?"

"Oh, much better than a par, it was," he said.

"So what the God damn hell was it, James Cagney?"

He said, "It was a very good score, sir. Your first of the round."

There is much to see in the neighborhood of Turnberry, and along the route to either Prestwick or Troon, like a castle here and there, or a birthplace of Robert Burns, of which there must be a dozen, but never should a visitor miss that hill— that thing—called the Electric Brae. Years ago, bicyclists discovered it, one learns. They found themselves forced to pedal sweatily to get uphill when it obviously looked as if the road were going downward into the woods. It is an optical illusion, and you would lose your wallet betting on it. The proof is this: stop the car at a point where you are certain you are headed uphill. Put a golf ball on the road, a shiny new Dunlop 65. It will roll uphill, that's all.

As mysterious as the Electric Brae is, it is no more mysterious than the course at Prestwick, the course where all of those early British Opens were staged beginning in 1860. Your first impression as you gaze out on a wasteland surrounded by an old stone fence is that this has to be the biggest practical joke in all of golf. I've got it, you say. You pay your green fee, put down a ball and aim at the world, take four or five steps and are never heard from again.

Consider the 1st hole, only 339 yards. On your right, the stone fence, about ten feet away, separating you from a train that will come chugging by at intervals. On your left: mounds of heather and whin. Directly in front: waste. Sheer waste. Small and large clumps of it, sheltered by thin layers of fog.

And the caddy hands you a driver. The fairway, presuming one is actually there, can't be more than twenty yards wide, but the caddy hands you a driver.

"*Where* is it?" I asked.

"Straightaway, sir," said Charles, who was distinguished from my caddy at Turnberry by two things. Charles wore a muffler and had his own cigarettes. "It's just there," he said. "Just to the left of the cemetery."

It is asking a lot, I know, to expect anyone to believe that you can bust a drive about 250 yards on a 339-yard hole, have a good lie in the fairway, and still not be able to see a green anywhere, but this is Prestwick.

The green was there, all right, as are all of the greens at Prestwick, but you never see them until you are on them, which is usually eight or ten strokes after leaving the tee. They sit behind little hills, or the terrain simply sinks ten or fifteen feet straight down to a mowed surface, or they are snuggled over behind tall wood fences over which you have nothing to aim at but a distant church steeple.

You would like to gather up several holes from Prestwick and mail them to your top ten enemies. I guess my all-time favorite love-hate golf hole must be the 3rd hole on this course. Like most of the holes at Prestwick, it is unchanged from the day in 1860 when Willie Park, Sr., shot 174 to become the first Open champion. Quite a score, I have since decided.

First of all, without a caddy, it would take you a week and a half to find the third tee. It is a little patch of ground roughly three yards wide perched atop a stream, a burn, rather, with the cemetery to your back and nothing up ahead except fine mist. Well, dimly in the distance, you can see a rising dune with a fence crawling across it—"the Sleepers," the caddy says. But nothing more. Nothing.

"I'll be frank, Charles," I said. "I have no idea which way to go, or what with."

"Have a go with the spoon, sir," he said.

"The *spoon?*" I shrieked. "Where the hell am I going with a spoon?"

"A spoon'll get you across the burn, sir, but it'll na get you to the Sleepers," he said.

"Hold it," I said. "Just wait a minute." My body was sort of slumped over, and I was holding the bridge of my nose with my thumb and forefinger. "These, uh, Sleepers. They're out there somewhere?"

"Aye, the Sleepers," he said.

"And, uh, they just kind of hang around, right?"

"Aye," he said. "The Sleepers have took many a golfer."

Somehow, I kept the three-wood in play and when I reached the shot, Charles casually handed me the four-wood. I took the club and addressed the ball, hoping to hit quickly and get on past the Sleepers, wherever they were. But Charles stopped me.

"Not that way, sir," he said.

"This *is* the way I was headed when we left the tee," I said.

"We go a bit right here, sir," he said. "The Sleepers is there just below the old fence. You want to go over the Sleepers and over the fence as well, but na too far right because of the burn. Just a nice stroke, sir, with the four-wood."

Happily, I got the shot up and in the general direction Charles ordered, and walking toward the flight of the ball, I finally came to the Sleepers. They were a series of bunkers about as deep as the Grand Canyon. A driver off the tee would have found them, and so would any kind of second shot that didn't get up high enough to clear the fence on the dune. A worn path led through the Sleepers, and then some ancient wooden steps led up the hill and around the fence to what was supposed to be more fairway on the other side.

It wasn't a fairway at all. It was a group of grass moguls going off into infinity. It looked like a carefully arranged assortment of tiny green Astrodomes. When Charles handed me the pitching wedge, I almost hit him with it because there was no green in sight.

I got the wedge onto the green that was, sure enough, nestled down in one of those dips, and two-putted for a five that I figured wasn't a par just because the hole was 505 yards long. Charles said I had played the hole perfectly, thanks to him, and that I could play it a thousand times and probably never play it as well.

I said, "Charles, do you know what this hole would be called in America?"

"Sir?" he said.

"This is one of those holes where your suitcase flies open and you don't know what's liable to come out," I said.

"Aye, 'tis that," he said.

"One bad shot and you're S.O.L. on this mother," I said.

"Sir?" said Charles.

"Shit out of luck," I said.

"Aye," said Charles. "At Prestwick, we call it the Sleepers."

Prestwick has a number of other charming atrocities. There is a 201-yard 5th hole which the caddies call the "Himalayas" which one plays with anything from a five-iron to a driver, depending on the wind. You flog the shot over a mountainous dune and discover, on the other side, about a hundred feet down, a green. You ring a bell when you've putted out. There is a wonderful 15th hole of only 329 yards, straight-away, but the fairway is total heather except for the width of an umbrella, and there is no green at all that I could find. All in all, I would say that Prestwick is the most unique course in the world. There are eighteen holes but I dare any visitor to find more than, say, twelve fairways and seven or eight greens.

Only a couple of graveyards and trash piles away from Prestwick lies. Troon. In fact, from the 10th tee at Prestwick you can see Troon better than you can see Prestwick. The course is on the Firth, not so much as Turnberry but more so than Prestwick, and the town is filled with small resort hotels and rooming houses which advertise bed-and-breakfast. Troon is the seaside getaway on weekends for the inhabitants of Glasgow. You can fish there, and hike, and go camping in the drizzle. But the best thing you can do if you are privileged enough is play Old Troon, the championship course of the snootiest club on the West Coast. Mr. A. Sweet, sektry, will arrange the round if he approves of the cut of your blazer.

Old Troon is the only Scottish links on the West Coast that the R&A keep on what Keith Mackenzie terms "the championship rota." These are courses fit to host the British Open. In Scotland, they have been narrowed down to St. Andrews, Muirfield, Carnoustie and Troon. And in England they are Birkdale, Lytham and Hoylake. Troon takes immense pride in the fact that it is the jewel of the west, and even more pride in the fact that it was the scene of one of Arnold Palmer's most glorious weeks. Palmer, of course, captured his second British Open at Troon in 1962 by six strokes (276) on a course that Gary Player declared "unfair" before walking off in a rage, and a course that drew such horrid individual holes out of Jack Nicklaus as tens and eights.

For the full haul of eighteen holes, Troon is not all that memorable. The rough, for one thing, is more like rugged American rough; you *can* escape from it in one hearty swing if the waist of your trousers is cinched up. Troon, I found, is what you would call a very pleasant course and perhaps more modern than most Scottish courses if any layout without the hint of a tree can look modern to an American.

This is not to say that Troon is void of character. It has several holes, as a matter of fact, which are as good as any to be found, including the single hardest hole I have ever seen— the 11th—not to forget two others which have been architectural landmarks since they were constructed.

The 8th, for example. This is the famed "postage stamp."

It is so named because the green, which clings to nothing but the lower half of a heather-covered mound, is not much larger than a stamp. The hole measures only 125 yards, but it can play up to a four-iron if the wind is whipping out of the north. Mr. A. Sweet likes to tell about a member who made a hole in one at the "postage stamp" in a most unusual way. His tee shot came to rest atop the mound. He swung at the ball with a wedge from up there, and missed it. But the sweep of the clubhead through the grass dislodged the ball and it trickled down the hill and into the cup.

"Rightly, of course, the chap made a two," said Mr. Sweet.

It did not harm the fame of the "postage stamp" that in 1923 when Troon was first used to stage the Open championship, none other than Walter Hagen made a double bogey five there to blow the title by a stroke to a Mr. Arthur Havers.

All over Scotland one continually finds par-four holes where, at one time or another, according to the caddies, Jack Nicklaus was on in one. The hole before the "postage stamp," Troon's 7th, is such a hole. It is renowned for two other reasons; first, it is supposed to be one of the original doglegs, since the fairway curves sharply to the right, and it is also considered one of the most beautiful holes.

With the tee up on a bluff furnishing a wide view of the sea, and with the wind usually helping, you can envision how Nicklaus might have driven it those 385 yards. He caught one just right and strung it out over the sandhills, hit a downslope and burned a path through the whin up to the putting surface.

It might well have been this good fortune back in 1962 that encouraged Jack to take out the driver at Troon's 11th the day he had to sink a fifty-foot putt for a ten. The 11th hole is 485 yards of railroad track on the right and clusters of whin on the left. The fairway is nothing but moguls all the way with the tiny green hard by another of those old stone fences. This is the hole Palmer won the Open on, for

he played it with two threes and a four and five—five under—
by using a one-iron off the tee and a two-iron to the green.

Nicklaus, however, tried to go with the driver. First, he
got acquainted with the whin for a few shots, and once he
made it to the fairway, he put a couple over the wall. Here,
too, was the point from which Gary Player left for the clubhouse, thence to the airport.

My caddy at Troon, Peter McNeil, who happened to have
toted Sam Snead's bag in the 1962 Open, gave me the driver
at the 11th, and when we lost sight of it soaring out over the
whin, he consoled me the way a good caddy should.

"You're just not with it today, sir," he said.

Troon makes no claim to being among the oldest clubs in
Scotland, seeing as how it wasn't built until just the other
day—1878—but like any other self-respecting private domain
for gentlemen golfers, it has a set of relics that are said to be
the oldest in Britain. Mr. A. Sweet proudly pointed to the
trophy case and said those clubs were found in a cupboard
wrapped in a newspaper dated 1741.

"I think Laurie Auchterlonie at St. Andrews is getting ready
to discover a set from 1740," I said.

Mr. A. Sweet did not laugh.

The crass American would not think much of a clubhouse
at a Scottish links, be it Troon or Prestwick, or most anywhere.
There are no tennis courts, of course, and no swimming pool.
There is no Mixed Foursome Grill because there is no Mixed.
Which means no women or pros allowed inside. The pro stays
in his wooden shack nearby, selling rainsuits and mending
clubs. The main clubhouse itself is for ex-wing commanders
to eat lunch in—no smoking until after two P.M.—to change
socks in before or after their daily thirty-six holes, and to
slump over their *Financial Times* in. If there is a shower stall
down some creaking corridor, the water is chilled and hits you
with all the force of a leak in the roof. On the walls of the
dining room and the reading room, both of which are likely
to offer a close-up view of the 18th green, will be portraits of

a lot of men who look like George Washington but would rather be dead first. They will be ex-secretaries and ex-captains of the club who not only invented the mashie-niblick but were survivors of the Black Hole of Calcutta.

If you are as poor at geography as I, you have to divide Scotland like this. The West Coast, where Troon and Prestwick and Turnberry are, and where I had been, is the Ireland side. From almost any point on those three courses, in other words, if you could see far enough, you would see Northern Ireland. This is also known to me as the Glasgow side, which, even to the Scots, is not exactly Sutton Place. Where I was headed now was to the East Coast, the Edinburgh side, to the North Sea, to the more posh area of the country where St. Andrews, Muirfield and Carnoustie are. There is a great deal more to Scotland than just this "golf belt," which embraces the land across the mid-section from Troon to Muirfield. There is, for instance, way up north, the links of Dornoch. As good a test as any, according to Keith Mackenzie, but too far away for the R&A to transport its people, chestnut palings, gallery rope, scoreboards and tens for the Open championship. Thanks, Dornoch, but Carnoustie is as far north as the R&A cares to travel.

Actually, if one could grease himself up and swim like Florence Chadwick, he could get to Carnoustie from St. Andrews in about thirty minutes. It is just across a bay. Driving, however, takes a couple of hours because cars have to go through Dundee, which is Yonkers with, as they say, less glamor.

From the viewpoint of providing difficulty for the top professional golfers, Carnoustie is surely the toughest course in Scotland. It is long and windy and wet. It is also smoky, dreary and somber. It is a course with more of a sameness to it throughout than any other. Every hole begins to look like the one you've just played—unreachable. Even the names of the holes are unimaginative. The 2nd: Gulley. The 4th: Hillocks. The 6th: Long. The 11th: Dyke. The 18th: Home.

Carnoustie began to develop a distinction around the 5th hole, I thought. But maybe I felt this because my caddy had me primed. Here was the hole where the Wee Icemon, Ben Hogan, had chipped in for a birdie three in 1953 during the last round. It was where he had made the stroke, from the lower-left bunker, that launched him toward the British Open title the one and only time he ever played in the tournament.

"He stood right here," said Phillip, the caddy. "Aye, it was only a short flick of the wrist."

The 6th, too, had character, most of it provided by an electrical fence down the left-hand side of the fairway. Periodically, a sign in red letters hung on the fence which said: DO NOT TOUCH ANYTHING. IT MAY EXPLODE AND KILL YOU. On the other side of the wire, as you might guess, was a firing range used by the Ministry of Defense. The hole is 565 yards long, and the Scots named it Hogan's Alley in '53, for Ben birdied it the last two rounds.

Phillip stopped at a point far beyond my tee shot down the fairway. "Here," he said, digging his shoe into the turf. "And here." He moved it a couple of inches. "Then here." He moved it another inch. "And over here." He moved his shoe about a foot.

"That's where the Icemon drove it," he said.

From here until near the finish Carnoustie became something of a blur. The wind wouldn't give my four-wood a rest, and the steady drizzle turned my under and over cashmeres into about seven hundred pounds of inconvenient weight. The most fascinating landmark near the course, after the firing range, was Anderson Cranes and Stone-Cutting Machinery.

"Phillip," I said. "Did anyone ever suggest to you that Carnoustie is *not* Antibes?"

Somewhere near the end, I vaguely recall, there is a Barry Burn that you have to cross about thirty times on the last three holes, which happen to be a 243-yard three par into the gale that Jack Nicklaus finally reached with a driver in 1968, a 438-yard par four that you are forced to lay up on off the tee, and a 453-yard par four 18th that I judged to be a driver, spoon and full eight-iron. With dry grips, maybe less.

As it turned out, I finished with a flourish. Good driver, good spoon, good eight-iron, four feet from the cup. Of course in my haste to have Phillip show me the spot where Hogan used to go to wring out his sweaters, I blew the putt. And with a number of people staring at me through the clubhouse window, too.

Later on, I was safely indoors trying to dry off and get one of those wonderful hot beers when a tall Britisher in a coat with a crest approached me.

"I say, you're the chap who was out there on the eighteenth a while ago," he said.

"Afraid so," I said.

"Bit dodgey that putt," he said. "Breaks left."

"Sure does," I said.

"Good for me, though," he said. "Took four shillings off a mate at the bar."

Yeah, I thought, well, Hogan won the Open here and he's from my town, and lend lease and—ah, screw it.

Muirfield from St. Andrews is in precisely the opposite direction of Carnoustie, and it is everything Carnoustie isn't. Muirfield is elegance and class, charm and dignity, convenience and pleasure. There is not a true distance on it, nor a fixed par, nor a name for a hole, but it is a course with a championship quality in the purest sense. There is not a tree or a bush or a burn, but there are 165 bunkers and they are trouble enough. It is the only course in Scotland that takes advantage and disadvantage of the full cycle of the wind, for the outgoing nine goes clockwise and back to the clubhouse, and the back nine runs counterclockwise and returns. Par is probably 72, but it is easy to envision days when the winds would make it 76.

Muirfield is on the Firth of Forth between Gullane and North Berwick, not painfully far from Edinburgh. It is on a fine shore surrounded by estates, and one gets the idea that this area is to Edinburgh what the Hamptons are to New York City. Muirfield's clubhouse is noted for its spaciousness in comparison with other Scottish clubhouses, and its kitchen is noted for its cuisine. This, after all, is where The Honourable Company of Edinburgh Golfers hangs out.

Directly next door to the huge stone clubhouse with its sprawling veranda and putting green is the Greywalls Hotel, where a member of The Honourable Company would stay. Greywalls fronts on the 9th green, and the Scots have long felt that part of the vast charm of Muirfield is that a fellow can stop after nine holes and grab a tap at Greywalls—the way Americans do at their courses everywhere.

The real charm of Muirfield is in its amazing fairness and its splendid pacing, both of which are much on the order of Merion, that gem of a battleground on Philadelphia's Main Line where every club comes out of the bag every time you play it. Muirfield has short fives and long fives, short, bending fours, and long, narrow fours, short, tricky threes and long but reachable threes. Its fairways are skinny but the lies are perfect, and there are shortcuts to be taken by the brave or long-hitting who wish to flirt with more bunkers than the eye can count.

Because of the eccentricities of the wind, for example, as well as the roll of the fairway, Jack Nicklaus was able to drive the 407-yard 15th hole when he won the British Open there in 1966. But he had to lean on a three-wood coming back to reach the 198-yard 16th. It would be difficult to imagine a more implausible course on which Nicklaus could win a tournament because the tightness would practically render his big drive useless. But as they say at Muirfield, "He one-ironed her."

The highest complement anyone could pay Muirfield, I suppose, would be to say that it is a Hogan type of course. Distances are meaningless because of the wind, and Hogan always said they were meaningless, anyhow. Every shot has a look to it, he said, a certain feel. "I might hit a two-iron a hundred fifty yards," he often said.

I played Muirfield that way. My two-irons went exactly 150 yards, and frequently off the shank of the club to the right.

"This is the course," my caddy said, over and over. "This is the best of the lot."

"I'd like to see it sometime," I said.

There are a number of spectacular holes at Muirfield, but the 6th is perhaps its finest. It is a par four—sometimes a par five—of 475 yards or thereabouts, an uphill-downhill dogleg left which curls around a battered rock wall which separates the course from an archery field. The landing area for the tee shot is no more than twenty yards across, and deep bunkers patrol it. With a career drive you can then get close to home with a career three-wood to a rolling green, again framed by bunkers.

"What a hole," I said to the caddy as I stood there considering the three-wood.

"Have a good go with the spoon," he said. "But a word of caution, sir. A ball played into Archerfield Wood is irrecoverable."

The mystique of Muirfield lingers on. So does the memory of Carnoustie's foreboding. So does the scenic wonder of Turnberry, and the haunting incredibility of Prestwick, and the pleasant deception of Troon. But put them all together and St. Andrews can play their low ball for atmosphere.

To begin with, St. Andrews is an old university town. Spires rise up over narrow streets littered with shops and cozy pubs. Students wearing red cloaks are bicycling around. Statues confront the stroller. An inn is here and there, and the North Sea just beyond.

There are four golf courses at St. Andrews: Old, New, Eton and Jubilee, and they are all available to the public. The *new* course is over seventy years old. Try that on for nostalgia. But no one, of course, is ever concerned about anything but The Old. The Old Course *is* St. Andrews, the R&A, all of those famed hazards. It is Jones, Vardon, Hagen, and old and young Tom Morris, and Keith Mackenzie standing on the balcony of his office in the R&A building just above the first tee surveying the entirety of the layout through a pair of mounted German submarine binoculars.

I was fortunate enough to secure lodging in The Old Course Hotel. Thus, I could walk out on my terrace and it was all there directly below me. To my left, the course stretching out to the 11th green—the short hole, of course—and to my right, a matchless view of the 18th fairway leading up through the Valley of Sin with Rusacks Hotel standing there as it is supposed to be, and with the great gray edifice of the Royal & Ancient clubhouse forming a backdrop.

The Old Course has been called a lot of things because, at first glance, it looks like nothing more than a flat green city park. Some Americans have labeled it a "third-rate municipal course," and a "football field," but Bob Jones knew its subtleties better. It was, he said, the one course he would play forever if he could choose just one.

Two things strike the first-timer at St. Andrews immediately. First, the double greens. No fewer than fourteen holes share enormous putting surfaces, the 2nd also being the 16th, and that sort of thing. There are two flags, naturally, and often they will be as far apart as perhaps eighty yards, with many a dip and turn between them. The erring shotmaker is apt to find the longest putts in golf at St. Andrews. Secondly, The Old Course is something of a paradise for one with a chronic hook. The first nine goes straight out, you see, with all of the heather and the sea on your right. And the back nine returns, parallel, giving the hooker all of those outgoing fairways to land on.

The mystery of why no golfer has ever been able to tear apart The Old Course—278 is the lowest a winner has shot in the British Open there—lies in the wind and the putting, and the fantastically perfect location of such hazards as Hell Bunker, a deep and somewhat inescapable pit at the 14th, the Swilken Burn, a small brook which rushes right up against the green of the 1st hole and catches many a soft nine-iron, and the Valley of Sin, the cavernous lower level of the 18th green from which three-putts and even four-putts are commonplace.

I attacked The Old Course in the company of Ginger Johnson who had merely been caddying there for forty-five years. For a few holes, he thought he had Henry Cotton again. The wind was behind and my shank, my top, my slice and my putting jerk seemed to have disappeared. Through the 10th, I was only one over par, and I said to Ginger:

"I don't know, but I think I'm bringing The Old Course to its knees."

And Ginger said, "Aye, ya made a putt or two, sir. But now we go home into the wind."

In rapid order, I was lost in the Elysian Fields, lost in the Beardies, trapped in Hell Bunker, gouged in the Principal's Nose, over the fence, smothered in heather, and even out of bounds on an overhang of The Old Course Hotel at the Road Hole. Finally, I limped up the 18th fairway en route to the Valley of Sin. Par for 86.

"You had a wee bit of hard luck," Ginger said. "But it can't spoil the fact that as we cum up the eighteenth, we sense a wee bit of tradition, don't we?"

Keith Mackenzie peered down from his balcony as I walked onto the green. I putted out. One final insult: a straight-in four-footer which broke six inches. The secretary motioned me up for lunch in the R&A dining room—no smoking at all. I toured the club and reread the letter that Isaac Grainger, then the president of the USGA, had written to the R&A on the occasion of its two-hundredth birthday.

He had said, in part, "What golf has of honor, what it has of justice, of fair play, of good fellowship and sportsmanship—in a word, what is best in golf—is almost surely traceable to the inspiration of the Royal and Ancient."

I thought of those words again as I strolled back outside to stand and look at the sea, and at the town, and all across the gentle green sweep of The Old Course—the oldest course. I had been there forever.

The Doggedest Victim

Fancy seeing you here.

—ARNOLD PALMER,
winning the U.S. Open

He first came to golf as a muscular young man who could not keep his shirttail in, who smoked a lot, perspired a lot and who hit the ball with all of the finesse of a dock worker lifting a crate of auto parts. Arnold Palmer did not play golf, we thought. He nailed up beams, reupholstered sofas, repaired air-conditioning units. Sure, he made birdies by the streaks in his eccentric way—driving through forests, lacing hooks around sharp corners, spewing wild slices over prodigious hills, and then, all hunched up and pigeon-toed, staring putts into the cups. But he made just as many bogeys in his stubborn way. Anyhow, a guy whose slacks are too long and turned up at the cuffs, who matches green shirts with orange sweaters, a guy who sweats so much, is *not* going to rush past the Gene Littlers, Ken Venturis and Dow Finsterwalds, the stylists, to fill the hero gap created by the further graying and balding of Ben Hogan and Sam Snead. This is what most of us believed around 1960, even after Palmer had won his second Masters, even after he had begun to drown everyone in money winnings.

This was a suave new godlet of the fairways, a guy out of Latrobe Dry Goods?

We were, of course, as wrong about him as the break on a downhill six-footer, as wrong as his method seemed to us to be wrong: hit it hard, go find it, hit it hard again. We knew we were wrong one day when the bogeys suddenly went away. No one understood why or how, except that Palmer willed them to. And now he had become a winner like none we had ever known. He was a *nice* guy, of all things. He was honestly and naturally gracious, untemperamental, talkative, helpful and advising, unselfish of his time, marvelously good-humored; he had a special feeling for golf's history and he was honored by its traditions; and with all of this he remained the gut fighter we insisted he be, a man so willing to accept the agonies of pressure and the burdens of fame that for a few years we absolutely forgot that anyone else played the game he was dominating and changing.

He actually started *being* Arnold Palmer in that summer of 1960, a stupidly short time ago it seems. He became the Arnie of whoo-ha, go-get-'em Arnie on a searingly hot afternoon in Denver when, during the last round of the U.S. Open, he exploded from seven strokes and fourteen players behind to win. Two months earlier he had finished birdie-birdie on national television to win the Masters and now he had created another miracle—again on national television.

Much has been written into the lore of golf of how it was that day, of the epic 65 he shot in the final round at Cherry Hills, of the day that really made him, but not by anyone who had lunched with him, kidded him, and then happily marched inside the gallery ropes with him, scurrying after Cokes, furnishing cigarettes, and hoping to put him at ease.

During lunch in a quiet corner of the Cherry Hills locker room before that round, Arnold was cheerful and joking as he ate a hamburger, drank iced tea, and made small talk with a couple of other players, Bob Rosburg and Ken Venturi, a writer named Bob Drum, and myself. He talked to no one else who might win. All he seemed concerned about was Cherry Hills' 1st hole, a comparatively short, downhill, downwind, par four. It bugged him. He thought he could drive the green, but in three previous rounds he had not done it.

"It really makes me hot," he said. "A man ought to drive that green."

"Why not?" I said. "It's only three hundred and forty-six yards through a ditch and a lot of high grass."

"If I drive that green I might shoot a hell of a score," he said. "I might even shoot a sixty-five if I get started good. What'll that bring?"

"About seventh place. You're too far back."

"Well, that would be two-eighty," Arnold said. "Doesn't two-eighty always win the Open?"

"Yeah," I said. "When Hogan shoots it."

Arnold laughed and walked out to the first tee.

For a while I loitered around the big clubhouse waiting for the leaders to go out, as a good journalist should. In the process of milling around, however, I overheard a couple of fans talking about an amazing thing they had just seen. Palmer, they said, had driven the first green. Just killed a low one that hung up there straight toward the mountains and then burned its way through the USGA trash and onto the putting surface. Got a two-putt birdie.

I smiled to myself and walked out onto the veranda and began edging my way through the spectators toward the 1st tee where the leader, Mike Souchak, would be going off presently. But about that time a pretty good roar came up from down on the front nine, and seconds later, a man sprinted by panting the news that Palmer was three under through three.

"Drove the first, chipped in on two and hit it stiff on three," he said, pulling away and darting off to join Arnie's Army. Like the spectator and a few thousand others who got the same notion at the same time, I tried to break all records for the Cherry Hills Clubhouse-to-Fourth Fairway Dash. We got there just in time to see Arnold hole his fourth straight birdie.

Wringing wet and perishing from thirst, I staggered toward the fifth tee, stopping to grab a Coke at a concession stand. I ducked under the ropes as an armband permitted and stood there puffing but excited.

Arnold came in briskly, squinted down the fairway and walked over. He took the Coke out of my hand, the cigarettes out of my shirt pocket and broke into a smile.

"Fancy seeing you here," he said. "Who's winning the Open?"

Palmer birdied two more holes through the 7th to go an incredible six under, working on an incorrigible twenty-nine out. But he bogeyed the 8th and had to settle for a 30. Even so, the challengers were falling all around him like wounded soldiers, and their crowds were bolting toward him, and the title would be his. Everything would be his now.

Later on, somewhere on the back nine holes, I remember sizing up a leader board with him and saying, "You've got it. They're all taking gas."

"Aw, maybe," he said, quietly. "But damn it, I wanted that twenty-nine."

There have been other major victories, as we know, and scores of lesser ones, and precisely because of him the professional tour has tripled, quadrupled in prize money. He has become, they say, something immeasurable in champions, something more than life-size, even though he has turned into his forties, the hip hurts, and a lot of other big ones have slipped away.

This is true, I think. He is the most immeasurable of all golf champions. But this is not entirely true because of all that he has won, or because of that mysterious fury with which he has managed to rally himself. It is partly because of the nobility he has brought to losing. And more than anything, it is true because of the pure, unmixed joy he has brought to trying.

He has been, after all, the doggedest victim of us all.

About the Author

DAN JENKINS has been a sportswriter all his life and in 1972 he became a best-selling novelist as well. His writing career began at *The Fort Worth Press* in 1948. He became sports editor of the *Press* in 1957. He moved to *The Dallas Times Herald* as sports editor and columnist in 1960. He joined the staff of *Sports Illustrated* in New York in 1962 and wrote over 500 articles for the magazine through 1984. He now writes a monthly sports column for *Playboy* and contributes essays and covers major golf championships for *Golf Digest*.

His best-selling novels are *Semi-Tough* (1972), *Dead Solid Perfect* (1974), *Limo* (with Bud Shrake, 1976), *Baja Oklahoma* (1981), *Life Its Ownself* (1984), and *Fast Copy* (1988). Jenkins also co-wrote the screenplays for the HBO productions of *Baja Oklahoma* and *Dead Solid Perfect*.

A native Texan, Jenkins is currently at work on a new novel for Simon & Schuster and divides his time between New York City and Ponte Vedra, Fla.